THE DEEDS OF
LOUIS THE FAT

THE DEEDS OF
LOUIS THE FAT

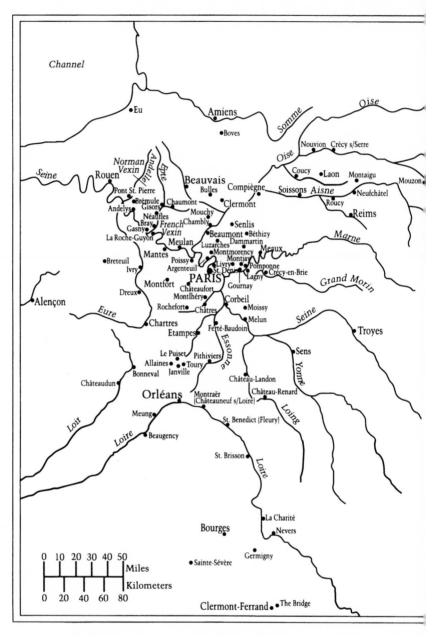

The towns, estates, and castles of central France mentioned in the *Deeds*.

Suger

THE DEEDS OF
LOUIS THE FAT

Translated with Introduction

and Notes by Richard Cusimano and

John Moorhead

The Catholic University of America Press
Washington, D.C.

The paper used in this publication meets the minimum
requirements of American National Standards for Information
Science—Permanence of Paper for Printed Library materials,
ANSI Z39.48–1984.

∞

LIBRARY OF CONGRESS CATALOGING-IN-PUBLICATION DATA
Suger, Abbot of Saint Denis, 1081–1151.
    [Vita Ludovici Grossi Regis. English]
    The deeds of Louis the Fat / Suger ; translated with
introduction and notes by Richard Cusimano and John
Moorhead.
        p. cm.
    Translation of: Vita Ludovici Grossi Regis.
    Includes bibliographical references and index.
    1. Louis VI, King of France, 1078–1137. 2. France—
History—Louis VI, 1108–1137. 3. France—Kings and rulers—
Biography.
    I. Cusimano, Richard, 1939–   . II. Moorhead, John, 1948–   .
III. Title.
DC88.5.S813   1991
944'.022'092—dc20
[B]   91-25427
ISBN 0-8132-0757-6.—ISBN 0-8132-0758-4 (pbk.)

Contents

Preface

Suger's *Deeds of Louis the Fat* is a key source for twelfth-century French history, and it was in the conviction that it should be made available to students and other readers who do not wish tackle the author's demanding Latin that we began, unbeknownst to each other, to translate it some years ago. On discovering that we were working independently on the same text we decided to combine forces, and the work here presented is the result of a happy collaboration. The introduction and notes to the text have been written primarily with the needs of students in mind. We have felt exonerated from going into great detail by the recent appearance of some excellent writing in English, in particular the papers read at the symposium held in New York in 1981 to commemorate the nine-hundredth anniversary of Suger's birth.

The notes to the text have been divided: those supplying lengthier commentary and additional sources are the endnotes; those giving parenthetical comments and identifications of important persons and places are footnotes. In addition, we have wished to provide as many references to other primary sources as possible, in particular those which amplify Suger's account; and with the interests of students in mind, we have cited translations, even though we realize that these are not satisfactory in all respects. Finally, we have not attempted consistency in the way we have translated personal names—for example, Theobald and Matthew are English forms, whereas Garlande is French, and Pagan and Drogo are forms close to the Latin. In selecting the forms, we have sought simply to represent personal names as they are most often seen in English, or in a manner that seemed most natural.

We wish to thank Gabrielle M. Spiegel, Andrew W. Lewis, and Charles T. Wood, who read the manuscript for The Catholic University of America Press. Their comments and suggestions for change have been a great help to us in the preparation of this work. And without the assistance and support of Mary Kooyman, Doris Theall, Pamela Stroup, and Jeff Rogers, our efforts in completing our task would have been much more difficult.

Abbreviations

WORKS BY AND EDITIONS OF SUGER

De admin. and *De consec.*	*De administratione* and *De consecratione*; see Panofsky for edition used; the portions of the *De admin.* not contained in Panofsky are cited from Lecoy.
Lecoy	A. Lecoy de la Marche, ed., *Oeuvres complètes de Suger*, Paris, 1887
Molinier	Auguste Molinier, ed., *Vie de Louis le Gros par Suger*, Paris, 1887
Panofsky	Erwin Panofsky, *Abbot Suger on the Abbey Church of St. Denis and Its Art Treasures*, rev. ed. by Gerda Panofsky-Soergel, Princeton, 1979
Waquet	Henri Waquet, ed., *Vie de Louis VI le Gros*, Paris, 1929

PRIMARY SOURCES AND SERIES

Abelard	*The Letters of Abelard and Heloise*, trans. Betty Radice, Harmondsworth, 1974
A-S Chron.	*The Anglo-Saxon Chronicle*, trans. Dorothy Whitelock, David C. Douglas and Susie I. Tucker, London, 1961
Bernard, *ep.*	*The Letters of St. Bernard of Clairvaux*, trans. Bruno Scott James, London, 1953
Chron. Mor.	*La Chronique de Morigny (1095–1152)*, ed. Leon Mirot, 2d ed., Paris, 1912
Galbert	Galbert of Bruges, *The Murder of Charles the Good, Count of Flanders*, trans. James Bruce Ross, rev. ed., New York, 1967

Gesta Francorum	*Gesta Francorum et aliorum Hierosolimitanorum*, ed. and trans. Rosalind Hill, London, 1962
Guibert	*Self and Society in Medieval France: The Memoirs of Abbot Guibert of Nogent*, ed. and rev. trans. John F. Benton, New York, 1970
Henry of Huntingdon	*The Chronicle of Henry of Huntingdon*, trans. T. Forester, London, 1847
J-W	P. Jaffé and G. Wattenbach, *Regesta Pontificum Romanorum*, vol. 1, Leipzig, 1885
MGH	Monumenta Germaniae Historica
Odo of Deuil	Odo of Deuil, *De Profectione Ludovici VII in Orientem*, ed. and trans. Virginia Gingerick Berry, New York, 1948
OV	*The Ecclesiastical History of Orderic Vitalis*, ed. and trans. Marjorie Chibnall, Oxford, 1969–80 (references are to the volume and page number of the old edition by Le Prévost, supplied in the margin to Chibnall's text)
PL	Patrologia Latina, ed. J. P. Migne, Paris, 1844–55
Tardif	Jules Tardif, *Monuments Historiques*, Paris, 1866
Walter Map	Walter Map, *De Nugis Curialium* (Courtiers' Trifles), ed. and trans. M. R. James, rev. by C. N. L. Brooke and R. A. B. Mynors, Oxford, 1983
William of Malmesbury	*William of Malmesbury's Chronicle*, trans. J. A. Giles, London, 1847

SECONDARY WORKS

Abbot Suger	Paula Lieber Gerson, ed., *Abbot Suger and St. Denis*, New York, 1986

Barlow	Frank Barlow, *William Rufus*, Berkeley, 1983
Bournazel	Eric Bournazel, *Le Gouvernement capétien au XIIe siècle*, Paris, 1975
Bur	Michel Bur, *La Formation du compté de Champagne v. 950–v. 1150*, Nancy, 1977
Cartellieri	Otto Cartellieri, *Abt Suger von Saint-Denis, 1081–1151*, Berlin, 1898 (=Historische Studien 11)
Dunbabin	Jean Dunbabin, *France in the Making, 843–1180*, Oxford, 1985
Fliche	Augustin Fliche, *Le règne de Philippe I, roi de France*, Paris, 1912
Hallam	Elizabeth M. Hallam, *Capetian France, 987–1328*, London, 1980
Lewis	Andrew W. Lewis, *Royal Succession in Capetian France*, Cambridge, Mass., 1981
Luchaire	Achille Luchaire, *Louis VI le Gros, annales de sa vie et de son règne, 1081–1137*, Paris, 1890
Monarchy	C. Warren Hollister, *Monarchy, Magnates and Institutions in the Anglo-Norman World*, London, 1986
Spiegel	Gabrielle M. Spiegel, *The Chronicle Tradition of Saint-Denis: A Survey*, Brookline, Mass., and Leyden, 1978
von Simson	Otto von Simson, *The Gothic Cathedral*, London, 1956

Chapter Titles in the Text

Introduction

Suger, abbot of St. Denis, has won a lasting place in European history as the man responsible for the rebuilding of the great abbey church of St. Denis, a reconstruction crucial in the transition from Romanesque to Gothic architecture.[1] But at the very time that work was proceeding on the great abbey (portions of which were completed in 1140 and 1144) Suger employed himself as well in writing a notable account of the deeds of King Louis VI (1108–37). The work has an evident value, for Louis's reign has been seen as marking a turning point in the fortunes of French monarchy, beginning a trend of augmented royal power that culminated in the monarchy of Louis XIV.[2] But Suger's work has an interest quite apart from its being an important account of the deeds of a significant king. Like Einhard, who had written his life of Charlemagne some three centuries earlier, Suger was a man of literary bent. Both were enthusiastic about their subject, and each produced a work that is a prime source of information about that person; but there remains an important difference between the historians. Einhard closely followed a classical prototype, Suetonius, and readers of his work often find his own thought elusive, submerged beneath the figure of the ancient author. Suger, however, although subjected to various influences, lacked a model. Doubtless his work is more confused and less subtle than Einhard's, but to this degree it also reveals more about its author. The careful reader of Suger's text feels that he knows not only the deeds of Louis but the ideas of its writer as well.

Little is known of the early life of Suger, who was born in 1080, or perhaps 1081. He described himself as having been of humble birth, as does his friend and biographer William; but modern work has suggested that members of his family were knights, and it may be that he came from a moderately well-to-do family. At the age of ten Suger was placed, presumably by his parents, as an oblate in the abbey of St. Denis, a few miles north of Paris.[3]

One of the wealthiest in France and a burial place of royalty, the abbey of St. Denis owed much of its status to a curious process whereby three different individuals had come to be seen as one man. According to the Bible, St. Paul numbered among his Athenian converts one Dionysius (French *Denis*) the Areopagite (Acts 17:34). Then, in the third century, another Dionysius, who seems to have been bishop of Paris, was martyred. It was later believed that Clement, one of the early popes, had sent this Dionysius to preach the gospel in Gaul, and by Suger's time an identification between him and Dionysius the Areopagite, which had been proposed in the ninth century by the abbot and translator Hilduin, was generally accepted. Meanwhile, in about A.D. 500, an eastern author of texts on such themes as the unknowability of God and the hierarchy of the angels affixed the name of Dionysius the Areopagite to his work, a misattribution that deceived most people until modern times. So, when Suger and his fellow monks contemplated the patron saint of their abbey, they saw him as a particularly impressive figure: a man in contact with St. Paul who had become the author of important theological work in his own right, who had been sent as a missionary to Gaul by a pope, and who had closed his life in glorious martyrdom. In addition, the abbey had been benefitting from royal generosity since the Merovingian period, with various Merovingian, Carolingian, and Capetian sovereigns having been buried there, so that by the twelfth century many people felt that the blessed Dionysius was in some way the patron saint of France, and that the abbey had special ties with French royalty.[4] Thus, when Peter Abelard denied the claim of the monks that their patron was the Areopagite, they said that he was a "traitor to the whole country"; those who sacked the abbey during the

French revolution similarly identified it with the French *regnum*.[5]

The young Suger seems to have been happy there, and as a man in his sixties he looked back on the monastery as having been a mother to him. He eagerly read the old charters, which documented the rights of the monastery to various possessions. He maintained this early interest throughout his life, and his rise within the community was quick.[6] Having completed his studies, he went with Abbot Adam of St. Denis to a council presided over by Pope Paschal II at Poitiers in 1106; in the following year he argued the claims of his monastery against the bishop of Paris before the pope; on a later occasion, he again accompanied Adam to discussions being held between Paschal and representatives of the emperor Henry V. He became provost of a dependency of St. Denis at Berneval in Normandy, and in 1109 provost of Toury.[7] We gain the picture of a scholarly monk who enjoyed the confidence of his abbot, who was coming to move in high circles, and who was rapidly gaining administrative experience.

Suger tells us that the church of St. Denis solemnly set him "among the princes of the kingdom and the church," and from an early age he must have been an associate of his contemporary, Prince Louis, who was educated at the abbey.[8] Despite being the eldest son of King Philip I (1060–1108), Louis's path to the throne was not entirely straightforward. His father, Philip, dismissed his mother, Bertha of Holland, while Louis was still a young boy, and began a liaison with Bertrada of Montfort, the wife of Count Fulk IV of Anjou, from which union were born two sons, Philip and Florus. Tension about the succession was inevitable, and Suger alludes to it in general terms. But at some time during the years 1098–1100, Louis became associated with Philip on the throne with the title "king-designate"; and in 1108, following his father's death, Louis went in haste to gain the crown in a ceremony at Orléans.[9] Louis and Suger enjoyed a developing relationship, documented in the pages of the *Deeds*. As early as 1104 we find Suger in Louis's company; Suger overheard Philip give advice to Louis about the castle of Montlhéry, just as in 1112 Suger was present at an important discussion between Louis and Hugh of Le Puiset, one of the barons of the royal principality. In 1118 and again in 1122 he travelled on Louis's behalf to meet popes. While returning from Rome on the second of these occasions he learned of Abbot Adam's death and his own election as abbot. Louis was irate because of a lapse in procedure, for the electors had failed to request the *licentia eligendi*, and the importance of St. Denis made the election of its abbot a political question. Any animosity, however, was short-lived, for Louis quickly accepted the election and confirmed the monastery's privileges, leaving Suger in the office he held until his death (January 13, 1151) and free for another trip to Italy.[10] The relationship between the two men had reached a new plateau.

As abbot of St. Denis, Suger found himself even more involved in high affairs of state. He was present in 1124 when Louis, his kingdom threatened by a planned German attack, came to St. Denis to seek the assistance of the kingdom's patron saints, the blessed Dionysius and his companions, and a document issued by Louis on that occasion refers to Suger as a man familiar and faithful in his councils.[11] Indeed, Suger travelled to Reims where the French awaited the Germans, and the successful outcome of this fracas can only have strengthened the ties between Suger and the king, for many believed that the blessed Dionysius had played an important role in the results. And a later series of events, known to us only in outline, must have had a similar benefit for Suger. For some time Stephen of Garlande had been building up his power until he became seneschal and chancellor; but in 1127 he lost his position and left court. His departure created a power vacuum, a situation from which the abbot of St. Denis profited, for the witness lists to charters issued by Louis indicate that during the late years of Louis's reign, Suger could frequently be found in the king's circle. With precise reference to 1129, the *Chronicle of Morigny* states that Suger was then a man outstanding in the king's court and an excellent pleader of causes.[12]

Suger's book, *The Deeds of Louis the Fat*, allows his close involvement in other important affairs of state toward the end of Louis's reign to be followed. Louis sent him to greet Pope Innocent II at Cluny in 1130; the *intimi et familiares* who advised the king to have his second son, Louis, anointed and crowned following the death in 1131 of the elder son, Philip, included Suger among them; and the king sent him as a *familiaris* in the party he dispatched to Aquitaine in 1137 to fetch Eleanor, who had been entrusted to the royal care by her dying father, Duke William X.[13] His absence from court on this occasion caused Suger to miss the death and burial of the man whom he later described as "our dearest friend and lord."[14] The younger Louis experienced a smooth accession to the throne; but some individuals who had played a leading role during his father's reign, such as his mother, Adelaide of Maurienne, and his cousin Ralph, count of Vermandois, found their influence at least temporarily in eclipse. So too Suger, for he apparently withdrew from court in 1139 and became less involved in royal activities. He later returned and, as the dominant figure in the regency during Louis VII's participation in the Second Crusade, enjoyed more power than he had had before. But during the interval Suger retired somewhat from affairs of state, and gave his attention to rebuilding the abbey of St. Denis and composing his account of the deeds of his friend and lord.[15]

What kind of book did Suger see himself as writing? As far as we know he did not give his work a title, and the manuscripts that preserve the text bestow several names on it. But in his prefatory letter to Bishop Josselin of Soissons, Suger states that he is forwarding for his friend's comments "the deeds (*gesta*) of

Louis, the most serene king of the French," just as he elsewhere refers to his account of "the deeds of the aforesaid king."[16] Similarly, Suger's successor as abbot of St. Denis, Odo, referred to him as having written the deeds of Louis; and his biographer, William, refers on three occasions to Suger's account of Louis's deeds.[17] We see no reason to dispute the description of the work provided by both Suger and his contemporaries; and so we have not followed Henri Waquet, who published his edition and translation under the title *Vie de Louis VI le gros*. We believe that Suger sought to compose not a life of Louis but an account of his deeds.[18]

It may be worth going into some detail at this point. Portions of the *Deeds*, those that describe the last illness, death and burial of King Louis and that may owe something to the influence of traditional hagiography, have come down to us in a separate manuscript; it seems possible to identify them with a series of lessons which Suger is known to have composed for the liturgical office at St. Denis on the anniversary of Louis's death.[19] Two of Suger's editors have suggested that these lessons are extracts from the *Deeds*; but it may well be that, on the contrary, the *Deeds* represent an expansion of the lessons. We know that as early as 1124 Suger was providing for Louis's anniversary to be celebrated at St. Denis, and that a passage of the *Chronicle of Morigny* that refers to Suger's having composed lessons was written during the period 1139–42. A passage in the *Deeds*, however, implies that its author wrote it after the death of Pope Innocent II in 1143, and the earliest reference to the *Deeds* occurs shortly after that date. Perhaps, then, Suger worked up his book from the lessons, but as it turned out, the work described not Louis's life as much as his deeds, particularly those of battle. Once this is understood it becomes easier to locate the *Deeds* in its proper genre.[20]

Suger's *The Deeds of Louis the Fat* can be set beside such writings of eleventh- and twelfth-century provenance as Wipo's

The Deeds of the Emperor Conrad, William of Poitiers's *The Deeds of William the Conqueror,* William of Apulia's *The Deeds of Robert Guiscard,* the anonymous English *The Deeds of Stephen,* and *The Deeds of Frederick Barbarossa* of Otto of Freising. In works of this kind the narrating of deeds takes precedence over the provision of biographical data. It is even tempting to compare Suger's book with writings on the First Crusade that contain the word *Gesta* in their titles, and at a further remove perhaps with the Old French *chansons de geste* as well. This is not to suggest that Suger played any part in the creation of the Old French literature that has come down to us.[21] But he was a lover of stories. We know Suger could relate the deeds of any king or prince of the Franks who might be named, and when he was in a very good mood he loved to stay up to the middle of the night telling of the deeds of heroic men.[22] Louis was one of the brave men whose deeds Suger enjoyed recounting, and it may be suggested that the curiously episodic character of the book he produced owes something to the technique of a raconteur.

But it would be wrong to see Suger's *Deeds* as merely a collection of incidents chronologically arranged, for an analysis of the individual chapters reveals an internal structure.[23] We frequently find that quarrels, disputes, disturbances, or attacks have upset a peaceful order. These violent acts can be small in scale—especially those done by the petty barons of the Ile-de-France—or large, such as the invasion of France that Emperor Henry V planned; they may be directed against either lay people or churches. The innocent parties come before Louis to seek his help, often casting themselves at his feet.[24] Louis hastens to put matters straight; his proud opponents learn to their cost that, in one of Suger's favorite expressions, they have been "deceived by a vain hope," and the peace that had earlier prevailed is restored or improved upon. Read in this way, the *Deeds* reveal a definite structure. Its chapters are more or less autonomous units, laid out in a sequence whose movement is reiterative rather than strictly linear.[25] They constitute the building blocks of a text not as disordered as it may first appear. It is simply structured on principles foreign to our notion of historical writing.

Suger concerned himself, then, with recounting the deeds of Louis rather than presenting a biography of him. With this in mind, the reader may readily accept his leaving out details that an author of a modern biography would have included. One would never know from reading Suger that Louis received his knighthood away from home following an apparent falling-out with his father, that he was present at the court of his future enemy Henry I of England in 1100, or that his stepmother, Bertrada, asked Henry to hold Louis in perpetual confinement and thereafter tried to poison him, as other contemporaries of Suger reported.[26] There is only a fleeting reference to Louis's marriage to Adelaide of Maurienne, and Philip, his eldest son by the marriage, is introduced only to die. Similarly, Suger has little to say concerning what some scholars would regard as the most important features of Louis's reign, such as his activities in bestowing charters and building castles. The growing importance of St. Bernard and the currents of ecclesiastical opinion he represented are likewise ignored.[27] Indeed, Suger recorded only a few grudging words about the house of St. Victor in Paris, which Louis himself founded and which became prominent in twelfth-century spiritual and intellectual life; he is suspiciously silent about Louis's involvement with any religious house other than St. Denis.[28] The Louis described by Suger was a man of deeds, and it will be worth our while to ask why Suger found him so attractive.

Suger emerges from his book as a staunch royalist, perhaps not surprisingly, in view of his enthusiasm for the writings of pseudo-Dionysius. He had no difficulty in seeing French society in hierarchical terms, with the monarchy at the top.[29] It was a view that provided a theoretical model for a strong monarchy, but, as can easily be seen from the *Deeds*, Louis VI was not a particularly powerful king, for his interests were largely concentrated in the area around Paris, the Ile-de-France. Here was located the royal demesne, or domain—the cluster of lands and rights that the king himself held—and the somewhat wider block of territory termed the royal principality where the king's direct rule prevailed. Even in his own domain, however, the position of the king was not strong; a story later told in England depicted the young Louis unable to proceed three miles beyond Paris without the permission and safe-conduct of the neighboring princes.[30]

Distinguished work done by French scholars since World War II has drawn attention to a widespread breakdown in authority in France around the year 1000. Power passed from major feudatories and the holders of public power to those who held castles and were able to gather bands of knights around themselves, so that early twelfth-century France was "less an age of fiefs than an age of castles."[31] Just as Henry I of England, in his capacity as duke of Normandy, devoted himself to the towers and castles of that area, so Louis turned his attention to settling affairs and reducing the power of the greater and lesser castellans of the Ile-de-France. From the pages of the Deeds one gains the picture of a monarch continually marshalling his forces for action throughout his principality, from the Norman frontier to the lower Marne valley to the region of Orléans. Indeed, as seen by Suger, a chief task of the king was to impose his will on the turbulent barons around Paris and thereby keep peace for the churches and villagers of his lands.

But Suger's Louis does more, for on several occasions he intervenes directly in districts outside the royal principality. Since "a king's power should never be thought of as being limited only to the narrow boundaries of any part of his lands," Louis led a large host south of the Loire into Berry in 1109 in answer to a plea of a lack of justice.[32] He subdued the fortress of Germigny, brought its holder, Haimo II, lord of Bourbon, back into the Ile-de-France for trial, and kept the castle for his own disposition. In 1122 and once more in 1126 the king led major expeditions into the Auvergne in response to petitions for help from the bishop of Clermont-Ferrand against Count William VI. In restoring peace to the land and the churches, Louis accepted fealty, a sworn oath, and a sufficient number of hostages from Duke William X of Aquitaine, who had interceded on behalf of his vassal the count. The duke rebuked the king for his direct interference, but he guaranteed that all concerned would settle these affairs at Orléans within the royal principality. Then, in one of his most dramatic efforts the king eagerly entered Flanders in 1127 burning with a desire to avenge the foul murder of a kinsman, Count Charles; he is represented as having accomplished the vengeance fairly easily.[33] He installed a new count, helped capture the conspirators, and saw them condemned to a demeaning death after he had taken possession of the castle of Ypres. Suger describes every one of these interventions of the king of France as the lawful action of a monarch rightly concerned with dispensing justice throughout the realm, something that he felt had not been done during the previous reign.

In various passages of the *Deeds* Suger mentions Louis's father, Philip I, and he makes it clear that he had very little time for this king. Philip emerges as an adulterer who neglected his kingdom for a woman, and a man who sensibly decides to be buried away from other kings. His most striking characteristic is indolence, for even during Philip's lifetime Louis was the "defender of his father's kingdom"; and according to Suger, the interest the son took in the welfare of those who prayed, those who worked, and the poor was something to which they had not been accustomed for a long time. Significantly, people are described as having complained to Philip a hundred times about Ebles of Roucy, whereas only two or three complaints brought action from Louis. Suger found this idleness in Philip easy to explain, for after he took up with Bertrada he gave himself up to lust, lost interest in affairs of state, and became utterly self-indulgent. Although the *Chronicle of Morigny* describes Philip as a "man of wisdom," there may be some truth in the account of Suger, the emphasis of which is similar to that of William of Malmesbury.[34]

But what a contrast with Louis! As early as chapter 3, Hugh of Clermont hastens to him to seek justice over the wrongful loss of a castle. Louis quickly sets the legal process into motion, and when it fails he rushes to take vengeance. In the following chapter his forces flee, whereupon the young lord leaps on his horse and hastens after them. The Louis of Suger lives in a world of constant motion, and the narrative of his deeds is full of verbs and adverbs of speed. Doubtless the king slowed down toward the end, but his pattern of robust activity remains. In the final chapters of his book, within the space of a few pages, Suger sums up the conclusion of several of Louis's expeditions with a neat phrase he may have borrowed from Ovid: "He returned home a victor."[35] And even as his strength failed him, Louis continued to fight against the king of England, Count Theobald, and all his enemies. The contrast with his father Philip could hardly be more plain.

What was the attraction of this busy king for the author of the *Deeds*? We are in a good position to say, for toward the end of his life Suger, aware that his death was approaching, wrote a letter to the king's son and successor, Louis VII, in which he made it clear what he felt the younger Louis should be doing:

With due care I entreat Your Nobility on behalf of the noble church of St. Denis, which is the greatest part of the kingdom and your crown, that in all things, among all things, and before all things you foster and support it, as is proper for a good and pious lord, and that you extend to it the hand of counsel and aid. The loftiness of Your Majesty will recall the way in which, as a young man, you departed from your land, placed the noble kingdom of the French in the hand of the church of God and, after many dangers and the deaths of many people, you visited the eastern church. Look out, and think carefully, so that you do not lose the fruit of such a great effort! Love the church of God, defend orphans and widows, and in this way you will be able to resist every power, spiritual and worldly, and, God being your helper, the plots of however many enemies you may have. This is my counsel.[36]

A healthy respect for the abbey of St. Denis and a concern for the churches, orphans, and widows were the qualities that Suger deemed desirable in the younger Louis; and his father Louis VI, at least in the story the abbot chose to tell, had displayed them both to a high degree.

The centrality of the abbey of St. Denis and its traditions in the life of Suger is difficult for us to understand. But monks of the middle ages felt such loyalty toward their houses, which they so often entered in boyhood, that they were willing to accept traditions for them on the basis of what we would consider very slender evidence. Guibert of Nogent, for example, in other respects a good historian, believed that the church of Nogent, which later developed into a monastery, was founded by a king of Britain who had spoken with St. Peter, the other apostles, and the Virgin Mary in Jerusalem shortly after the Ascension of Jesus Christ.[37] Similarly, Suger believed that Dionysius, the martyred bishop over whose relics the monastery of St. Denis had been built, was none other than Dionysius the Areopagite, who had been converted to Christianity by St. Paul. Suger became passionately devoted to this patron; and as we have seen, he applied himself to rebuilding the great abbey church at the very time he was raising to Louis his "monument more lasting than bronze," the *Deeds*, in the prologue of which he describes himself as "abbot of blessed Dionysius the Areopagite."[38]

But Suger was in no position to be exultant. To the east, the church of Reims was promoting the cult of St. Remigius, a rival to that of Dionysius; and in 1090 the young prince Louis had subscribed to a document issued by his father that confirmed the possessions and immunities of the competing saint's house in that city. In addition, the claim that Dionysius the Areopagite was the patron of the abbey of St. Denis had recently been challenged by Peter Abelard.[39] And the attitude of King Philip had given Suger no cause for satisfaction, for he had chosen to be buried at the abbey of St. Benedict on the Loire river. It has been suggested that Suger's chagrin even led him, shortly after Philip's death, to draft a document that established at St. Denis a solemn commemoration of the death of King Dagobert, who significantly had not only chosen to be buried at St. Denis but had been a good friend of that church.[40] King Louis, on the other hand, had behaved well; this is made particularly clear in the passages Suger originally wrote for the liturgical commemoration of him. They describe Louis as a close friend of the church from boyhood, explain that his response to serious ailment was the generous disbursement of treasure, much of it to St. Denis, and show him riding to the abbey church despite being mortally ill. More than once in the text of the *Deeds*, Suger states that Louis conducted himself at St. Denis "with great humility." His response to a threatened German invasion in 1124 partly took the form of hastening to St. Denis, asking the blessed Dionysius for help, and taking from the altar a battle standard in a ceremony that, as depicted by Suger, implied that Louis was the vassal of the abbey. Then, when the threat of the invasion had ended, Louis returned to St. Denis to give thanks for the protection of the kingdom. Suger's description of these events is open to question in several respects, but behind the embellishment one can nevertheless detect a king who was devoted to St. Denis.

Louis's devotion to St. Denis was not his only characteristic to receive Suger's approbation. A circular letter written on the occasion of the abbot's death mentions his task of bringing before the king the pleas of the churches and the requests of widows, orphans, and the poor.[41] With minor variants, Louis's care for the churches and the unfortunate runs like a leitmotiv throughout the *Deeds*. In the lessons composed for the liturgical commemoration of Louis at St. Denis, Suger linked the account of Louis's youth with the description of his final illness, death, and burial by a few words summing up two characteristics of his thirty-year administration: "A splendid defense of the churches and a continual oversight of the poor and orphans."[42] The theme is reiterated, in an understated way, in the first paragraph of chapter 2; then it makes a notable appearance at the end of the book when, among the things the dying Louis urges on his son and successor, the first is care for the church of God, the poor, and orphans, which had been a royal duty for several centuries.

Louis's concern for the welfare of churches seems to be a main motive, according to Suger, behind many of the king's actions. The author of the *Deeds* persistently describes the royal intervention on behalf of churches being troubled by lay magnates: the church of Reims by Ebles of Roucy, that of Orléans by Leo of Meung, and that of Clermont-Ferrand by the count of the Auvergne. The depredations of Hugh of Le Puiset led to the formation of a formidable ecclesiastical coalition against him, which included among its members the archbishop of Sens, the bishops of Orléans and Chartres, and Suger himself. The most evil character in Suger's gallery of scoundrels, Thomas of Marle, is described as having owed his successes to the devil; one of the most powerful passages of the book shows him dying without communion. Suger makes it perfectly clear that Louis's two campaigns against him were fought at the behest of churches. In his encomium of King Robert, written around 1033, Helgaud represented this king as being bid farewell by "the monks, the clerks, the widows, the orphans and all Christ's poor."[43] Suger's thought is in the same tradition, which indeed had been expressed by authors writing long before Helgaud; for him a good king will intervene on behalf of churches (a term which includes their estates), both episcopal and monastic.

Moreover, Suger generally, although not always, describes

Louis's interventions as being on behalf of churches rather than "the church." Students of the middle ages are frequently taught to interpret the events of the period in terms of a battle between the two amorphous abstractions of Church and State; but such a schema, while it may have some limited pedagogical value, scarcely does justice to the complex reality. It ignores the subtle ties of belief, interest, and often family relationship that bound together the holders of power in both "church" and "state," and tends to gloss over tensions between the representatives of the various groups within the church, as between bishops and abbots. More importantly, the characteristics that made wealthy churches favorite targets for Vikings in the ninth and tenth centuries made the Hughs and Thomases of the eleventh and twelfth cast envious eyes on them as well. The old French epic cycle of poems concerning William, count of Orange, has as a chief theme the weakness of monarchy, and at one stage the hero states:

> I saw the whole country full of demons who were burning cities, desecrating churches, destroying chapels, overturning belfries, and twisting the breasts of noble women so that I felt great pity for them in my heart and wept bitterly. And there I swore to the Glorious One in Heaven and St. Giles, to whom I had just been praying, that I would go and help the people in that land with as many men as I could have under my command.[44]

Small wonder that Peter the Venerable, the abbot of Cluny, complained more than once in his correspondence, whether metaphorically or not, that his abbey was located in an area "without a king and without a prince."[45] Twelfth-century ecclesiastics were frequently grateful for whatever security a strong rule could offer; and in this regard Suger felt that Louis had behaved admirably.

Suger's fellow monk and biographer William favorably compared his abbot's writing style with the masterful prose of Ci-

cero, but modern scholars have been less kind, and Waquet's
charge that he was totally lacking in taste may stand as representative of their opinions.[46] Suger's wording is awkward and continually creates difficulties for those who would translate him.
We have occasionally had to content ourselves with giving the
apparent meaning of passages rather than a translation in the
strict sense; when we have consulted the French version that
accompanies Waquet's edition, we have found ourselves not
alone in this policy. The moralizing observations with which
numerous chapters commence and the descriptions of places, in
particular, are often labored. Furthermore, Suger was a lover of
repetition.[47] In the hands of a master like St. Bernard this trait
can be impressive, but the reader of our author is more likely to
find it irritating, and we have not always sought to bring it out in
our translation. There are problems even with the vocabulary,
for the work is packed with words used with unusual meanings.[48] Variant readings in the manuscript tradition indicate not
so much carelessness on the part of scribes as intelligent and,
one sometimes suspects, desperate efforts to make sense out of
passages. Suger's translators are frequently tempted to conclude
that their author was simply not in control of his language. In
addition, as the most casual perusal of the *Deeds* shows, his
style abounds in needless repetitions and apparently indiscrimi-
nate use of superlatives. But just when the temptation to despair
is strongest, the reader comes upon a witty turn of phrase or pun
that alerts one to the fact that, at least sometimes, Suger knew
very well what he was doing. Rather surprisingly, the abbot
emerges from his work as an author with classical tastes. In
addition to numerous quotations from and allusions to Lucan
and other classical authors, which occur frequently in passages
describing war, there are references to Hector and the giants, and
Hercules and his pillars, and a comparison of Louis with "a
powerful wrestler and admirable gladiator."[49] Yet, our author is
medieval at heart. For example, he consistently terms the city of

Louis's residence *Parisius*. The authors of the *Chronicle of Morigny* do the same, but in their work the term is glossed with its classical equivalent, *Lutecia*, on its first occurrence.[50]

To say that Suger would have failed to win first prize for classical Latin prose does not imply any lack of subtlety in his method of presenting historical material. His approach can best be understood from his ideas about beauty. Suger lavished care and money on the rebuilding and decoration of the church of St. Denis at a time when powerful currents in western monastic thought, represented by such divergent figures as St. Bernard and Peter Abelard, were noted for insisting on the need for simplicity. Against his critics, Suger held that beauty had a function in heightening Christian experience:

> When—out of my delight at the beauty of the house of God—the loveliness of the many-colored gems has called me away from external cares, and worthy meditation has caused me to reflect, transferring that which is material to that which is immaterial, on the diversity of the sacred virtues: then it seems to me that I see myself dwelling, as it were, in some strange region of the universe which exists neither entirely in the slime of earth nor entirely in the purity of heaven; and that, by the grace of God, I can be transported from this inferior to that higher world in an anagogical manner.[51]

Suger can be seen as a particularly strong advocate of a way of looking at reality that strongly colored the period we now know as the middle ages: "Things that are signified give more pleasure than that which signifies them;" and so, in a famous formulation, Suger states that the teaching of Christ reveals what Moses veils.[52] He would certainly have agreed with Peter the Venerable that, while dreams were often vain, not all of them were to be despised, since the accomplishment of what they signified showed that they were often true, as twice in the *Deeds* significant dreams occur just before important changes in the dreamers' lives.[53] Similarly, Suger points out that the consecration of the future King Louis VII by Pope Innocent at a council attended by many important prelates presaged a growth in royal power, and he is sympathetic to an interpretation of the slaying of William Rufus, which he emphasizes was an accident humanly speaking, as being an incident that allowed the vengeance of God to be divined. His world is full of things that point to realities greater than themselves, and it is easy to understand his devoting several pages of the *Deeds* to the alleged prophecy of Merlin.

When a man of this bent turned his attention to writing an account of the deeds of a king, his purpose was not merely to explain how things had happened. He was naturally alive to readings of events that transcended the events themselves; for as he mentioned in another work, "The setting down of things past is the showing forth of things to come."[54] In addition, as the notes to the following text show, Suger's description of Louis's ventures continually tries to put the best face on things. Louis was by no means an outstanding king; but as has well been said in a slightly different connection, Suger waved his wand over small beer and turned it into champagne.[55] In another of his writings, Suger uses a striking phrase in connection with problems that arose in the construction of the new abbey church: "Because we could not do what we wanted we settled for wanting to do what we could."[56] One has the feeling that, similarly, compromise underlay much of Louis's activity, and that Suger's portrait of him as a strong and victorious king is the product of some tailoring of his material. But Suger, the custodian of the burial places of many French kings and the abbot of a house with monarchist traditions, looked beyond the trivia that characterized so much of Louis's tenure of office and perceived a *rex Francorum* in the tradition of Charlemagne, Louis the Pious, and Charles the Bald.[57] Just as the accoutrements of the church of St. Denis could lead people toward God, so the small change of Louis's wars against the troublemakers of the Ile-de-France reveals what monarchy really is. For example, Suger's description of a drawn out and ultimately inconclusive struggle with Thomas of Marle begins with reflections on the office of kingship and concludes, with the help of a text from St. Paul, by explaining that Louis had indeed been fulfilling that office. However minor and banal, Louis's deeds point beyond themselves to a concept of French and Christian monarchy.

Suger's text of the *Deeds of Louis the Fat*, then, allows the careful reader an opportunity to discern the author's ideas and values. However, although certain themes and emphases develop as the events unfold, the man himself remains elusive, as one senses he did for his contemporaries. After Suger died in 1151, the monk William wrote his biography, in which he sought the intercession of his departed abbot. But although William believed that Suger was still praying, significantly he did not deduce this from Suger's character; rather, it was simply the abbot's *officium* to pray. Perhaps Suger was seen by those around him in terms of his function rather than his personality. But we are left with the impression of genuine achievement. Suger was a particularly small man; but as William commented, "Good Jesus, what strength, how much spirit was in him!"[58]

A COMMENT ON THE TEXT

The Latin text of the *Deeds* is fairly straightforward. Eight manuscripts were at the disposal of Waquet when he produced his edition, including several full texts of the twelfth century, and it is usually clear what Suger wrote.[59] Such problems as there are stem from Suger's vocabulary and his style, which copyists tried to improve. In general we have sought to translate the text as written by Suger, avoiding it only where grammatical mistakes render it impossible or difficult. Such cases are indicated in the notes.

One manuscript, ms. f, presents additional problems, for it differs from all other manuscripts in certain ways. Frequently it changes the style of the Latin, and more importantly it adds material. It now seems impossible to determine whether Suger stands in some manner behind this manuscript. We note in it a persistent tendency to style Louis *rex Francie*, in contrast to the *rex Francorum* frequently found in Waquet's edition of the *Deeds*, although there occur in both Waquet's edition and ms. f certain odd expressions, such as "arms as powerful as Hector's." It is true that ms. f contains a reference to "we who wrote the history of the lord Louis," but elsewhere it refers to Suger in the third person. Suger may well have been involved in the process that led to the composition of ms. f, but the position is not clear, and so we have ignored it.[60]

THE DEEDS OF
LOUIS THE FAT

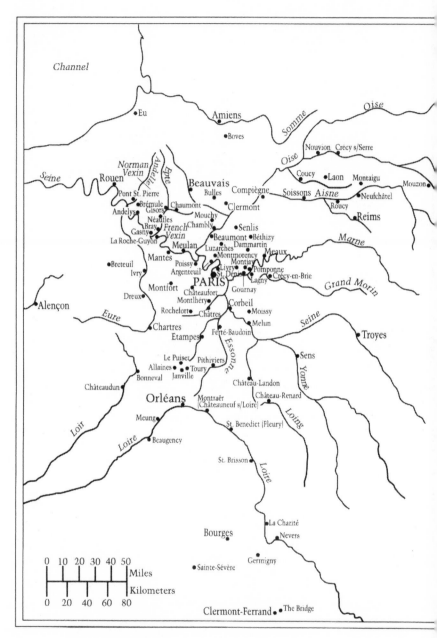

The towns, estates, and castles of central France mentioned in the *Deeds*.

Prologue

To Lord Josselin, the duly revered bishop of Soissons, from Suger, an unworthy servant of Jesus Christ, whom God suffered to be called abbot of blessed Dionysius the Areopagite: may he be united as a bishop with the bishop of bishops.[a]

Both we and our works will profit from review and judgment by those who will pronounce at the Last Judgment sentences of hatred and love, each according to the merits of the case, when "the noble man will sit at the gates among the senators of the land."[2] And you would be among the best of these, even without the office of bishop, to which I am as dedicated as you are yourself. But do not expect more from me, for I have no more. That is why we are sending the deeds of Louis, the most serene king of the French, to be judged by your excellent learning.[b] Let me write and you correct, and together let us sing praises and shed tears for him whom together we loved, for our lord showed himself most kind both while he was advancing us and after he had done so. And friendship that arises from favors received puts no barrier in the way of love, for he who commanded us to love our enemies would not forbid us to love our friends.[3]

We owe him a double debt of gratitude and love, different but not divergent sentiments. Therefore, let us fashion for him "a monument more lasting than bronze,"[4] recounting with our pen his zealous care for the churches of God and his wonderful valor in administering the affairs of the kingdom. May the fortunes of time never succeed in effacing memory of him; and, in return for

a. The Vulgate Bible refers to Christ as a bishop (1 Pet. 2:25); presumably he is the "bishop of bishops" in this sentence. See further endnote 1.

b. It was common for medieval authors to write prefaces offering their work to friends and expressing the hope of receiving corrections and stylistic improvements, but such amendment was not expected.

benefits received, may the unrelenting prayers of the church never cease interceding for him from generation to generation.

May your highness sit joyfully as a bishop amid the senators of heaven.[c]

[1]
His valor as a youth and how he valiantly drove back William Rufus, the very powerful king of the English, who was making trouble for his father's kingdom

To begin, the splendid and renowned Louis, king of the French and son of the stately King Philip, was distinguished and handsome in the very flower of early age, when he was hardly twelve or thirteen years old.[a] He showed so much zeal in forming virtuous habits, and his graceful body was growing so tall that his future reign held immediate promise that the kingdom would be honorably enlarged, fostering hope that our prayers for the protection of the churches and the poor would be answered. This highborn stripling followed the ancient custom of Charles the Great and other excellent kings, evidence of which is contained in the imperial charters, and clung to the holy martyrs of St. Denis and their monks with innate tenderness.[b] He maintained

c. A good example of Suger's ability to turn a phrase, recalling to mind the "senators of the land" quoted in the second paragraph above.

---

a. The greater portion of this first paragraph was also part of a series of lessons composed by Suger for the observance of the anniversary of Louis's death at St. Denis. See further endnote 1 and Introduction above.

b. The designation of Louis as "highborn" (*altus*) and the reference to Charlemagne and other kings bring out a theme of the book, a concern to

throughout his life, with much generosity and the bestowing of honor, that friendship toward their church that had been born in him as a child. And coming to his end, he placed his highest hopes, after God, in them, and he delivered himself body and soul to them, freely and very devoutly, so that if it had been possible he would have become a monk there.[c]

At the age already mentioned, valor was growing, maturing, and beginning to flourish in the spirit of this young man, and he could no longer endure hunting and the amusements of boys at a stage of life when most tend to be playful and neglect their practice with weapons. At that very time many magnates of the kingdom, but especially that mettlesome William, king of the English and son of that even more mettlesome King William, conqueror of the English, launched an attack against him.[d] The force of the young man's prowess inflamed him, and his valor smiled at the task at hand. It took away his idleness, opened his eyes to good sense, destroyed his leisure, and aroused his sense of duty. For William, king of the English, was as skillful in knightly practice as he was greedy for praise and a seeker of fame.[3] After his older brother Robert had been disinherited, he happily succeeded his father William on the throne; and after the same brother had departed for Jerusalem, he came into possession of the duchy of Normandy. Since the duchy adjoined the realm and

---

locate Louis's achievements against the glories of pre-Capetian monarchy. See further endnote 2.

c. The short extract from the lessons concludes here. The reference to Louis's end makes more sense when seen as part of these lessons, which resume at chapter 33 of the *Deeds*.

d. King William II (William Rufus, 1087–1100) gained the kingship of England upon the death of his father, King William I (William the Conqueror, 1066–87), a donor to the abbey of St. Denis (Guibert, p. 228). Suger has scant praise for either king, but he tends to praise William Rufus more than most writers of the time, for by emphasizing his merits he could explain the young Louis's lack of success against him.

extended to its very borderlands, he strove to attack the renowned young man by whatever means he could.[e]

In their way of fighting they were both alike and not alike.
They were alike in that neither would yield, and not alike in that
one was a grown man and the other a youth. The one, being
wealthy, squandered the treasures of the English, hiring and
paying knights splendidly; the other lacked estates and used the
resources of his father's realm sparingly.[5] But the lord Louis
gathered a force of knights by zeal and talent alone, and fought
back boldly. This young man could be seen riding swiftly with
his band of knights, sometimes across the district of Berry,
sometimes the Auvergne, and sometimes Burgundy; and he led
them back into the Vexin no less swiftly when notified that he
was needed. With his meager three hundred or five hundred
knights he bravely withstood the same King William with his
ten thousand; and as the outcome of battle is an uncertain thing,
sometimes he withdrew, and sometimes he put him to flight.[6]

Both sides took many prisoners in these clashes. The renowned young man and his followers seized a large number, and
among them were the noble Count Simon, the noble Baron
Gilbert of L'Aigle, who was equally respected in England and
Normandy, and Pagan of Gisors, for whose sake the castle of
Gisors was first fortified.[7] On his side the king of England captured the valiant and noble Count Matthew of Beaumont, the
distinguished baron Simon of Montfort of great fame, and the
lord Pagan of Montjay.[8] But King William, concerned at his need
to hire more knights, quickly ransomed the English prisoners,
while the French wasted away during lengthy captivity, and

e. On the death of William the Conqueror, his eldest son Robert inherited
Normandy; the second son, William, took England, and the youngest, Henry,
received treasure with which he acquired land in Normandy. Robert's government of Normandy was by no means successful, and in 1096 he pledged
his duchy to William for ten thousand silver marks and set off on the First
Crusade. See further endnote 4.

there was only one way to get free. They had to undertake knightly service for the king of England, bind themselves to him by homage, and swear on oath to attack and make trouble for the kingdom and the king.

It was commonly said that this proud and headstrong king aspired to the throne of the French, for the renowned young man was the only son of his father by his very noble wife, the sister of Count Robert of Flanders.[f] Two other sons, Philip and Florus, had been born of the irregular union to Countess Bertrada of Anjou.[g] But they would not be considered for the succession even if the only heir met with some misfortune and died first. However, since it is neither right nor natural that the French be subject to the English, but rather the English to the French,[10] the outcome of events made sport of William's detestable ambition. He stirred himself and his men up for three years or more with this madness, and calmed down only when both the English and the French who were bound to him in homage could not help him accomplish his goal. So he crossed back into England and gave himself over lustfully to the desires of his heart. And one day while he was hotly pursuing game in the New Forest, he was struck suddenly by an untimely arrow and died.[h]

Some people, believing their opinion to be true, judged that divine vengeance had struck the man down, for he had burdened the poor beyond endurance and had cruelly extorted from churches. Whenever bishops or prelates died, he kept their pos-

---

f. Philip's wife, Bertha, was the daughter of Count Florence of Holland and Gertrude of Saxony. Following the death of Florence, Gertrude had married Count Robert I "the Frisian" of Flanders (1071–93), the father of Count Robert II "the Jerusalemite" (1093–1111). Bertha was Robert II's uterine sister.

g. In 1092, after he had repudiated Bertha, the mother of Louis, King Philip I eloped with Bertrada of Montfort, the wife of Count Fulk IV of Anjou. See further endnote 9.

h. William Rufus was killed while hunting on August 2, 1100.

sessions for himself and squandered them, showing no respect. Several people claimed that the very noble Walter Tirel shot him with the arrow; but we have quite often heard Walter Tirel, when he had nothing to fear or gain, affirm on oath as if he were swearing on a holy relic, that he had not come into that part of the forest where the king was hunting on that day, and that he had never even seen the king in the forest.[11] How fitting it was that the great madness of so great a man was reduced to ashes by the divine power so suddenly, and that he who needlessly harassed others was even more endlessly harassed, and that he who coveted all was himself shamefully despoiled of all. Kingdoms and their laws are under the power of God, who loosens the sword belts of kings.[12]

William's very alert younger brother Henry succeeded him on the throne as quickly as he could, for the older brother Robert was busy on that grand expedition to the Holy Sepulcher.[i] Henry's valor of mind and body, as well as learning, was both amazing and worthy of praise, and would offer good material for writing. But this is not our purpose, for in our work we have proposed to entrust to history selected deeds of the French, not the English. However, it will sometimes be appropriate for us to examine briefly something only incidentally relevant to our theme, such as the affairs of the kingdom of the Lotharingians.

i. Robert's misfortune continued, for at the time when he could reasonably hold expectations of the throne he was still in the East. See further endnote 13.

[2]
How he prevented the noble
Burchard of Montmorency and his accomplices
from attacking St. Denis

In his youth the renowned Louis was so cheerful, pleasant, and friendly that some even thought him simple; but when he grew more mature he became a renowned and spirited defender of his father's kingdom.ᵃ He took care that the churches prospered and zealously sought peace for those who prayed, those who toiled, and the poor, which had not been done for a long while.[1]

At that time a controversy over some customary rights arose between Adam, the venerable abbot of St. Denis, and the noble Burchard, the lord of Montmorency.ᵇ This dispute boiled over into an irritating quarrel; all ties of homage were broken, and the former allies fought bitterly with weapons, warfare, and fires. But news of the conflict, when it reached him, bothered the lord Louis and made him angry. With no delay he summoned Burchard before his father's court at the castle of Poissy for judgment. However, when Burchard lost his case and refused to comply with the decision against him, he was not arrested there and then, for that is not the custom of the French.[2] He withdrew from court and quickly learned how much trouble and how

a. The next eleven chapters of Suger's text give an account of Louis's deeds as "king-designate" in the years before his father Philip's death in 1108. At some time between 1098 and 1100, Philip had formally associated Louis with him on the throne (see Luchaire, no. 8; Lewis, p. 51).

b. Montmorency, Seine-et-Oise, is a few miles north of St. Denis and about seven miles north of Paris. Significantly, Louis's first expedition outside the Vexin described in the *Deeds* was undertaken against an enemy of Suger's predecessor, Abbot Adam (1099–1122). It probably occured in 1101 (Luchaire, no. 16).

much misfortune the insolence of subjects deserves from his royal majesty. The renowned young man made war against him and the accomplices who joined him, namely Count Matthew of Beaumont and Drogo of Mouchy, valiant and warlike men. He laid waste the land of Burchard, overturning and tearing down all his enclosures and entrenchments except those of the castle. He wore him down with fire, famine, and sword. When those in the castle made equal efforts to fight back, he besieged it on all sides with his own French forces and the Flemings of his uncle Robert. With these and other bruising blows, the lord Louis bent the humiliated man to his will and pleasure and, taking compensation, pacified the quarrel that had caused the trouble.[3]

On another occasion, he responded to these and other wrongs, but especially those perpetrated against the church of Beauvais, when he maneuvered against Drogo of Mouchy and found him amid a large force of knights, archers, and crossbowmen. They had advanced only a short distance from their castle so that their retreat, if necessary, would be quite short.[c] Rushing upon him, the lord Louis allowed him no way to escape back into the fortress amid the crush of arms. His charge against the enemy carried him with them through the gate; and being a marvelous swordsman and brave champion, he kept striking and sustaining blows until he had made his way to the middle of the castle. He considered it would have been unworthy if anyone had ousted him or forced him to withdraw before he burned the entire place with its furnishings all the way up to the precinct of the tower. In his great heroic fervor he gave no thought to turning aside from the blazing fire, even though it was dangerous for him and his host, and made him very hoarse for a long time. Thus he humbled the man beneath the powerful arm of God, whose affair it was, and made Drogo subject to the dominion of his will like some bedridden patient.[4]

c. Mouchy-le-Châtel is about fifteen miles northwest of Beaumont in the French Vexin and about forty miles north of Paris.

How the lord Louis forced Count Matthew of Beaumont to restore the castle of Luzarches to Hugh of Clermont, after he himself had attacked the same castle with great force

Meanwhile, a long-standing grudge led Count Matthew of Beaumont to quarrel with Hugh of Clermont, a noble but inconstant and simple man whose daughter he had married. Matthew took full possession of the castle of Luzarches, half of which he held by reason of his marriage, and with arms and armed men attempted to fortify the tower in his own interest.ᵃ What could Hugh do but rush to the defender of the kingdom, throw himself at his feet, and pour forth his tears? He beseeched him to comply with the request of an old man and bring help to a person seriously wronged. "I would rather, most beloved lord," he said, "that you took possession of all my land, since I hold it of you, than that my dishonorable son-in-law get control over it.[1] Death would be better than dispossession by him." Struck by sorrow for a misfortune that would make one weep, the lord Louis extended his hand in alliance, promised to give aid, and sent away the man whom hope had made joyful; and this "hope did not disappoint him."[2]

In fact, messengers swiftly went forth from the court and summoned the count. They instructed him, by order of Hugh's defender, to restore in proper form what he had improperly despoiled; and, concerning his right, they set a day for him to plead his case at court. But when Matthew failed to appear, the defender quickly took his vengeance. He assembled a large host,

a. Luzarches, Seine-et-Oise, is about six miles southeast of Beaumont and about nineteen miles north of Paris. The events described in this chapter occurred in 1102 (Luchaire, no. 19).

moved swiftly against him, and attacked the castle of Luzarches, assailing it now with arms, now with fire. He took it by assault after a great struggle, fortified its keep with a guard of knights, and restored the fortress to Hugh as he had promised.

[4]
How, when he had besieged Chambly, another castle of the same Matthew, a sudden storm forced his host to flee, so that if Louis himself had not bravely fought back, the host would have nearly been destroyed; and how Matthew himself gave satisfaction to him with humility

In like manner he marshalled the host for action against Chambly, another castle held by the same count.[a] He pitched his tents and ordered that siege engines be brought into position; but things turned out very differently from what he had hoped. The very pleasant weather suddenly became unpleasant and stormy; and a huge downpour of rain, with terrifying flashes of lightning and thunder, threw the entire land into disorder during the night. The horses were knocked down and the host was so frightened that some of the men hardly hoped to survive.

In their state of unbearable fear some members of the host were getting ready at dawn for flight early in the morning. But while the defender of the kingdom was still asleep under his

a. Chambly, Oise, is about three miles northwest of Beaumont and about twenty-eight miles north of Paris. The siege of Chambly also occured in 1102 (Luchaire, no. 19).

pavilion, someone treacherously set fire to the tents. Since this was a signal to pull back, the host suddenly made haste to leave; but no one had taken precautions, and everything was in disarray. Thrown into terror by the unanticipated need to escape, everyone rushed together, each paying no heed to the others; and the lord himself was bewildered by their headlong dash and loud shouting. To find out what was happening, he jumped on his horse and hurried after the host, but his men were now spread about and could not be marshalled for action. What else could this renowned young man do but rush back into battle with the few men he could bring along? Putting himself up as a wall to protect those who were in flight ahead of him, he took and gave frequent blows; and this wall so protected those behind it that his men were able to withdraw in peace and safety. Many of them, however, were fleeing in small groups scattered far from him, and for this reason were seized by the enemy. The distinguished Hugh of Clermont was himself among those captured, along with Guy of Senlis, Herluin of Paris and very many common knights of undistinguished name from the host, as well as many foot soldiers.[1]

The lord Louis took this affront very badly, for he had never experienced or known this sort of setback before. On his return to Paris he felt an unusual passion welling up in him; and he did the customary thing for one his age who seeks to do worthy deeds. He stirred up his anger; and it stirred him into action. His desire to get swift revenge for the insult consumed him as he shrewdly and cautiously summoned men from all sides and tripled the size of his host. He frequently groaned and sighed that it would be better to die than suffer such shame. Count Matthew heard report of all this from friends; and this distinguished and courteous man could not bear this unintended affront to his lord. Using many mediators he made every effort to find a way for peace and, applying a great deal of charm and flattery, he worked to settle the young man down. He explained away the insult, plausibly enough, as one of those unfortunate but unintentional accidents that happen, and presented himself ready to give satisfaction as the lord Louis wished. And so the pleas of many men, the advice of intimate counsellors, and the repeated but belated request of his father calmed his fighting spirit. He spared the man who had repented, pardoned the affront, and restored the possessions that could be recovered after the count had returned them. He freed the captives and reinstated peace for Hugh of Clermont, handing back in firm peace what was his in the castle that had been seized earlier.

[5]
Ebles, count of Roucy

The very powerful and turbulent Baron Ebles of Roucy and his son Guichard were brutally attacking and robbing the noble church of Reims and its dependent churches of their possessions.[a] Ebles's great arrogance had even prompted him once to set out for Spain with a host of a size proper to kings alone.[b] And the more he roamed about with his host of knights, the more rabid and greedy he grew as he took his fill of pillage, plunder, and the pursuit of every wickedness.

A hundred complaints against this forceful and criminal man had been tearfully lodged with the lord king Philip, but the son heard only two or three before he angrily assembled a medium-

a. Roucy is on the river Aisne about twelve miles northwest of Reims; Louis will now be operating further from home, about one hundred miles northeast of Paris. See further endnote 1.

b. The second half of the eleventh century saw a good deal of French involvement in wars being waged against the Muslims in Spain. See further endnote 2.

sized host of about seven hundred knights, selected from the noble and powerful magnates of France, and hurried to Reims.[c] During two months of hard fighting he took revenge for the grievances suffered by the churches in the past. He ravaged the lands of the tyrant and his accomplices, destroyed them with fire, and laid them open for raids. What a splendid deed! The plunderers themselves were plundered and the torturers tortured with the same or even more pain than they had used to torture others. Indeed, the great fervor of the lord Louis and his host hardly allowed them to rest while on campaign except on Saturday and Sunday.[d] They were constantly taking up lances and swords to engage in combat, or they were busying themselves laying waste the lands of Ebles to avenge the wrongs done by him.

He campaigned there against Ebles and all the barons of those regions. They formed a distinguished host of many columns, which marriage alliances with the magnates of Lorraine had made possible. And while numerous attempts at peace were being made, this young lord found himself called away to other regions to address a variety of concerns and dangerous problems. So he took counsel with his advisors, ordered and obtained[4] peace for the churches from the tyrant, and made him affirm the accord on oath after he himself had taken hostages. Having welcomed and whipped Ebles in this way, he sent him away, putting off for another day his claims concerning Neufchâtel.[e]

c. "France" here refers to the Ile-de-France.

d. Under the guidance of the church, the great movement of the Truce of God had sought to prevent fighting on such days as Saturday and Sunday. But its provisions were frequently ignored, the Battle of Hastings, for example, being fought on a Saturday; and so Louis's conduct was commendable in Suger's eyes. See further endnote 3.

e. Neufchâtel-sur-Aisne is upstream from Roucy, about twelve miles north of Reims. Reading between the lines of this and the following chapters, it is clear that Louis was not doing particularly well in these encounters; and it may well be that he was coming off worse (Bur, p. 257).

[6]
The castle of Meung

And he won no less renown when he brought a force of knights to help the church of Orléans against Leo, a nobleman of the castle of Meung and vassal of the bishop of Orléans, who had taken away from that church the greater part of the same castle and lordship over another.[a] The lord Louis curbed him with his mighty hand and shut him up in the same castle with many others. When the castle had been lost, Leo took refuge in a church next to his own residence. Siege engines were set up, and he strove to defend himself. But, as the strong is always subdued by the stronger, he could not withstand the pressure of arms and fire directed against him. And he was not alone in paying the penalty of a long-standing excommunication when he and many others, about sixty, were engulfed by the flames. They tumbled down from the tower and became stuck on the points of the standing lances. With arrows flying into them, they breathed their last and carried off their miserable souls in sorrow to hell.[1]

a. Meung-sur-Loire is downstream about eight miles southwest of Orléans and about eighty miles south of Paris. This expedition probably occurred in 1103 (Luchaire, no. 25).

[7]
The castle of Montaigu

The very strong castle of Montaigu in the district of Laon came by reason of marriage into the possession of Thomas of Marle, the vilest of men and a plague to God and men alike.[a] All his neighbors in that region lived in terror of this unbearable madman who, like some monstrous wolf, had become fearless in his impregnable stronghold. The very man said to be his father, the venerable and honorable Enguerrand of Boves, made more effort than anyone to drive Thomas from his castle because of his seditious tyranny.[b] A group of men, namely the same Enguerrand, Ebles of Roucy, and all the others whom they could win over to their side, agreed to besiege the castle and Thomas in it. They enclosed him with a palisade made from stakes and interwoven branches, planning to force his surrender at some later time under the threat of starvation; if possible they would overthrow the castle and condemn him to imprisonment forever. But the wretch saw that there were still gaps in the palisade even though the siege towers had been firmly secured. So he slipped out under the cover of darkness, went immediately to the renowned youth, bribed his intimate counsellors with gifts and promises, and very swiftly gained the aid of knights to help him.

The young man assembled a host of seven hundred knights and hurriedly approached the district. His youth and compliant nature had led him to make this decision.[2]

a. Montaigu, Aisne, is about ten miles southeast of Laon and about 110 miles northeast of Paris. See further endnote 1.

b. It was doubtful whether Enguerrand was Thomas's father, because of the notorious infidelity of his wife Ada (see also Guibert, pp. 170, 184). Suger provides us with another example of bad relations between a father and a son. Boves is about five miles southeast of Amiens and about seventy-five miles north of Paris.

As he drew near Montaigu, the men besieging the castle sent messengers. They petitioned him as their lord-designate to spare them the shame of being forced to lift their siege. They argued that he should not lose the service of men like themselves for the sake of a reprobate and declared, truthfully enough, that he would suffer greater ruin than they if this vile man were left safe. But when flattery and threats could not sway him from his intention, the barons still hesitated to do battle with their lord-designate. Planning to renew their siege and return to war when he departed, they withdrew and put up with whatever he wished to do. With a powerful hand he tore down and dug up the entrenchments all around, set the castle of Montaigu free, and furnished it with a good supply of weapons and foodstuffs. In this way he showed his contempt for the sophistic arguments of the barons. But the magnates, who had withdrawn out of love and fear of him, grew angry when he spared nothing. Regretting their decision, they threatened on oath to honor him no longer; and when they saw him leaving, they moved camp, drew up their warriors in battlelines, and followed after him as if to engage in combat.

But one thing hindered their coming together in battle. A roaring stream, which had to be crossed slowly, lay between each side's lines and so prevented an encounter. They stared at each other for one day and then another as battle trumpets blared on each side and as "javelins menaced javelins."[3] Then suddenly a jongleur, an experienced knight, came before the French from the other side and convinced them that the magnates would join battle as soon as they found a suitable crossing.[c] They would take up lances and swords to avenge the affront they had suffered in defense of their liberty. They had let him go,

c. "French" seems to indicate nothing more than Louis's followers, as even its use restricted to his principality would also cover his opponents here.

he said, to fight for the one who had been his lord by virtue of birth. News of the impending battle now spread from tent to tent, and the knights grew bold and began to dance about. They adorned themselves with gleaming hauberks and helmets, encouraged each other in valor, and made ready to rush through the roaring stream if they had the luck to find a way to cross. They deemed it more honorable to charge against the foe than defend themselves.

Seeing this, the men of highest nobility, Enguerrand of Boves, Ebles of Roucy, Count Andrew of Ramerupt, Hugh the White of La Ferté, Robert of Cappy, and other wise and discerning men, came together for deliberation. They admired the valor of their lord-designate and chose to defer to him.[d] Coming to him in peace, they took into consideration his young age, extended their right hands in alliance, and pledged themselves and their men to his service. Not long afterward, in order that the defeat of wicked men be ascribed to the divine will, Thomas of Marle lost through an annulment both his castle and a marriage defiled by an incestuous relationship.

[8]
How Milo gained entrance into the castle of Montlhéry

Encounters like these helped the lord-designate grow more manly in his actions, and he made a valiant effort to provide wisely for the administration and government of the kingdom at

---

d. Andrew was the brother of Ebles, and Robert the brother of Enguerrand. The importance of family in the building up of such alliances is clear.

every available opportunity. He subdued the disobedient and either seized troublesome castles or made them submissive by any means possible.

For example, Guy Trousseau, son of that turbulent man and disturber of the kingdom Milo of Montlhéry, made his way home from the expedition to the Holy Sepulcher.[1] He had been broken by the stress of a long trip and the irritation that comes from various afflictions, and by guilt for his unusual behavior at Antioch when, in fear of Corbaran, he escaped over the wall and deserted God's host besieged within. Now wasting away and devoid of all bodily strength, he feared that his only daughter might be disinherited. So he met the wishes of the lord king Philip and his son Louis who greatly coveted his castle, and gave his daughter in marriage to Philip, the son of the king by his irregular union with the countess of Anjou.[2] And at his father's request the older brother, the lord Louis, confirmed Philip in possession of the castle of Mantes on the occasion of his marriage, in order to join him most firmly in his affection.[a]

When the castle of Montlhéry had come into their custody for this reason, they rejoiced as if they had plucked a mote from their eyes or had broken down barriers that had enclosed them. Indeed, we heard the father tell his son Louis that he had been heavily burdened to the point of exhaustion by that place. He said, "Beware, my son, keep watch and guard that tower; the distress I have suffered from it has nearly made an old man out of me. Its plots and vile treachery have never allowed me good peace and quiet."

Its bad faith made loyal men disloyal, and disloyal men treacherous. It coupled together faithless men from far and near, and nothing evil was done in the entire kingdom without their con-

---

a. Mantes, Seine-et-Oise, is on the Seine about thirty-five miles northwest of Paris, on the southern boundary of the French Vexin. See further endnote 3.

sent or assistance. For, Corbeil on the river Seine, Châteaufort on the right, and Montlhéry on the road midway between them encircle the countryside around Paris.[b] And the chaos and confusion that took hold between Paris and Orléans had made it impossible for the inhabitants of either city to travel to the other without the permission of those faithless men, unless they went under strong guard.[c] But the aforesaid marriage broke down this barrier and restored welcome access to each for both groups.[4]

In addition, Count Guy of Rochefort, a man of experience and a veteran knight, the paternal uncle of Guy Trousseau, had returned from the expedition to Jerusalem renowned and rich.[5] He gladly bound himself to King Philip, for they were old friends and Guy had formerly been his seneschal. So the king himself and his son, the lord Louis, again appointed him seneschal for administering the realm. They wished to take calm possession thereafter of the castle of Montlhéry and lawfully demand peace and service from the county that adjoined theirs, namely from the castles of Rochefort, Châteaufort, and others nearby, which had not been a customary thing.[d] Their friendship with Guy continued to grow, and the father soon persuaded the son, the lord Louis, to take the daughter of the count in solemn marriage, even though she was not yet of an age to wed. But although he took her as his betrothed, he never had her as his wife; and some years later the marriage was dissolved on grounds of consanguinity before it had been consummated.[6] The alliance continued for three years, and both father and son had the utmost faith in

b. Montlhéry, Seine-et-Oise, is about fifteen miles south of Paris on the road to Orléans. Corbeil, Seine-et-Oise, is some ten miles southeast of Montlhéry while Châteaufort, Seine-et-Oise, is about the same distance to the northwest.

c. A startling illustration of the weakness of the French monarchy in the period.

d. Rochefort and Châteaufort are about twenty-five and twelve miles southwest of Paris respectively.

Count Guy, who, together with his son Hugh of Crécy, did all he could for the defense and honor of the kingdom.

But "a jar will long preserve the odor of what filled it when it was new."[7] So the men of Montlhéry, seeking to live up to their usual treachery, hatched a plot with the Garlande brothers who had at that time run afoul of the king and his son. Accordingly, Viscount Milo of Troyes, the younger brother of Guy Trousseau, arrived there in the company of his mother the viscountess and a large band of knights, and they were let into the castle by all those who had perjured their oath.[e] Milo then tearfully recalled the many benefits given them by his father, extolled their noble hereditary service, and praised their wonderful fealty. He thanked them for reinstating him, fell down at their knees, and humbly pleaded with them to finish well what they had well begun. Being bent by such a plaintive bending of the knees, they rushed to arms, hurried to the tower, and engaged its defenders in very bitter battle with swords, lances, fire, stakes, and stones. They hoped to pierce the outer rampart of the tower in many places and inflict deadly wounds on many of its defenders.

Present in that very tower were the wife of Guy and his daughter, who was betrothed to the lord Louis. Being a singularly brave man, the seneschal started out promptly when he heard what was happening, and boldly approached the castle with as many knights as he had at hand. He had already swiftly dispatched messengers to gather up others quickly from all sides. The enemy saw him coming from the top of the hill where they were attacking the tower, and they grew afraid that the sudden arrival of the lord Louis would mean the noose for them, for they had not yet conquered the stronghold. So they pulled back and wavered between making a stand and taking off in flight. But Guy was a bold-spirited man who knew what to do in a tight spot.

e. The following events seem to have occurred in 1105 (Luchaire, no. 34). See further endnote 8.

Taking counsel, he summoned the Garlandes from the castle and swore on oath that they would have peace and favor with the king and the lord Louis; and in this way he turned them and their accomplices from their undertaking. After their defection, Milo himself defected and, his plot undone, fled swiftly weeping and wailing.

At this news the lord Louis rushed to the castle. Having gained a true report of the events, he rejoiced that he had lost nothing, but he regretted not finding any seditious men to fix to a gibbet. He kept peace with those still there because of the oath which Guy had given; but to keep them from undertaking anything similar in the future, he tore down all the defenses of the castle except the tower.

[9]
Bohemond, prince of Antioch

About that time Bohemond, the famous prince of Antioch, came down to the regions of the Gauls.[a] As the great siege of that city ended, the garrison there admired his valor and chose to surrender to him alone. He had won fame and renown among the people of the East, and the Saracens themselves praised his noble deeds, which could never have been done without the help of God.

In addition, Bohemond and his father, Robert Guiscard, had besieged the fortress of Durazzo on the other side of the sea. The riches of Thessalonica, the treasures of Constantinople, and the

a. One of the heroes of the First Crusade, Bohemond had become prince of Antioch following its capture in 1098. See further endnote 1.

whole of Greece itself had not been enough to ward them off.[b] But suddenly, legates of the lord pope Alexander crossed the sea after them, stood in their presence, and summoned them to return to Italy out of love of God and in fulfillment of their sworn ties of homage. They pleaded with them to rescue the Roman church and the lord pope who had been confined in the tower of Crescentius by the emperor; and they swore on oath that the City and the church, indeed the lord pope himself, would be ruined if they did not bring aid quickly.[c]

The princes hesitated over what to do. Should they abandon a great and costly expedition without hope of recovering their losses? Or should they allow the lord pope, the City and the church to be cast into slavery, or rather destroyed? They had anxious moments of discussion but made an excellent choice, deciding to do the one without abandoning the other. Leaving Bohemond behind at the siege, the father crossed the sea and returned to Apulia.[4] He gathered together warriors and weapons from wherever he could, from Sicily, Apulia, Calabria, and Campania. With great speed and great daring he hurried to Rome; and the way things turned out seemed to be an amazing portent of the divine will. The emperor of Constantinople had heard that Robert had departed for Rome; so he united his army of Greeks and brought them up on land and sea to assault Bohemond at Durazzo. Then, on one and the same day, Guiscard the father joined in battle with the emperor at Rome, and Bohemond fought valiantly against the emperor of the Greeks. Marvellous

b. Across the Adriatic Sea from Italy stood Dyrrachium, the modern Durazzo, at the end of the classical Via Egnatia, which proceeded east to Constantinople. Robert Guiscard, duke of Apulia, besieged it in the company of his son Bohemond in the summer of 1081. "Greece" here refers to the Byzantine empire. See further endnote 2.

c. The tower of Crescentius is the classical mausoleum of Hadrian, now known as the Castel San' Angelo; the Crescenti had been an important Roman family. See further endnote 3.

to say, each prince triumphed while each emperor suffered defeat.[5]

Bohemond had come into these regions seeking a way to marry the very noble Constance, the sister of the lord-designate Louis, who was courteous in her manners, charming in character, and beautiful in appearance.[6] The threat of this union frightened even the Saracens themselves, for the great valor of the kingdom of the French and of the lord Louis was well known abroad. The noble lady was free; but having put aside Count Hugh of Troyes, she was not seeking another marriage with someone unworthy of her.[7] However, the prince of Antioch was a man of experience whose lavish gifts and promises showed that he perhaps fully deserved to be united to that noble lady. So, a grand wedding was celebrated at Chartres in the presence of the king and the lord Louis, with many archbishops, bishops, and magnates of the kingdom in attendance.[d]

Among those present was the legate of the apostolic Roman see, the lord Bruno, bishop of Segni. The lord pope Paschal had sent him in the company of the lord Bohemond to summon and urge people to make an expedition to the Holy Sepulcher. For this reason the legate held a solemn plenary council at Poitiers; and, having just returned from our studies, we were able to attend it.[e] He conducted the varied business of the synod but especially made sure that zeal for the journey to Jerusalem not grow lukewarm, for both he and Bohemond aroused many of those present to make it.[8] Then, supported by a large company of these people and a large force of knights, the lord Bohemond, the lady Constance and the legate himself returned home with success and glory.[f] The lady Constance bore to the lord Bohe-

d. The wedding took place after Easter in 1106 (OV 4:213).

e. Here, as elsewhere, Suger introduces matters of which he has personal knowledge, not strictly relevant to his theme.

f. By "home" we are to understand Bohemond's possessions in southern Italy, not the crusader territories in the East. See further endnote 9.

mond two sons, John and Bohemond. John died in Apulia before
the age of knighthood; but Bohemond, a handsome youth well
suited to be a knight, became the prince of Antioch. He once
pressed too vehemently against the Saracens in battle and,
thinking little of their eagerness to fight, chased after them with
too little caution. Because of his reckless courage he was caught
in an ambush, and had the misfortune to be beheaded along with
one hundred of his knights. He lost Antioch and his life, along
with Apulia.g

[10]

The arrival of Pope Paschal in France, his quarrel over investitures with the emperor, Henry, and his arrest at Rome by the emperora

During the year after Bohemond returned home, the universal
and supreme pontiff Paschal, of venerable memory, approached
the western regions with a large number of very wise men,
bishops, cardinals and a company of Roman nobles.[1] He wished
to confer with the king of the French and his son, the king-
designate Louis, and with the Gallic church about the recent
quarrels over ecclesiastical investiture and several other problems. The emperor Henry was making trouble for the pope over

g. Bohemond's son Bohemond arrived in the East in 1126, and was killed
in battle in 1130.

a. A title for this chapter is missing in the manuscripts, so we have
supplied one. Pope Paschal II arrived in France in early 1107.

these issues and was threatening to trouble him even more. Lacking all human feeling or any affection for his parent, the emperor had cruelly persecuted his own father, Henry, and had despoiled him of his hereditary rights. There were reports that he confined his parent in a miserable prison and shamefully forced him, by means of wrongs and blows inflicted by enemies, to surrender the royal insignia, namely the crown, scepter, and the lance of St. Maurice.[b] He left him in possession of nothing in the entire kingdom as his own.

Since the treachery of the Roman people could be bought, these matters and all others besides would be settled more safely with the help of the king, the king's son, and the Gallic church, in France rather than in the City.[3] So the pope came to Cluny, and from Cluny he went to La Charité, where he performed the sacred ceremony of dedication for that noble monastery amid a large gathering of archbishops, bishops, and men of the monastic order.[c] The noblest magnates of the kingdom were present, and among them was the seneschal of the king of France, the noble count of Rochefort, who had been sent to meet the lord pope. It would be the count's task to serve the pleasure of the pope throughout the kingdom in recognition of his office of spiritual father. Being present at that consecration ourselves, we stood manfully in the sight of the lord pope and with clear evidence and in conformity to canon law won our case against the lord Galo, bishop of Paris, who was harassing the church of St. Denis with many complaints.[4]

Wearing the Phrygian mitre, as is the Roman custom, the pope celebrated *Letare Jerusalem* in the church of St. Martin of Tours, and then arrived with friendship and devotion at the venerable

b. St. Maurice is believed to have been a soldier who became a martyr in Gaul in the third century. See further endnote 2.

c. La Charité-sur-Loire, Niève, is downstream about fifteen miles north of Nevers and about thirty miles east of Bourges.

abbey of the blessed Dionysius as if the place were his very own see of the blessed Peter.[d] He received a splendid welcome worthy of a bishop, and he left to posterity a notable model of behavior, something to which the Romans were unaccustomed. Not only did he make no attempt to carry off the gold, silver, and precious pearls of the monastery as people greatly feared he would, but he did not even deign to look upon them. Having prostrated himself before the relics of the saints, he offered tears of remorse and presented himself with his whole heart as a burnt offering to the Lord and his saints.[6] As a suppliant he prayed that a small portion of the episcopal vestments soaked with the blood of the blessed Dionysius be given him for his protection, saying, "May it not displease you to return only a small part of his vestments to us who, without a murmur, sent that distinguished person to you as the apostle of Gaul."[7]

King Philip and his son the lord Louis came there with joy to meet him as they had promised. For the love of God they humbled their royal majesty before his feet, in the way that kings bow down with lowered diadem before the tomb of the fisherman Peter. The lord pope lifted them up and made them sit before him like devout sons of the apostles. In the manner of a wise man acting wisely, he conferred with them privately on the present condition of the church. Softening them with compliments, he petitioned them to bring aid to the blessed Peter and to himself, his vicar, and to lend support to the church. He asked that they follow the established custom of their predecessors, Charles the Great and other kings of the French, and make a bold stand against tyrants, enemies of the church, and above all the emperor Henry. They extended their right hands to him as a sign of alliance, aid, and counsel, and put the kingdom at his dis-

d. The Phyrgian mitre is special papal headgear. *Letare Jerusalem* ("Rejoice Jerusalem") is the beginning of the introit of the mass for the fourth Sunday in Lent. See further endnote 5.

posal.[8] They then joined company with archbishops, bishops, and Abbot Adam of St. Denis, whom we also accompanied, and travelled swiftly to Châlons to meet the legates of the emperor.

The lord pope had been lingering there for some time before the legates of the emperor Henry lived up to the agreement and arrived; but far from being humble, they showed themselves unyielding and stubborn. The chancellor Adalbert, whose word and spirit the emperor himself closely followed, stayed behind in their lodging at Saint-Menge while the others put on their finest garments and came to the papal court in a pompous throng.[e] Making up this crowd were the archbishop of Trèves, the bishop of Halberstadt, the bishop of Münster, very many counts and Duke Welf, a corpulent man who was remarkably tall and round. Being a continual brawler, he had his sword carried before him everywhere he went. These legates created quite a disturbance and seemed to have been sent more to terrify than to conduct rational discourse.[10]

The archbishop of Trèves, a distinguished, wise, cheerful, and eloquent man who knew French well, stood alone and apart from the others and delivered an elegant speech. He brought to the lord pope and his court greetings and service on the part of the lord emperor, saving the right of his realm; and then, proceeding to his commission, he said: "Our lord the emperor sent us for the following reason. During the time of our predecessors[f] and holy popes such as Gregory the Great and others, the empire had a recognized right that the following order be observed in every election. Before carrying out the election in public, the name of the candidate would be communicated to the lord emperor; and if the person were fitting, he gained his assent before

e. St. Menge is St. Memmie, a few miles east of Châlons in central eastern France. See further endnote 9.

f. The archbishop is speaking in Henry's name, so the predecessors were earlier emperors. See further endnote 11.

the actual election. Thereafter, in a general assembly and in accordance with the canons, the procedure continued at the petition of the people, with the election of the clergy and the assent of the lord. Then, freely and without simony, the one who had been consecrated returned to the lord emperor for the regalia, to be invested with ring and staff, to pledge his fealty and perform his homage. No one questioned this procedure, for in no other way could the elected person hold the cities, castles, marches, tolls, and every other thing belonging to the imperial dignity. If the lord pope would support these procedures, the kingdom and the church would be joined together in good fortune and good peace to the honor of God."

The lord pope consulted his advisers and responded through the voice of his spokesman the bishop of Piacenza:[g] "The church has been redeemed and set free by the precious blood of Jesus Christ; it is by no means proper for it to be enslaved a second time. If the church were not able to elect a prelate without consulting the emperor, it would be subject to him as a slave, and Christ's death brought to nothing. Investiture with the staff and ring, things that pertain to the altar, is a usurpation of God's own rights. If hands made holy by the body and blood of the Lord are placed in homage beneath a laymen's hands which reek with blood from a sword, then the holy orders and sacred anointing are degraded."

When those stiff-necked legates heard these and like things, they gnashed their teeth violently as Germans do, and went on a rampage. If it had been safe for them to have risked it, they would have belched forth vile abuse and assaulted those present. "This quarrel will be ended," they said, "not here but at Rome, with swords." But the pope sent a large number of reliable and experienced men to the imperial chancellor to meet in an orderly and calm manner with him about these affairs. They were

g. Aldo Gabrielli, bishop of Piacenza (1096–1118).

to speak with him and listen to him but strenuously insist that he work for the peace of the kingdom. After their departure, the lord pope came to Troyes and held a solemn universal council whose members had been summoned a long time before. Then, with love for the French who had done him great service, and with fear and loathing for the Germans, he returned home with success to the see of the blessed Peter.[12]

But some two years after the lord pope's return, the emperor assembled an astonishing host of 30,000 knights; and "finding no path pleasant to take unless covered with blood," he headed for Rome.[h] In an amazingly skillful way he feigned peace, laid aside the quarrel over investitures, and promised a good outcome for these and other disputes. He then entered the city by doing the only thing he could. He resorted to flattery and did not hesitate to deceive the supreme pontiff, the whole church, and even the King of kings himself. When the Roman citizens heard that this issue, so great and so dangerous for the church, had been laid to rest, they were overjoyed even more than they should have been. The clergy too were full of glee and, in their delight, argued about the best way to welcome the emperor with proper honor and high distinction.

Meanwhile, the lord pope found himself amid a tight throng of bishops and cardinals. Wearing fine capes, they rode horses draped with white cloths and hastened to meet the emperor, and the Roman people were trailing behind. The pope had already sent ahead envoys who received the emperor's oath, taken on the most holy Gospels, that he would preserve the peace and put aside the quarrel over investitures. That pledge was given a second time in the place called Mount of Joy,[i] where pilgrims

---

h. The emperor Henry V crossed the Alps into Italy in August 1110. See further endnote 13.

i. *Mons Gaudii,* so called because of the circumstance Suger relates. Generally known as Monte Mario, it is just to the north of the Vatican. See further endnote 14.

arriving at Rome first encounter the sight of the church of the blessed apostles. And the Romans enjoyed a wonderful scene when the emperor himself and his magnates extended their hands and swore it a third time on the very porch of the church.

There next took place a ceremony more splendid by far than if someone were being graced by a triumphal arch after winning a victory in Africa.[15] The most holy hands of the lord pope placed the imperial diadem on the emperor's head in the style of the Augusti amid triumphal hymns of praise. And with a large crowd devoutly looking on, the emperor was led with great solemnity to the most holy altar of the apostles while the clergy sang hymns before him and the Germans shouted out frightening chants that pierced the heavens. Then, saying a mass of thanksgiving, the lord pope consecrated the body and blood of Jesus Christ, and the emperor partook of the Eucharist, which they divided between themselves. In this way he solemnly pledged to the church a wonderful guarantee that they would be joined in undivided love and that the agreement would be kept.

But before the lord pope had even put aside his episcopal vestments after mass, the mad Germans[16] invented a pretext for a quarrel, gnashed their teeth in fury, and began to rage out of control. Their treachery caught everyone by surprise. With drawn swords they rushed about like men who were out of their minds and attacked the Romans who, properly in such a place, were not armed. The Germans shouted threats that all the Roman clergy, bishops as well as cardinals, would be seized or slaughtered; and going even beyond the limits of insanity, they did not fear to lay their wicked hands on the lord pope himself. The Roman nobles and people mourned with unspeakable distress and deep sorrow of heart. Only at this late stage did they become aware of the plot. Some rushed to arms while others fled like fools and were surprised by an attack from their foes. They found their only escape behind wooden beams torn down from the portico, and its ruin became their defense. Tormented by the bad conscience that comes with a criminal act, the emperor found himself terribly disturbed and departed from the City as quickly as possible. But a Christian took away as prey that which no Christian had ever before been heard to take, namely the lord pope and as many cardinals and bishops as he could. He took up residence at Città Castellana, a place well fortified by nature and human skill.[j] He treated the cardinals vilely as he shamefully disrobed them; and, something horrible to say, he rudely stripped even the lord pope himself of his pluvial and mitre. He carried away whatever insignia of the apostolic office he could and did not hesitate to lay hands on the anointed of the Lord.[17] He abused and shamed his prisoners greatly, and refused to release the clergy or the pope until he had forced him to annul the pact and return the privilege that had been granted. He also extorted another privilege, which he stole from the hand of the lord pope: that he might continue to perform investitures. But we heard the same lord pope in a grand council of three hundred or more bishops invalidate that privilege by judgment of the church and render it null and void by his eternal anathema.[18]

But if someone should ask why the lord pope acted so half-heartedly, he should know that the church was growing listless. Its shepherd and his associates had been beaten down, and a tyrant nearly enslaved and made her his own property, for no one would resist him. The pope's actions were sure proof of this. He took the steps necessary to secure the release of his brothers, the pillars of the church, for the church's protection and renewal. He also restored peace of some kind or other to it, but he then took refuge in a secluded desert and would have stayed there forever if the outrage of the whole church and the Romans had not forced him to return.[19]

But the lord Jesus Christ, the redeemer and defender of his church, did not allow her to be trampled under foot any longer.

j. Città Castellana is about twenty-five miles north of Rome.

Nor did he permit the emperor to go unpunished, for even those who were not bound or obliged by fealty to do so took up the cause of the storm-tossed church. With the help and counsel of the lord-designate Louis, the Gallic church came together in a well-attended council and bound the tyrannical emperor with anathema, running him through with the sword of the blessed Peter.[20] Then, devoting their attention to the German realm, they stirred up the magnates and the greatest part of the kingdom against him and deposed his accomplices, including Burchard the Red, the bishop of Münster.[21] They did not stop harassing him or seizing his possessions until his vile life and tyrannical regime were suitably extinguished; and his evil deeds received their just reward when God took his revenge and transferred the imperial rule. Duke Lothar of Saxony, a warlike man and a heroic defender of the state, succeeded to the throne on the emperor's death.[k] Campaigning with the lord pope Innocent, he subdued and plundered disobedient Italy, Campania, and Apulia up to the Adriatic Sea, right before the eyes of Count Roger of Sicily, because he had made himself king. But when he was returning home in triumph and victory, the victor himself succumbed to death.[23]

But we shall let their writers record these events and others like them. Let us now turn our pen back to describing the deeds of the French as we intended.[l]

k. Henry V died in 1125. See further endnote 22.

l. The greater part of this chapter seems irrelevant to a book on the deeds of Louis, and judging by its concluding sentence Suger was aware of this.

The capture of the castle of Gournay

Count Guy of Rochefort allowed hard feelings to inflame his mind, and he now "fanned a tiny spark into a roaring fire."[1] After jealous men set their schemes into motion, the marriage between the lord-designate and the count's daughter was dissolved by annulment in the very presence of the lord pope on the grounds of consanguinity.[2]

But the lord-designate continued to hold the count in the same high regard until suddenly the Garlandes mixed themselves up in the affair. They tore apart the friendship, broke up the alliance, and heightened the ill will. And the lord-designate found a reason for making war when Hugh of Pomponne, a valiant knight who was castellan of Gournay, startled some merchants on the royal highway, stole their horses, and led them off to his castle on the banks of the river Marne.[a] Almost beside himself at this rash insult, Louis assembled the host and suddenly besieged the castle, surrounding it swiftly to cut off its defenders from a good supply of foodstuffs.

Close to the castle lies a charming little island where a fair number of horses and cattle graze in pleasant pasturage. Its moderate width and greater length are particularly helpful to the men of the garrison. Its flowing waters put radiant smiles on their faces as they stroll about, and its meadows, sometimes flower covered, sometimes green, present their eyes with a delightful and brilliant sight. The river itself, which flows around the island, provides them with a safe place to live. The lord Louis

---

a. Gournay-sur-Marne (Seine-et-Oise) and Pomponne (Seine-et-Marne) are both on the Marne, about ten and fifteen miles east of Paris respectively. Hugh of Pomponne is the same person as Hugh of Crécy, the son of Guy of Rochefort, already introduced by Suger (above, cap. 8). See further endnote 3.

therefore assembled a flotilla and swiftly launched his attack. He made some of his knights and many foot soldiers strip down so that they could enter the water freely and spring up quickly should they happen to sink. Boldly entering the river himself, he ordered his men to seize the island, instructing some to swim and others to ride across as best they could, even though the deep waters made this dangerous. The men of the garrison fought back bravely; and being higher up on a steep bank, they hurled down rocks, lances, and even stakes as they forcibly drove back those who were beneath them in the boats amid the waves. The attackers were just driven back, but they regained their fighting spirit and strove to drive back those who had driven them back. They forced the crossbowmen and archers to stop firing and fought hand-to-hand when they could engage the enemy. Wearing hauberks and helmets and fighting daringly like pirates, the men in the flotilla joined battle and drove back the very men who had earlier been driving them back. And as the valorous do not allow themselves to be shamed, they captured and took control of the island by armed might, forcing the defenders to withdraw under duress into the castle.

But the lord Louis, when he could not quickly force those caught in his tight siege to surrender, grew tired of delay. So one day, carried away by fervor, he assembled the host and attacked the castle which, being well fortified with a stout rampart, was nearly impregnable, with its oak wall on top and the deep roaring stream below. He climbed up through the noisy river to the palisade beyond the moat, made his way to the oak wall and, commanding his men to fight by fighting himself, engaged the enemy in serious and bitter battle. On the other side, the defenders found boldness preferable to life and quickly strove to protect themselves, not even sparing their lord. They met his attack with force, drove back their foes, and regained the higher and even the lower bank by hurling their assailants into the water. Thus in turn, some gained glory while others unwillingly went down to defeat.

One after another, engines of war were made ready for the overthrow of the stronghold. A lofty machine towering three stories high over the combatants was raised up, and its elevation above the castle prevented the enemy archers and crossbowmen of the front line on the inside from moving about or even being seen. This tight confinement, without relief day or night, made it impossible for them to maintain their positions. Wisely seeking shelter in holes in the ground, they found protection for themselves and set ambushes from which their archers could fire. They were awaiting a deadly attack from the combatants on the top story of the engine. A wooden bridge was attached to the towering machine; it reached out at a height that would enable it to be let down a little above the oak wall and thus provide easy entry into the castle for those coming across it.[4] But men experienced in these matters stuck out various wooden staves to tumble the bridge and those on it down into ditches planted with sharp stakes cleverly hidden with straw. The men attacking from the engine would have to risk their lives and sustain many deaths.

Meanwhile, Guy of Rochefort, an experienced and valiant warrior, stirred his relatives and friends into action, petitioned and rallied the lords, and sped relief to the besieged. He negotiated with the palatine count Theobald, a most distinguished young man well versed in the pursuits of the knightly order, and set a date for him to bring force and break the siege of the castle quickly, for the besieged were running out of foodstuffs.[b] At the same time Guy himself took pains to lift the blockade by raiding and burning.

Then, on the day they had chosen for Count Theobald to bring help and lift the siege with his band of knights, the lord-designate, calling upon no one from afar, assembled as large a host as he could from those at hand. Mindful of the high station

b. Count Theobald of Blois and Brie and, from 1125, of Champagne, was Louis's chief enemy among the aristocracy. See further endnote 5.

of a king and of the honor paid to the valiant, he left his tents and camp guards, and went out onto the field in a happy mood. Having already sent ahead someone to report when the enemy was approaching or wished to do battle, he assembled his barons, put his knights and foot soldiers into fighting formations, and separated his bowmen and spearmen into their positions. Sounding the bugles to make themselves noticed, they aroused the fervor of the horses and horsemen, and battle was very swiftly joined. Well trained from continual fighting, the French attacked and slaughtered the men of Brie who had grown soft from long peace.[6] Striving for victory, they struck them down with lances and swords; the knights and foot soldiers did not stop their valiant attacks until the enemy turned their backs and sought safety in flight. To avoid capture, the count himself preferred to be found among the first rather than the last to flee. He abandoned his host and hurried back home.[c]

Some were killed, many were wounded, and a great number captured in this engagement, and so the fame and renown of the victory spread throughout the lands. Having gained a timely and mighty triumph, the lord Louis headed back to his tents. He banished the men of the garrison, who had been deceived by vain hope, and kept the castle for himself, entrusting it to the care of the Garlandes.[d]

c. Count Theobald here flees, just as in a later encounter he will abandon his allies (below, cap. 21). Suger takes delight in implying that he was a coward.

d. The handing over of Gournay to the Garlandes indicates their rise to favor. The siege occurred in 1107; Guy of Rochefort died in 1108.

[12]
The capture of the castle of Sainte-Sévère

Laziness, the companion of idleness, makes noble men lose their nobility and glorious men their glory. It plunges them into the depths. But valor of spirit stimulated by strenuous bodily effort gives noble men more nobility and glorious men more glory. It lifts them up to the heights and awards them the chance to do splendid deeds, in which their valor takes delight and finds pleasure, everywhere in the land.

There came before the lord Louis petitioners who, promising him many services that would cost them dearly, sought to prevail upon him to cross over into Berry, into that part lying next to the boundary of the Limousin, namely to the castle of Sainte-Sévère.[a] The castle had been rendered very noble and famous by the knights who held it by hereditary right, and by its large garrison of foot soldiers. The petitioners asked that he force its lord, the noble Humbald, to give good justice or, in accordance with the Salic law, make him justly forfeit his castle for his lack of justice.[b]

Having been asked, he entered those districts, without a host but with a band of household knights.[c] And while the lord Louis was hurrying toward the fortress, the castellan went out to encounter him with a large company of knights, for he was high-

a. This is the modern Sainte-Sévère-sur-Indre, about fifty miles southwest of Bourges in south-central France. The events described in this chapter occurred in June/July 1108 (Luchaire, no. 55).

b. The Salic law was the law of the old Salian Franks, but here it merely has the sense of old law. The Humbald in question seems to have been a former bishop of Limoges (1087–95).

c. On this occasion Louis rode out with some members of his household, presumably unmarried knights eager for battle. Suger refers to such people a number of times.

born by blood and a free-handed man who took precautions. Taking up a position behind a stream filled with logs and other snags, he awaited the French forces along the only road by which they could come. Each side paused there with the stream in the middle, but the lord Louis became angry when he saw one of the enemy who took more risks than the others break through the obstacles. Having greater courage than his followers, the lord Louis spurred his horse on, leapt to the attack, and struck his foe with his lance. With one blow he knocked him into another man behind him and brought them both down. Thus, although it little befitted a king to do such a thing, he arranged a splendid bath for his foe all the way up to his helmet in that stream. He did not delay to follow up his successes, but entered the narrow space from which the other had come out and, fighting like a champion in single combat, kept on pushing back the enemy. When the French saw this, they found amazing courage. They broke through the obstacles, rushed across the stream, and began to slaughter their foes, pursuing and driving them under duress all the way back to the castle.

The quickly spreading news stunned the men of the garrison and the whole neighborhood. They knew that the lord Louis and his men were very bold knights who would not see fit to withdraw until they had destroyed the castle down to its foundations; and they would either fix its noble men to a gibbet or rip out their eyes. So, after some discussion, the lord of the castle promptly surrendered to his royal majesty and placed the fortress and his land under the king's authority. And on his return the lord Louis took the lord of the castle as a hostage and, leaving him behind at Etampes, came back home to Paris with a quick victory and a happy outcome.

[13]
The death of King Philip

Meanwhile, as the son made headway from day to day, his father, King Philip, was from day to day losing ground. After his irregular union with the countess of Anjou he did nothing worthy of the royal majesty, for he was carried away by lust for the married woman he had carried off and gave himself over to gratifying his desires. He indulged himself too much and did not take care of either his kingdom or the health of his noble and handsome body. The condition of the realm prospered only because others both feared and loved his son and successor. Finally, when he was nearly sixty years old, he put aside his kingship and brought his last day to a close at the castle of Melun on the river Seine, with the lord Louis at his side.[a]

Many revered men took part in his stately funeral, namely Bishop Galo of Paris, the bishops of Senlis and Orléans, Abbot Adam of St. Denis of good memory, and very many monastic clergy.[2] They carried the noble body of his royal majesty to the church of the blessed Mary and spent the night celebrating his solemn funeral rites. On the following morning the son placed the bier on the shoulders of his chief servitors; silk coverings and all other funeral accoutrements properly adorned it. He then wept with appropriate filial affection and did all he could to help, as, sometimes walking, sometimes riding, he accompanied the barons whom he had with him. Once again he displayed his wonderful nobility of spirit; for, despite the repudiation of his mother and the irregular union with the Angevin woman, he

a. One wonders whether the negative portrayal of Philip in this paragraph has been heightened to make the contrast with Louis more effective. Melun is upstream on the Seine about twenty-eight miles southeast of Paris. See further endnote 1.

had taken care never to displease his father in any way while he lived. Nor had he upset his father's lordship over the kingdom by any sort of plot, as other young men customarily do.

They carried the body in a grand procession to the noble monastery of the blessed Benedict on the river Loire, for King Philip had expressed a strong desire to be buried there.[b] Some people said they had heard him explain his decision to be separated from the burial place of the kings, his forefathers, who are buried as if by natural right in the church of the blessed Dionysius. He felt that he had been less benevolent than his predecessors toward that church, and that no one would consider his tomb important among so many noble kings.[3] So they placed him as properly as they could before the altar of the same monastery, commended his soul to the Lord with hymns and prayers, and covered his body with decorative stones.[4]

[14]
His accession to the kingship

In his youth Louis had merited the friendship of the church by his generous defense of it, for he had taken up the cause of the poor and orphans, and had subdued tyrants with powerful force.[a]

b. The abbey of St. Benedict at Fleury, which is upstream on the river Loire about twenty miles east of Orléans, was a house with some royal traditions, for it was there that Helgaud had written his account of King Robert (996–1031). The abbey claimed to possess the relics of its patron.

a. At this important point in his narrative Suger pauses to restate what is by now a familiar theme, a variant of which occurs at the beginning of the next chapter. He is a firm believer in repetition.

With God assenting, the agreement of good men now summoned him to the highest dignity of the kingdom, just as a conspiracy of wicked and evil men would have excluded him from it had it been possible.[b]

During the discussion that was held, the venerable and most wise Ivo, bishop of Chartres, was the main person to urge that they meet without delay at Orléans and quickly accomplish his elevation to the throne in order to foil the schemes of those evil men.[2] And so Archbishop Daimbert of Sens came to Orléans. He had been invited along with his suffragans, namely Bishops Galo of Paris, Manasses of Meaux, John of Orléans, Ivo of Chartres, Hugh of Nevers, and the bishop of Auxerre.[3] And on the day of the discovery of the relics of the holy protomartyr Stephen, he anointed him with the oil of the most sacred unction and said the mass of thanksgiving.[c] He took from him the sword of secular knighthood, girded him with the ecclesiastical sword for the punishment of evildoers, and joyfully crowned him with the diadem of the kingdom. With the approval of the clergy and the people, he devoutly handed him, along with the other royal insignia, the scepter and the rod that symbolize the defense of the churches and the poor.

The archbishop then had no time even to take off his festive clothing after divine service when bearers of bad news from the church of Reims suddenly came before him. They brought letters of objection which, if they had arrived in time, would have prevented the royal anointing under the force of apostolic authority. The letters alleged that the first stages in the crowning

b. The "evil men" were almost certainly a group around Philip, the older of Louis's half-brothers, and his stepmother, Bertrada of Montfort. See further endnote 1.

c. Since Louis was anointed and crowned on August 3, 1108, the feast of the discovery of the relics of St. Stephen, and Philip had died on July 29, one gets a picture of great speed.

of a king belonged by right to the church of Reims, and that this prerogative had stood unimpaired and undisturbed from the time of Clovis, the first king of the French, whom the blessed Remigius had baptized.[d] And the letters further claimed that anyone who tried to violate this right by some rash enterprise would fall under perpetual anathema. By this pretext they hoped either to stop the royal coronation or bring about peace for their archbishop, the venerable and worthy Ralph the Green, for he had incurred the severest and most dire enmity of the lord king when he had been elected and enthroned on the see of Reims without royal assent.[5] However, the messengers came too late; so they were speechless at Orléans, but when they returned home they found their voices. Nevertheless, whatever they said, they reported nothing useful.[e]

[15]
The capture of Ferté-Baudouin and the rescue of the count of Corbeil and Anselm of Garlande

Louis, king of the French by the grace of God, could not put aside what he had grown accustomed to do in his youth, namely safeguarding the churches, protecting the poor and the needy, and working for the peace and defense of the kingdom.

For instance, Hugh of Crécy, the son of Guy the Red, was a skilled and valiant young warrior, equally adept at plundering

d. The claim of the church of Reims to anoint and crown kings was based on the baptism of Clovis, the first Christian king of the Franks, by St. Remigius, the bishop of Reims. See further endnote 4.

e. As usual, one cannot help noting that Reims comes out badly in Suger's telling of the story.

and burning and very quick to make trouble for the whole king-dom.[1] When they lost the castle of Gournay, however, both father and son reddened with shame; their resentment deep-ened, and they did not stop belittling the royal majesty.[a] Hugh chose not to spare even his own brother, Count Odo of Corbeil, because he had given him no help against the king.[2] He laid a snare for his simplicity, for one day when Count Odo had de-cided to go hunting in the safety of his own land, the foolish man learned what kinship really means and what happens when it is corrupted by envy. Kidnapped by his own brother Hugh, he was bound with shackles and chains in the castle called Ferté-Baudouin, to be freed only if he showed himself willing to make war on the king if the chance arose.[b]

In the face of this unaccustomed lunacy, many men of the garrison of Corbeil, a castle rich in knights of old nobility, fled to the public refuge of his royal majesty. They threw themselves down at the knees of the king and, amid tearful sobs, reported the capture of the count and the cause of his captivity.[3] They begged him with many prayers to rescue him by force; and when the king promised to do so, they gained hope of the count's release. Their anger grew calm, and their sorrow found relief as they struggled with all the skill and strength they had to recover their lord. Hugh held Ferté-Baudouin not by hereditary right but by reason of his marriage to Countess Adelaide; but after he scornfully repudiated her, he kept the castle.[4] For this reason, a few of its men met with some men from Corbeil and swore on oath to admit them later with due caution into the castle.

The king hurried there at the urging of the men of Corbeil, but to avoid being discovered he took along only a small band of

a. Suger puns on Guy of Rochefort's nickname "the Red" (*Rubeus*) and his being "reddened with shame" (*erubescentia*) when he lost the castle.

b. Ferté-Baudouin is the modern La Ferté-Alais, Seine-et-Oise, about forty miles south of Paris on the river Essone.

knights from his court. The seneschal Anselm of Garlande, known to be a valiant knight, and about forty armed men had been sent on ahead. Late in the evening when people were still talking around the fires, Anselm and his men were let in through the gate which had been agreed upon and were fighting strenuously to secure it. But the men of the garrison, alerted by the snorting of the horses and the sudden shouting of the horsemen, rushed out against them. The street there was very narrow at its entrances on both ends, which prevented the men who had entered from either advancing or retreating as they wished. So the townsmen waiting outside it, emboldened by this advantage, slaughtered them without hindrance. The dark shadows of night and the unfortunate circumstance that they were fighting in an enclosed position finally forced the king's men to head back for the gate. But Anselm, still battling spiritedly as he fell back, was struck down; forestalled by the enemy, he could not reach the gate. Taken into custody along the way, he occupied the tower of that castle, not as its lord but as a captive, just like the count of Corbeil. They shared equal anguish but unequal fear, for one dreaded death but the other only disinheritance; and one could have applied to them that verse: "Carthage and Marius found comfort in their lot."[5]

The king advanced more quickly when he heard the shouts of the retreating men. Regarding any delay as unworthy, he did not shun the road although the night was dark and troublesome. He jumped upon a very fast horse and bravely tried to bring help to his men by rushing against the gate. But the gate was closed, and he pulled back, driven away by a hail of javelins, lances, and rocks. Overwhelmed by grief, the brothers and kinsmen of the captured seneschal collapsed before the feet of the king: "Have pity on us, O glorious king, and be valiant," they said, "for that accursed Hugh of Crécy, a most damnable man, is thirsty for human blood. He will come here or carry off our brother elsewhere, and do whatever he wants with him. He will slit his throat in a flash and, acting more wildly than the wildest beast, think little of the punishment awaiting him for condemning him to sudden death."

Fearing this very thing, the king quickly surrounded the castle and blocked the roads leading to the gates. He enclosed it with four or five entrenchments, and devoted the service of his kingdom and his own person to the recovery of the castle and the captives. Having first been overjoyed at their capture, Hugh now became terrified at the possibility of their rescue and the loss of his castle. He nervously toiled and schemed how he might enter the castle, taking various disguises as sometimes on horse, sometimes on foot, he pretended to be a jongleur or prostitute.

One day, when this matter was absorbing all Hugh's attention, the men in the king's encampment recognized him and, seeing that he could not withstand the continuous assaults of his attackers, he sought safety in flight. Then suddenly, the courtly knight and valiant warrior William, the brother of the captured seneschal, hotly pursued Hugh and tried to detain him. Having a quick spirit and a fast horse, William rode ahead of the others; but the very speed of his chase made Hugh take special notice of him. Brandishing his lance, Hugh turned toward him frequently; but fear of those following William allowed Hugh no delay; so he turned and fled again each time. Hugh too was an amazing and outstanding warrior; and if he could have stopped long enough for single combat, he would have put his dauntless courage on display. He would have gained great prestige either by winning the trophy of a duel or by facing death in the attempt. But Hugh had a further problem, for he could find no way to avoid the numerous villages situated on his route and the countless attacks he would encounter. So, resorting to trickery and deceitfully pretending to be William of Garlande, he shouted that Hugh was chasing him and invited the king's partisans to hinder his pursuer as if he were a foe. With tricks such as these, he slipped away in flight; and with a clever tongue and a stout heart, one man made fools out of many.

The king, however, did not pull back from the siege he had

begun for this or any other reason. He tightened his blockade of the castle and wore out the men of the garrison. Plotting with some of them but keeping it secret from the knights, he did not stop his attacks until he extracted the surrender of those under assault by powerful force. Amid all this confusion, the knights gave thought to their lives, not confinement, and fled to the keep of the castle. But once shut up inside, they could neither fully protect themselves nor find any way back out of the keep again. When some had been killed and even more of them wounded, they submitted to the will of his royal majesty and put themselves and the keep at his disposal, not without the counsel of their lord. Thus, in this one adventure, "there was someone dutiful and someone abominable."[c] For the king used good judgment and mercy, and restored a seneschal to himself, a brother to his brothers, and a count to the men of Corbeil. He disinherited some knights of the castle and ravaged their goods and, decreeing that others be severely punished, he burdened them with the pain of a long imprisonment, a lesson that would strike terror into people like them. By the gift of God, he gained an excellent victory and made the beginnings of his rule noble, contrary to the expectation of his rivals.

c. Ovid, *Metamorphoses* 3:5. We suggest that the king was dutiful and Hugh abominable.

[16]
The interview between King Louis and King Henry of the English at Néaufles

About that time[a] King Henry of the English, a very brave man who was renowned in peace and war, came into the districts of the Normans.[1] Nearly the whole world had heard of his superior merit, and even that rustic prophet Merlin, a marvelous visionary who foretold the whole future of the English, spoke well of him in a mighty proclamation with a fine and truthful style. Breaking forth abruptly as seers usually do, he praised him with prophetic voice: "There will come to the throne a lion of justice," he said. "At his roar the Gallic towers and the dragons of the island will tremble. In his days gold will be squeezed from the lily and the nettle, and silver will flow from the hooves of mooing cattle. Men with curled locks will put on different fleeces because their exterior dress will signify their interior states. The feet of those who bark will be cut off; wild beasts will enjoy peace; mankind will grieve at its punishment. The token of commerce will be split in half; the half will be round. The greediness of kites will perish, and the teeth of wolves will be blunted. The cubs of the lion will be changed into fish of the sea, and the eagle will build its nest on top of Mount Aravius."[2]

Every part of this great and ancient prophecy exactly fits the valor of his person and the management of his kingdom. Neither one iota nor one word detracts from its aptness; and the prophecy seems verified beyond doubt from what is said at the end about the lion cubs. His sons and daughter were shipwrecked, and they changed their physical forms after being eaten by the fish of the sea.[b]

a. February or early March 1109 (Luchaire, no. 72).
b. An allusion to the disaster of the White Ship. Carrying Henry's heir,

King Henry happily succeeded his brother William to the throne.[c] Taking counsel with experienced and proven men, he gladly restored order to the kingdom of England according to the law of kings of old; and to win the good will of his people, he confirmed by oath the ancient customs of the realm. He then steered his ship to port in the duchy of Normandy; and relying on help from the lord king of the French, he calmed the land, renewed the laws, and imposed peace on the subdued.[5] To those who plundered he promised nothing but the ripping out of their eyes and the swing of the gibbet; and the swift enforcement of these and like promises astounded them, for "anyone can be rich in promises," but "the land grew silent in his sight."[6] Being warlike descendants of the Danes, the Normans are ignorant of the ways of peace and serve it unwillingly; and in this way they demonstrate the truth of the oracles of the rustic seer. The greediness of kites perishes, and the teeth of wolves are blunted, when neither the nobles nor the non-nobles dare pillage or plunder with any sort of foolhardiness. The words "at the roar of the lion of justice the Gallic towers and the dragons of the island will tremble" accord with King Henry's action in overturning nearly all the towers and strongest castles of Normandy, which is part of Gaul.[7] He introduced his own men and maintained them from his own treasury, or, if the castles had been destroyed, he made all submit to his personal will. "The dragons of the island trembled," because not a single baron of England dared even mutter during his entire administration.

"In his days gold" was being squeezed by him "from the lily," referring to monastic clergy of good behavior, and "from the nettle," referring to troublesome laymen. He had in mind that,

---

William, it sank on a crossing of the English Channel on November 25, 1120. See further endnote 3.

    c. Henry succeeded William Rufus as king of England in 1100. See further endnote 4.

just as he worked for the profit of all, so all should serve him. For there is more safety in the land if one man profits from all in order to defend all, than for all to perish if this one man fails to make his profit.[8] "Silver will flow from the hooves of mooing cattle" means that a safe countryside made the barns full, and full barns supplied an abundance of silver for his full coffers.[d]

For that reason he used flattery and threats and wrested the fortress of Gisors away from Pagan of Gisors. It was a strongly fortified castle conveniently sited at the common boundary between the French and the Normans where a river pleasantly full of fish, called the Epte, flows between them.[e] The river conforms to the old rope of alignment agreed to by the French and the Danes and serves as the border, but the castle itself offers easy entry for the Normans to rush into France while it hinders a French approach. Whenever the means to possess the castle became available, its location and the protection it afforded made it necessary, in accordance with the law of the kingdom, for the king of the French no less than the king of the English to covet it. Claims over the castle therefore quickly fomented a quarrel between the two kings. And after the king of the French had demanded in vain that King Henry either return Gisors or destroy it, he set a day and assigned a place for negotiating, but not before he reproached him for breaking a treaty.[9]

Meanwhile, as generally happens in these cases, slanderous remarks made by jealous men stirred up the anger of the kings to the point where nothing could calm them down. They gathered together their best knights in order to display both pride and wrath at their meeting. From a great part of the kingdom of

d. As provost of Berneval in Normandy, Suger would have had ample opportunity to learn of this first hand.

e. Since the tenth century the little river Epte had formed the border between the French Vexin and the Norman Vexin. It flows into the Seine midway between Paris and Rouen; Gisors is located on the Norman side in a small bulge of the river toward the east, about forty miles northwest of Paris.

the French the magnates assembled, namely Count Robert of Flanders with nearly four thousand knights, the palatine count Theobald, the count of Nevers, the duke of the Burgundians and many others, and a large number of archbishops and bishops. And the king of France led them across the land of the count of Meulan, ravaging it and giving it over to fires, for the count belonged to the party of the king of England. With such kind deeds so flattering to King Henry, he prepared him for their future meeting.[f]

Both sides had rallied great hosts, and they confronted each other at a place commonly called Planches-de-Néaufles, the site of an unfortunately located castle, for, as an old saying of the inhabitants warned, the men who assembled there could hardly ever or never find enough foodstuffs.[g] The French army took up its position on the bank of the river flowing between them but at a spot where neither side could cross. After holding a meeting the French elected their noblest and wisest men and sent them over to the English king. They crossed the river on an old, shaky bridge, which threatened to throw them one at a time or perhaps all together down into the water.

One of them, a skilled orator who took charge of this task, pleaded their case but without giving the king a salutation. Speaking on behalf of his companions he said: "Your efforts have gained for you the duchy of Normandy by the noble leave of the lord king of the French. But when the duchy was given in vassalage as fief by that same munificent right hand, the most important of the things agreed to and confirmed by oath con-

f. Louis's technique of ravaging (literally "depopulating") his enemy's land and giving it over to fires was a standard one, frequently mentioned by Suger. Ultimately it would destroy an enemy's productive capacity. See further endnote 10.

g. The modern Néaufles-Saint-Martin, Eure, is downstream on the Epte a few miles south of Gisors.

cerned Gisors and Bray.[h] If either of you should gain possession of them by any sort of pact, neither of you was to keep them: within forty days of gaining them, the possessor, submitting to this agreement, was to destroy those castles completely. And because you have not done this, the king orders that you do it now and make amends, as the law provides, for failing to do so. For it is unseemly for a king to transgress the law, because both the king and the law enjoy the same majesty of ruling. But if your men deny any of these provisions or in their deceit refuse to affirm them, then we are prepared to prove them by the formal witness of two or three barons, as the law of the duel allows."[i]

Having carried out their task, the French had no time even to report back to the king before some Normans who had followed them stood in his presence. They shamelessly denied whatever could injure their cause and demanded that the dispute be handled through the process of law. As this unresolved case had caught them by surprise, they turned their full attention to one tactic. They stalled for time in every way possible to conceal the truth of the matter from so many discerning magnates of the kingdom. The French again dispatched messengers along with men more powerful than those first sent; and, in addition, they boldly put forward Count Robert of Flanders, the Jerusalemite, a distinguished champion,[12] to prove their case. Refuting exaggerated words by the law of the duel, they would reveal by fighting on which side justice lay.

But when the Normans did not accept the offer or reject it in a suitable way, the high-spirited King Louis decided to rely upon his own stoutness of heart and body. He quickly dispatched

h. Bray is the modern Bray-et-Lu, Seine-et-Oise, downstream on the Epte some few miles south of Néaufles. See further endnote 11.

i. It emerges that the French had been sent across the bridge not to negotiate but to offer a challenge. The "law of the duel" refers to judicial combat, and is referred to again (below, cap. 19 at n. 13).

emissaries who enjoined King Henry either to destroy the castle of Gisors or to defend himself in person against him for having faithlessly broken his sworn word. "Come now," he said. "The one who fights hardest in combat should gain the glory given by truth and victory." Having come to as fair a decision as possible about the duelling place, he continued, "Let their host draw back from the bank of the river until we are able to cross, for a more secure position will make each side feel safer. Or, if he prefers, let each side take hostages from the most noble men of the entire host as a guarantee that we will fight in single combat. But he must permit us to cross the river safely after we have pulled back our own forces; otherwise no crossing will be possible." Some of them shouted out and jokingly suggested that the kings do battle on that flimsy bridge which would immediately tumble down; and being both reckless and brave, King Louis was eager to do this.

But the king of the English replied, "It would mean nothing to me[13] were I needlessly to lose a renowned and very useful castle because of remarks like these." Scorning these and other reproaches, he said, "When I see the lord king in a place where I may defend myself, I will not run away," and so he refused the offer of a fight in an untenable spot.

After that absurd response, implying that "favorable locations do the actual fighting for combatants,"[14] the French were stirred into action and rushed to arms, as did the Normans. Each side dashed to the river, and only their inability to cross prevented the tragedy of a great slaughter. They spent that day in discussion, and as night fell upon them, the Normans retired to Gisors, and our men to Chaumont.[j] The next morning, "when the early dawn put the stars to flight from the heavens,"[15] the French remembered the affront they had endured on the day before and became fired up by their knightly zeal. Taking to the road on the

---

j. The modern Chaumont-en-Vexin, Oise, about five miles east of Gisors.

swiftest horses, they rushed to the attack near Gisors and fought with amazing brashness and boldness. They forced the worn-out Normans back through the gate of the castle, endeavoring to teach them the superiority of those accustomed to war over those who had grown soft with long peace.[16]

The war caused by these and like beginnings continued for nearly two years, and the king of England was the one more seriously hurt when, in defense of his land, he girded nearly the entire Norman march, as far as his duchy extended, with many knights at heavy cost.[17] Ancient natural castles and fortresses, however, defended the king of the French; and the men of Flanders, Ponthieu, the Vexin, and other borderlands fought valiantly for him at no cost as they plundered and burned the land. But when William, the son of the English king, made his homage to King Louis, the king did a special favor and enlarged his fief by granting him the castle of Gisors as his own possession and brought him back on this occasion into the grace he had earlier enjoyed.[18]

Before this transpired, however, the abominable loss of men caused by this astonishing struggle was punished with astonishing vengeance.

The treachery committed at La Roche-Guyon by William, brother-in-law of Guy; the death of Guy and the swift revenge against the same William

Atop a steep bluff jutting up from a bank of the great river Seine there sits a dreadful and unstately castle, named La Roche-Guyon.[a] The ambitious hand of the builder dug it out of the lofty rock and kept its exterior hidden from sight; and while cutting the rock, he spread it on the slope of the mountain. It had the spaciousness of a very grand residence but only a few small entrances. You would think it was the cave of seers where the oracles of Apollo are received, or the place about which Lucan says: "For although the Thessalian prophetess plays havoc with destiny, when she inspects the Stygian shades, does she really allure them there, or does she descend into the shadows after them?"[2] From this place one does, perhaps, descend into the lower world.

This traitorous fortress, despised by gods and men alike, was held by Guy, a young man of good natural quality who had no part in the wicked ways of his ancestors. He broke with their tradition and decided to live honorably and free from the despicable gluttony of greed; but the misery associated with this wretched place finally caught up with him. And when he was beheaded through the most sordid treachery of his even more sordid father-in-law, he lost both the place and his person

a. La Roche-Guyon, Seine-et-Oise, is on the north bank of the Seine a few miles upstream from its junction with the Epte, about forty-two miles northwest of Paris. Suger's strong language immediately alerts the reader that evil is to follow. See further endnote 1.

through unexpected death. His brother-in-law William, a Norman by birth and a traitor beyond compare, was believed to be his intimate counsellor and closest friend, but he "conceived grief and gave birth to iniquity."[3] At dawn one Sunday, William found his chance for treachery when he mingled with the devout people who were gathering very early in the church, which was accessible from Guy's residence at an opening in the rock. But, wearing the mail of a knight beneath his cape, he met there with a handful of traitors for a purpose altogether different from theirs. While the others were at prayer, he pretended to pray for a short time while he kept an eye on the entrance where he would force himself on Guy. And in that very doorway where Guy was hurriedly entering the church, William rushed upon him with drawn sword and raged about like a madman with his usual depravity in the company of his most despicable companions. He struck, sacrificed, and slew the unsuspecting man who was smiling as if he had not even felt the sword.[b]

Struck dumb at seeing this, his noble spouse tore her cheeks and hair with wifely fury. She ran over to her husband and, caring nothing for death, tumbled down and covered him with her body: "Me," she said, "Behead me, you vilest of butchers, I am the miserable wretch that should die." Having thrown herself on top of her husband, she received the blows and wounds inflicted by the swordsmen: "Dearest spouse, what wrongs did you do these men? Weren't this son-in-law and father-in-law inseparable friends? What is this madness? You people are complete maniacs."[4] Twisting her by the hair, they dragged her away struggling as best she could, for she was stabbed and wounded over nearly her whole body. They condemned her husband to a

---

b. The murder of Guy and its sequel probably occurred in May 1109 (Luchaire, no. 75). There are a number of parallels between the events related in this chapter and the later murder of Count Charles of Flanders, which also occurred in a church, and its results (below, cap. 30).

shameful death, and those of their children they found they snuffed out with a wickedness worthy of Herod, dashing them against the rock.[5]

While the murderers raged and roamed about gnashing their teeth, the woman lay on the floor and, lifting up her piteous head, looked upon the mutilated body of her husband. In an outburst of love which her weakness hardly allowed, she slid along like a snake, dragging her own completely bloody body up beside the lifeless corpse. As if he were alive, she gave him as many sweet kisses as she could and broke out into a sorrowful song, so paying her respects to his sorrowful soul: "Why did you leave me behind, dearest husband?" she cried. "Has your wonderful fidelity toward me been so rewarded? Is this what comes of forsaking the wickedness of your father, grandfather, and ancestors? Is this what you get for giving up greed toward your neighbors and the poor, even though it meant keeping your own household in want?" "She said these things and collapsed in exhaustion, abandoned by her fury."[6] And no one could pull the totally dead man away from the half-alive woman, covered all over as they were with the same blood.

But that foul William put them on display as if they were pigs, and only after he had been sated with human blood like a wild beast did he finally calm down. He marveled at the extraordinary strength of the rock and found it suitable for his purposes. Although it was too late, he thought about how he might vehemently plunder everything around the place, and how he might strike fear into the French and Normans whenever he wished. Leaning that mad head of his out of a window, he called together the local inhabitants; and this man, devoid of good, promised them evil things if they would come over to his side. But not one of them entered the fortress.

In the morning the news of this monstrous crime spread quickly, and it upset not only the men of the neighborhood but even those far removed. The men of the Vexin, being valiant and very powerful warriors, were stirred to take severe reprisals. Each man gathered his knights and foot soldiers from all sides and joined them together into a force. Fearing that Henry, the formidable king of the English, was bringing help to the traitors, they rushed to the rock and positioned a large number of knights and foot soldiers on its slope to keep anyone from going in or out. They stationed the host on the road leading from the region of the Normans, and blocked it to prevent help from being brought in. Meanwhile, they sent to King Louis, informed him of the conspiracy, and inquired what his orders were in these matters.

He commanded, by virtue of his royal majesty, that the conspirators be punished by a carefully chosen and shameful death, sending word that he would bring support if necessary.[c] After the host had been in position for some days, that evil William, seeing it grow larger day by day, began to grow afraid. He finally realized what he had done in following the enticement of the devil, his teacher. So he summoned a few of the most noble men of the Vexin and promised them many things. He suggested how he might dwell in peace on the rock, how he might make an alliance with them, and how he might best serve the king of the French. But they rejected his proposals and hurried to avenge his treachery. Since William had now become careless, they persuaded him to exchange the fortress he had seized for their solemn pledge to surrender him some land and allow him to leave safely. With this agreement confirmed by sworn oath, William let a fairly large number of the French into his stronghold.

But the matter of the land delayed their departure, and the next morning a few besides those who had sworn the oath entered the fortress and others followed them, one behind the other. Then

c. In light of Louis's failure to become involved no further than this, Suger's inclusion of this chapter in the *Deeds* is hard to explain. See further endnote 7.

the shouting of those still outside grew louder as they yelled in a dreadful way for those inside to send out the traitors; otherwise they would be seen as accomplices and would suffer a penalty similar to theirs. Not wishing to yield to such effrontery or to fear, those who had sworn the oath made a stand; but those who had not sworn rushed against them and carried the day. Attacking them with swords, they piously slaughtered the impious, mutilated the limbs of some, disemboweled others with great pleasure, and piled even greater cruelty upon them, considering it still too kind. No one should doubt that the hand of God sped so swift a revenge when both the living and the dead were thrown through the windows. Bristling with countless arrows like hedgehogs, their bodies stopped short in the air, vibrating on the sharp points of lances as if the ground itself rejected them. The French hit upon the following unusual revenge for William's unusual deed. When alive he had lacked a brain, and now that he was dead he lacked a heart, for they ripped it from his entrails and impaled it on a stake, swollen as it was with fraud and evil. They left it set up in a conspicuous place for many days to make public their revenge for this wickedness.

The corpses of William and several of his companions were then tied with ropes to harrows and pieces of fences, which had been fitted for this purpose, and were cast upon the river Seine. And if nothing managed to keep them from floating all the way to Rouen, they would exhibit there how their treachery had been avenged. Those who had for a short time befouled France with their filth, now dead, would forever befoul Normandy, their native soil.[8]

[18]
How he took away the castles of Mantes and Montlhéry from his brother Philip, who made a stand against him

A lack of good faith leads to evil being returned for good more often than good for evil. The latter is proper to God, the former to neither God nor man: nevertheless, it is something that is done. And this mark of wickedness was on Philip, the brother of King Louis, who had been born of the irregular union with the Angevin woman. The lord Louis had yielded to the seductive flattery of his noble and most sycophantic stepmother and, at the insistence of his father, to whom he never refused anything, gave Philip lordship over Montlhéry and the castle of Mantes, which were located in the very bowels of the kingdom. Ungrateful for such favors, Philip placed his trust in the great nobility of his lineage and dared to rebel. His uncle was Amalric of Montfort, a distinguished knight and a very powerful baron, and his brother was Fulk, the count of Anjou who was later to become king of Jerusalem.[1] But his mother wielded greater power than all of these. A clever shrew, she had great skill in that amazing artifice women customarily use to trample boldly upon their husbands even after they have tormented them with abuse. She had so fully tamed her first husband, the Angevin, that he still venerated her as if she were his lady, even after he was totally rejected from the marriage bed. He often sat on a stool at her feet like someone under a spell, completely surrendering to her will. The mother, her sons, and the whole progeny had one chief interest: if, for any reason, disaster should befall the king, one of the brothers would succeed him; and in this way the whole family would joyfully raise its head to the throne of the kingdom and share in the honor and the lordship.[2]

Philip was frequently summoned to court but proudly refused to appear for a hearing and judgment. The king, however, grew tired of his plundering the poor, his burdening the churches, and his laying waste the whole countryside; and, in spite of a reluctance to do so, he went in haste after him. Philip and his party had the support of a very powerful band of knights, and they often boasted that the king would be driven back, but the cowards now stayed away from the castle. Wearing his hauberk, the king rushed against it without hindrance and, hurrying through the middle of the castle to the tower, surrounded it with a blockade. He then made ready various siege engines, ballistas and catapults; and after many days, when the besieged had despaired of life, he finally forced them to surrender.[3]

Meanwhile, Philip's mother and his uncle, Amalric of Montfort, dreading the loss of the other lordship, namely Montlhéry, conferred it on Hugh of Crécy by joining him in marriage to the daughter of Amalric.[4] They hoped to put a formidable barrier in the way of the king, for travel would be blocked by the castles of this lordship and by those of Guy of Rochefort, the brother of Hugh,[a] as well as by those of Amalric, whose jurisdiction extended without interruption all the way to Normandy. And besides the other trouble which they would be able to cause every day as far as Paris, it would now be impossible for the king to go to Dreux.[b] Having contracted his marriage, Hugh left in a hurry for Montlhéry; but the king followed at his heels even more hurriedly; for at the very hour, the very moment when he learned of the events, the king moved with great daring and swiftness to Châtres, a fortified place in the lordship.[c]

a. That is, Hugh's older brother Guy II, the eldest son of Guy the Red of Rochefort.

b. Another example of the feeble nature of royal power in the early twelfth century. Dreux is about thirty-five miles west-south-west of Paris.

c. Châtres is the modern Arpajon, Seine-et-Oise, about eighteen miles south of Paris on the river Orge.

The king won over the best men of the land, who had hope in his generosity and proven clemency, and rescued them from a tyranny and cruelty they had come to know and dread. Each side waited there for a few days as, in turn, Hugh strove to keep Montlhéry and the king strove to prevent him. But one scheme followed hard upon the other[5] when Hugh was duped by the following bit of shrewdness. After due consideration, Milo of Bray, the son of Milo the Great, came before the king and claimed the lordship by hereditary right. Having thrown himself at his feet, weeping and wailing he badgered the king with many petitions and badgered the royal counsellors. He begged as a suppliant that the king, in his munificence, return his lordship, restore his inheritance from his father, and in return receive him as a serf or tenant to be used as he wished.[6] Deigning to grant his tearful petition, the king summoned the men of the garrison and presented them with Milo as their lord. This action made up for every torment they had suffered in the past and made them as happy as if he had sent them the moon and stars from heaven. With no delay, they ordered Hugh to depart and promised him a very sudden death if he did not go as quickly as he could. They warned that neither fealty nor any sworn word would prevail against the person who was their lord by virtue of birth, but only power or the lack of it.

The dumbfounded Hugh took off in flight, thinking that he had been saved without his property being lost. But, for the momentary joy of a marriage, he carried away with him the long-lasting shame of a repudiation, as well as great pain and the loss of his horses and household goods. And this shameful expulsion taught him to reflect on what it meant to enter into alliance with his lord's enemies against his lord.

How he destroyed the castle of Le Puiset
after he captured Hugh

Just as very tasty fruit from a fruitful tree reproduces its fragrant taste if a shoot is transplanted or branches are grafted, in the same way evil and wickedness, qualities that should have been rooted out, continued to sprout forth and produced one man out of the branch of many wretched men. He was like a snake amid eels, which torments and stirs them up and enjoys the taste of its own sort of bitterness, as if it were absinthe. Hugh of Le Puiset was of such a kind, a wretched man, made rich only by virtue of his own tyranny and that of his ancestors. He succeeded his uncle Guy in the lordship of Le Puiset, for his father had taken up arms with amazing pride and had gone early on the expedition to Jerusalem. And Hugh proved to be a worthless shoot who took after his father with every kind of evil, but "those whom his father beat with whips, he, more despicable than his parent, beat with scorpions."[1]

Elated for having gone unpunished while he brutally tyrannized needy churches and monasteries, Hugh had reached the stage where "the workers of evil have fallen; they were cast out and could not stand."[2] Since he did not think much of either the King of the universe or the king of the French, he attacked the most noble countess of Chartres and her son Theobald, a very handsome youth and valiant warrior.[a] He ravaged their land all the way to Chartres, delivering it over to plunder and fires. When they could, the noble countess and her son fought back; but

---

a. Countess Adela, the daughter of William the Conqueror and thus the sister of kings William Rufus and Henry I of England, was indeed "most noble." She had married Count Stephen of Blois and Chartres in 1084, and Theobald was their second son. See further endnote 3.

their efforts were too little and too late for them to avenge themselves. They hardly ever or never approached within eight or ten miles of Le Puiset. So limitless was Hugh's daring, so cogent was the force of his powerful pride that, although few loved him, many came to his service. And although many strove to defend him, a large number of them longed for his destruction, for he was more feared than loved.

Count Theobald came to see that he could accomplish little against Hugh through his own efforts but much through those of the king. So, accompanied by his very noble mother, who had always served the king nobly, he hurried into the royal presence and begged the king with many pleas to give aid, showing how he had merited it for his great service.[b] He related some of the dishonorable deeds done by Hugh, his father, grandfather, and ancestors, saying: "As befits your royal majesty, lord king, remember the dishonor and shame inflicted on your father Philip by Hugh's grandfather, a man detestable for breaking his sworn word. He drove him away from Le Puiset in disgrace when he was striving to avenge the many crimes that had been committed. With the scornful contempt typical of a very wretched family and a seditious faction, Hugh's grandfather chased your father's host all the way back to Orléans. He dishonored the captured count of Nevers, Lancelin of Beaugency, nearly one hundred knights, and, what had never been heard of before, even some bishops, by throwing them into his prison."[4]

Continuing his reproaches, Count Theobald went on to discuss the purpose and the origin of the castle of Le Puiset, which had been built not too long ago by the venerable Queen Constance in the middle of the land of the saints for its protection.[c]

b. These events occurred before March 12, 1111 (Luchaire, no. 108). Theobald emerges in a more favorable light in this passage, presumably because he appears as a humble suppliant of Louis. But Suger will revert later in the chapter to his customary negative portrayal of Theobald.

c. Le Puiset is about twenty-five miles southeast of Chartres and about

He explained how Hugh's grandfather had afterward taken it all for himself and left nothing for the king but villainy. Now, if he wished, the king could easily avenge the insults done him and his father by overthrowing the castle and disinheriting Hugh, for the large host from Chartres, Blois, and Châteaudun, which usually helped Hugh oppose the king, would now not only desert him but stand against him. He could end the persecution of the churches, the plunderings of the poor, and the ungodly hardships endured by widows and orphans whenever Hugh ravaged the land of the saints and its cultivators. But if the king did not choose to punish the wrongs done to him personally and to those who deserved well of him, then he himself should share the blame for them.

Feeling the force of numerous complaints like these, the king set a day for taking counsel about them. We met at Melun where many archbishops, bishops, clerics, and monks flocked together, for Hugh had been more rapacious than a wolf in devouring their lands.[6] They cried out and threw themselves down at the feet of the king, against his will. They begged him to keep that greedy robber Hugh in check and snatch away from the jaw of the dragon their prebends, which the generosity of previous kings had granted the servants of God in the Beauce, a land fertile in grain. They prayed that he spare no effort in setting free the lands of the priests which, in a like way, were the only ones freed from the burdens imposed by Pharaoh.[7] They pleaded that the king, as the representative of God, render free the part that belonged to God, whose image he maintained and kept alive in his own person.

The king received their petition favorably and took appropri-

---

fifty miles south of Paris, a short distance to the west of the road to Orléans. The "saints" are the blessed Dionysius and his companions, SS Rusticus and Eleutherius; Suger terms the land theirs because of the dependencies of St. Denis there. See further endnote 5.

ate action. The prelates of the church, namely the archbishop of
Sens, the bishop of Orléans, and the venerable Ivo of Chartres,
departed. Ivo had formerly been held in prison when he had been
locked up by force in that very same castle for many days.[d] With
the consent of Abbot Adam, our predecessor of good memory,
the king sent me back to Toury, a profitable estate in the Beauce
belonging to St. Denis, where I was in charge. It was fertile in
grain but in no way fortified. While he summoned Hugh to court
to answer these charges, he ordered me to equip the estate and
strengthen it with a force of his and our knights as best I could.
He wanted me to keep Hugh from destroying it by fire, for he
planned to reinforce it and then attack the castle from it, as his
father had done.[e]

With the help of God, we filled the estate with a good supply of
knights and foot soldiers in a very short time. Then, after judgment was rendered against Hugh when he failed to appear in
court, the king came to us at Toury with a great host and demanded back from Hugh the castle whose possession he had lost
in the verdict. And, when Hugh refused to depart, he did not
delay. He quickly attacked the castle, directed his host of knights
and foot soldiers against it, and brought to bear different kinds of
crossbow, bow, "shield, sword, and war."[9] What a sight to behold!
Arrows were raining down, sparks of fire were flashing from
countless blows atop gleaming helmets, and shields were being
pierced and broken with amazing speed. The enemy were pushed
back through the gate into the castle; but once inside they hurled
down from the ramparts and the palisade a surprising volley of

d. Ivo, bishop of Chartres (1091–1116) had been imprisoned by Hugh I, the
grandfather of Hugh of Le Puiset, on the orders of King Philip in 1092,
apparently for having opposed Philip's liaison with Bertrada. See further
endnote 8.

e. Suger was then the provost of Toury, a few miles southeast of Le Puiset
and about fifty miles south of Paris on the road to Orléans; the description
that follows is that of an eyewitness.

missiles on our men, which even the boldest among them found almost unbearable. By dismantling roof timbers and throwing down the beams, the enemy began driving our men back, but they did not succeed, for the royal forces called upon their own valiant strength of body and spirit and fought bitterly against their foes. When their shields had been broken, they crouched behind shingles from the roof, doors, anything made of wood, and pushed against the gate. We had also loaded wagons with great piles of dry wood, greased with fat and lard, which would make them quickly burst into flames—a fitting end for the excommunicated within, who were devils through and through. A brave band of our men, taking cover behind these great heaps of wood, set the wagons up against the gate. They planned to turn them into a fire that no one could extinguish.

While our side took risks struggling to set the wagons afire, and theirs to put them out, Count Theobald led a great host of knights and foot soldiers in an attack against the castle from a different side, namely the one facing Chartres. Mindful of the wrongs he had suffered, the count hurried into battle, encouraging his men to climb up the steep slope of the embankment. But he lost heart when they fell back down again with even greater haste; to be precise, they tumbled down in a heap. He saw those whom he had urged to bend forward and creep up carefully plunge back down again on their backs recklessly. He did his best to find out whether they had breathed their last under the shower of rocks falling upon them. The knights who were defending and circling the castle on swift horses came unexpectedly upon the men clinging to the palisade with their hands and cut them down. They slaughtered them and sent them to the ground with thuds, from the top of the wall to the very bottom of the ditch.

With the hands of our men broken and their knees buckling, our attack had almost come to a standstill when almighty God willed that this great and just revenge be credited entirely to his

powerful, or rather almighty, hand. From the general levies of
the land that were present, God awakened the firm and courageous spirit of a bald priest; and, contrary to what men could
believe, it became possible for him to do what had been impossible for an armed count and his followers.[f] Carrying a flimsy
shingle, which left his front exposed, he swiftly climbed all the
way up and reached the palisade. Once there, he hid beneath the
coverings fitted to it and took them down little by little. Glad to
find no hindrance to his labor, he gave a signal for help to the
others who had been hanging back and taking a rest in the field.
When they saw an unarmed priest bravely tearing down the
enclosures, they surged forward with their weapons and began
striking the palisade with their axes and whatever iron tools
they had. They hacked it down and destroyed it; and, what was
an amazing sign of heaven's judgment, as if the walls of a second
Jericho had fallen, the hosts of the king and the count entered at
the very same hour through the chopped-down enclosures. A
large number of Hugh's men could find no place to escape the
assaults of their enemies, who were rushing in from all sides.
They were quickly surrounded and forcefully struck down.

Hugh himself was among the survivors, but seeing that the
interior wall of the castle would not give him enough protection,
he took himself off to the motte and the wooden tower on top of
it.[g] He cowered there before the menacing lances of the pursuing
host, and the man who had been beaten down surrendered without delay. Taken prisoner along with his men in his own residence, he was shackled with horrible chains and soon learned
what a fall such great pride prepares.[12]

f. During Louis's reign the bishops of France set up communities of the
people, so that the priests would accompany the king to a siege or battle with
their banners and all their parishoners (OV 4:285). See further endnote 10.

g. A motte was a large, circular, steep mound, artificially raised up if no
natural elevation existed. A tower or other fortification would be built on its
flat top. See further endnote 11.

Having won this victory, the king led away his noble captives, prey that suited his royal majesty. He ordered that all the castle's furnishings and costly things be appropriated, and that the castle itself be burned down; but the tower alone he delayed burning for a few days. Count Theobald had failed to remember the great advantage he had gained, which he would never have gained by himself, and devised a scheme to widen his borders by erecting a castle on an estate called Allaines, in the lordship of Le Puiset, which he held in fief from the king. But when the king would in no way approve of his action, the count offered to provide evidence through Andrew of Baudement, steward of his land, that they had made an agreement on this point. The king in return offered to support his case that he had never made such an agreement, by clear evidence and by the law of the duel, through Anselm, his seneschal, in any safe place chosen by the combatants. The valiant men in question frequently demanded that the court be convened for this battle, but nothing ever came of it.[13]

After the castle of Le Puiset had been totally demolished and Hugh imprisoned in the tower of Château-Landon, Count Theobald, relying on support from his eminent uncle Henry, the English king, made war with his accomplices against King Louis. Count Theobald threw the land into confusion, drew his barons into his party with promises and gifts, and jealously plotted every sort of harm for the state.[14] The king, however, being an adept knight, repeatedly sought to take revenge on him and despoiled his land in the company of many other barons, especially his uncle, Count Robert of Flanders, whom he had called to his side. Count Robert was a remarkable man who had initially won great renown among Christians and Saracens for his skill as a warrior during the expedition to Jerusalem.[15]

One day, when the king had brought his host to the city of Meaux to move against the count, he caught sight of the man and flew into a rage. He rushed against him and his men, and did not hesitate to pursue them as they fled back across the bridge.

With help from the swords of Count Robert and other magnates of the kingdom, he struck them down and drove into the water men who were already jumping in of their own free will. What a sight! This warrior was swinging arms as powerful as Hector's and launching attacks worthy of a giant on top of that trembling bridge, and no one was able to hinder him.[16] Despite heavy resistance he strove to seize the town right at its very dangerous approach, and not even the barrier of the great river Marne would have stopped him if a closed gate on the other side of the river had not stood in his way.

Equal was the renown for valor the king won in a distinguished action when he moved the host out of Lagny and turned his forces against the knights who were coming to encounter him on a plain covered with beautiful grass near Pomponne.[h] Under a hail of blows he forced them to beat a swift retreat, but the narrow approach to a nearby bridge became a dreadful prospect for them as they fled. Some feared for their lives like cowards, but nevertheless they did not fear to risk death by jumping into the river. Others rushed for the bridge, trampled each other under foot and, casting aside their weapons, became more dangerous to themselves than to their enemies. Only one man reached the bridge, even though all of them had the same desire at the same time. This disorderly knocking into one another threw them into confusion; and the more they hurried the more they were delayed. So it happened that the first found themselves last and the last first.[17] But the entrance to the bridge was enclosed by a ditch that gave them some protection, as it allowed the king's knights to pursue them only in single file. Although many of them tried, even at heavy cost to themselves, only a few were able to reach the bridge. When these gained entrance in whatever way they could, more often than not the

h. Pomponne, Seine-et-Marne, is north of the river Marne a few miles northwest of Lagny which is about seventeen miles east of Paris.

great crowd of our men and theirs threw them into confusion. Knocked to their knees unwillingly, they leapt back to their feet, causing others to be bumped down. The king and his men gave chase and hemmed them in amid much slaughter. Those he came up against he wiped out, and he wiped them out as much by the blow of his sword as by the very fierce charge of his horse, sending them splashing into the river Marne. The unarmed were light and managed to float, but those in hauberks were encumbered by their weight and went under for a first time. Dragged out by helpful companions before they sank three times, they did not escape the shame of a second baptism, if one could call it that.[18]

Tormenting the count with troubles like these, the king laid waste his lands everywhere, in Brie and in the countryside of Chartres; and it did not matter whether the count was more present than absent or more absent than present. Frightened by the slim numbers and inactivity of his men, the count became skillful in luring the king's barons away from him. He enticed them with gifts and promises, giving them hope that their various complaints would be satisfied before he would make peace with the king.

Among those who joined him were Pagan of Montjay and Lancelin of Bulles, the lord of Dammartin; their lands, located like a crossroads, allowed anyone who would make trouble for Paris to approach in safety. For the same reason Count Theobald lured to his side Ralph of Beaugency, whose wife was the daughter of Hugh the Great and first cousin to the king.[i] Prompted by a great deal of worry, for as the proverb says, "the prod speeds the old woman along," the count put the useful before the honorable

i. Montjay and Dammartin, Seine-et-Marne, are about fifteen and twenty-two miles east and northeast of Paris respectively. Bulles, Oise, is about five miles northwest of Clermont and about forty miles north of Paris. See further endnote 19.

and shamefully coupled his noble sister in an incestuous marriage to Milo of Montlhéry, whom we mentioned above when the king gave back his castle.[20]

By so doing the count made it difficult to travel about and, as it were, placed the old alarming storms and wars in the very center of France. With Milo on his side, Count Theobald secretly won over that man's relatives, Guy of Rochefort and Hugh of Crécy, the lord of Châteaufort; and he would have opened up the countryside around Paris and Etampes to hostilities if a force of knights had not prevented it. A wide area of approach to Paris and Senlis now lay open to Count Theobald and the men of Brie, as well as to his uncle, Hugh of Troyes,[j] and the men of Troyes on this side of the Seine, and to Milo on the other side; the ability to bring aid to each other was thus taken away from the inhabitants of the land. A similar thing happened to the residents of Orléans when the men of Chartres, Châteaudun, and Brie met no opposition and shut them in[21] with help from Ralph of Beaugency. The king was maneuvering often enough at their rear, but the abundant resources of both England and Normandy allowed him no rest when the illustrious King Henry expended all his effort and all his energy in raiding his land. He was hit so hard by these attacks that it seemed "as if the rivers threatened . . . to withdraw all their waters from the sea."[22]

j. Count Hugh of Champagne and Troyes, the brother of Theobald's father Stephen, had been married in earlier years to Constance, the sister of King Louis (above, cap. 9). The Guy of Rochefort mentioned a few lines above was Guy II, the son of Guy I the Red; Hugh of Crécy was his younger brother.

[20]
The release of Hugh of Le Puiset

Meanwhile, Count Odo of Corbeil died—a human being with no humanity, a beast with no reason.[a] He was the son of the extremely proud Count Burchard, himself a turbulent man of amazing bravery, the chief of evildoers. One day when he aspired to the throne and took up arms against the king, Count Burchard refused to take his sword from the hand of the person offering it and spoke reproachfully to his wife the countess, who was standing at his side: "Noble countess, hand this splendid sword to a noble count with joy, for the count who receives it from you will today return it to you as king." But on the contrary, as God willed it, he did not survive the day either as what he was or as what he wanted to be. He was struck down on that very day by the lance of Count Stephen who fought on the king's side.[b] And thus Count Burchard strengthened the peace of the kingdom by removing both himself and his war to the very bottom of hell, where he might do battle for eternity.

After the son, Count Odo, died, Count Theobald and his mother used the services of Milo and Hugh, and turned their full attention to taking hold of the castle of Corbeil. By giving every gift, present, and promise possible, they and their relatives sought to deprive the king of his very innards. The king and his party drove them back, spending much sweat themselves in a costly effort to take hold of the castle. But they could do very little without negotiating with Hugh, for he was the nephew of the count.[1]

a. Odo probably died in 1112 (Luchaire, no. 128).

b. Count Stephen of Blois and Chartres, the father of Count Theobald, died in the East in 1102. It is not clear on what basis Count Burchard aspired to the throne.

Therefore, a day and place were set for settling this business. An estate of the bishop of Paris at Moissy was chosen, and this was a clear sign of a bad outcome.c We came together, and the negotiations with Hugh turned out to be partly harmful and partly helpful. When we could not get what we wanted, we wanted what we could get.[2] He foreswore his claim to the castle of Corbeil which he boasted was his by right of inheritance; and he renounced in our favor every corvée, tallage, and annoying duty that had been imposed on the possessions of all the churches and monasteries. With hostages given to secure these pledges and to insure that he would never fortify Le Puiset without the consent of the lord king, we went home deceived by his treachery but not by his skill.

[21]
The attack on Toury and the rebuilding of Le Puiset

No time passed before Hugh's oath, sworn so recently it was like some liquid that had not yet set, was shown to be worthless. Enraged by his lengthy captivity, he was like a dog chained for a long time; it becomes mad and remains so as a result of the drawn-out interval spent in chains. When set free, it rages beyond all bounds; unchained it bites and tears things to pieces; and Hugh was no different. Setting his hardened wickedness

c. Moissy is the modern Moissy-Cramayel, Seine-et-Marne, about five miles east of Corbeil and about twenty-five miles southeast of Paris. Bishop Galo of Paris was an enemy of St. Denis (above, cap. 10 with n. 4), which may account for Suger's seeing the choice of this location as a presage of evils.

flowing, he stirred it up, put it into motion, and quickly turned it to deceit. And so he joined together with those who were pulling the kingdom apart, namely the palatine count Theobald and Henry, the distinguished king of the English. When he learned that the lord king Louis was about to depart into Flanders on business of the kingdom, Hugh gathered together as large a host of knights and foot soldiers as he could, decided to rebuild the castle of Le Puiset, and made haste either to throw the neighboring countryside into confusion or bring it under his control.[1]

One Saturday Hugh was passing through the ruins of the castle where a public market was being held by permission of the king.[2] Setting his amazing duplicity to work, he called out with the loud voice of a herald and pledged an oath of safe conduct for all. But then, in that very place, he suddenly cast into prison those whom he could see were the wealthiest men there. Next, like some wild beast gnashing its teeth and tearing to pieces whatever it met, he hurried on with Count Theobald and tried to demolish the fortified estate of Toury, a possession of St. Denis, down to its foundations. That man, so skillful at guile and wickedness, had met with us on the day before; in answer to his pleas we departed on that very day to intercede on his behalf with the lord king. He had decided to enter the estate when our absence would make this easy, and to destroy it utterly in the event of resistance being offered.[a]

However, those who fought for God and the blessed Dionysius had already entered the fortress and, with the help of God and the protection the place offered, were making a brave and very bold stand on its fortified ramparts. We, on the other hand, arrived at a spot on this side of Corbeil and met with the lord king, who had already heard the truth from Normandy about what was happening. Having soon learned why we had come, he

a. Again the reader is reminded of Suger's involvement in these events, which occurred in the spring and summer of 1112 (Luchaire, no. 134).

laughed at our naïveté and sent us back with all speed to help the estate, after he had angrily made known how Hugh had tricked us.

While the king himself was assembling his host on the road to Etampes, we travelled by the straighter and shorter road back to Toury. Persistently peering ahead, we beheld from afar one sure sign that the fortress had not yet been taken. Its three-storied tower could still be seen dominating the entire plain, whereas, if the fortress had fallen, the enemy would have immediately destroyed it by fire. But they were busily occupying the surrounding district, looting and destroying it; thus we could not, either by gifts or promises, persuade anyone we met to join our party.

But the smaller the group, the greater its safety. The sun was already sinking toward the west when the enemy finally found themselves exhausted and retired for a short rest. They had been throwing themselves against our men all day long without overthrowing them.[3] Seeing our chance we pretended to be part of their company and, risking great danger, rushed right into the middle of the estate. After we had given a sign to our men on the ramparts, they made ready the gate; and, with God permitting, we hurried into the fortress. Overjoyed at our presence, our men began to make fun of their enemy's sabbath,[b] provoking them with many jeers and insults; and although I did not approve and forbade them to do it, they shouted for their foes to attack again. But just as it had done after I had left, the divine hand continued to protect both the defenders and the defenses now that I had returned, for only a few from our small numbers died of their wounds, but from their multitude many. A large number of them were carried off on litters; others were shoved under a thin and very wretched covering of earth, stored up as a meal for wolves to eat the next day or some day later.

b. The "sabbath" of these enemies is probably a pun; they were so lazy they could have been observing the sabbath day, and in any case it was Saturday. For the expression, see Lam. 1:7.

The enemy, who had been driven away, had not even reached Le Puiset before William of Garlande and many of the most prompt and powerful warriors from the king's household hurried to the rescue of the estate.[4] They yearned wholeheartedly to find their enemies surrounding Toury so that they might display the valor of the royal knighthood. The lord king himself followed them at dawn; and when he learned that his men had been welcomed throughout the fortress, he made ready the revenge he had promised for his enemies. His face beamed with joy and good cheer, for he had a chance to avenge valiantly with sudden slaughter and surprising vengeance a wrong that had taken him by surprise.

Having become aware of his arrival, the king's foes were amazed that he had found out about their conspiracy, which they had kept secret until then. They were shocked that he had suddenly put off his expedition to Flanders and not so much come quickly as flown to bring help. Not daring to do anything else, they busied themselves with rebuilding the castle. But the king assembled what forces he could from nearby, for he was troubled with war in many other places as well; and early on Tuesday morning he led forth his host and set up his battle lines. He named the commanders, put the archers and crossbowmen into position, and step-by-step drew near the still-unfinished castle. He had heard that Count Theobald was boasting that he would fight against him in the field.[c] So with his usual greatness of spirit the king dismounted, went armed and on foot amid his armed warriors, and made them dismount with him. Ordering that the horses be taken away, he encouraged his knights to be bold, urged them to stand their ground, and shouted for them to do battle bravely. Seeing him coming so fearlessly, his foes were alarmed and became afraid to leave the outer zone of the castle.

c. Alert readers of Suger are by now aware that such a boast means trouble is in store for Theobald.

In a cowardly but cautious manner they chose to draw up their lines of battle behind the old moat of the ruined castle and await him there. Their plan was to confront the king's host when it struggled to climb up out of the ditch. His well-ordered battle lines would then be thrown into disorder, and being disordered would begin to waver, and this is largely what happened.

In the first shock of combat the king's knights were slaughtering and driving the enemy away from the moat with amazing boldness, as if victory were at hand. Then, throwing their battle lines into disorder, they set off in reckless pursuit of their foes. But Ralph of Beaugency, a man of great shrewdness and valor, had earlier been afraid of the very thing that was taking place.[5] So he had concealed his host in a part of the castle where the height of a church and shadows cast by neighboring houses would allow it to go unnoticed. Now, when he saw the men of his party going out through the gate, he sent forth his fresh forces against the exhausted knights of the king and attacked them harshly. Our men began fleeing in droves. Being on foot they were burdened by heavy hauberks and weapons, and could hardly withstand the ordered attack of knights on horse. After countless blows and lengthy fighting back and forth, they retreated through the moat they had taken, and the king, who was also on foot, went along with them. They realized too late that wisdom is superior to reckless courage, for if they had remained in battle order and had awaited the enemy in the field, they would have completely bent them to their will.

But, thrown into confusion by the disarray of their battle lines, they could neither find their horses nor decide what to do. The king mounted someone else's horse and returned to combat in a spirited fashion. He shouted and called his men back, urging the boldest by name not to flee. With sword unsheathed the king rushed amid the enemy ranks to help those whom he could and chase those who were fleeing. And something which little befitted the royal majesty, this veteran warrior fought hand-to-hand, fulfilling the office of a simple knight, not that of a king. But just when his mount became tired and he alone could not prevent the host from giving way, his squire suddenly appeared close at hand, leading up the king's own warhorse. He swiftly mounted and, holding his standard in front of him, led a few companions in another attack against his foes. With wonderful valor he rescued many of his men who had been captured and with a very powerful charge cut off some of the enemy. To prevent further harm to his host, he hurled back his foes and made them flee as if they had been dashing against the Pillars of Hercules at Cadiz or had been fended off by the great Ocean.[6]

Before returning to Le Puiset, the enemy joined up with a host of five hundred or more Norman knights who would have done the king greater damage if they had arrived sooner when the royal forces were pulling back. But the host of the king had now scattered in all directions, some heading for Orléans, others Etampes, and others Pithiviers.[d] So a very weary king came to Toury, "like a bull driven from the herd in the first struggle . . . testing his horns on tree trunks." Mustering strength in his very stout heart, "he gave no thought to a serious wound as he charged" through the iron weapon onto the enemy.[7] In just this way, the king reassembled his host, rekindled its valor, revived its fearless spirit, and attributed its defeat to folly, not a lack of foresight. He reminded them that knights were bound to encounter this kind of thing now and then. Using flatteries and threats, he began urging them to fight with greater daring and fervor, and to avenge the wrongs done them if a good chance arose. Meanwhile, the French and the Normans set about rebuilding the castle where Count Theobald, the Norman host, Milo of Montlhéry, and Hugh of Crécy, along with his brother Count Guy of Rochefort, had gathered. All in all, thirteen hun-

---

d. In other words, Louis's forces had fled about twenty miles in three different directions—south, north, and east.

dred knights were threatening to besiege Toury. But the king did not turn back because of fear of any kind; he worked night and day to harass and harm them as best he could, and to prevent them from foraging abroad for foodstuffs.

The castle was rebuilt after a week of steady work, and, although some of the Normans had left, Count Theobald and his sizable host were still there. The king, assembling the best men he had, started his war machine into motion, went back to Le Puiset with a strong force, and wore down the enemies he encountered. Fighting his way through the gate and avenging the wrongs done him, he shut them up in the castle and posted a guard of knights to keep them from leaving. He then took possession of an old motte only a stone's throw from the castle. It had been abandoned by his ancestors, but he now built his own castle there, with a great deal of work and a great deal of worry. For, although his men had tied posts together and put up a palisade, they still met with serious danger from the missiles launched by the slings, crossbowmen, and archers of the enemy who were harassing them from behind the secure enclosures of their castle. Their foes kept firing away with no concern for the retaliation their wrongdoing deserved; and as these rivals competed for victory, the struggle between those inside and those outside the new castle grew dangerous and vehement. The king's knights who had been wounded remembered the pains they had suffered and strove very bitterly to return the favor. They did not stop the work they had begun until they had installed many knights and much equipment in their fortress, which had been built so quickly that it seemed enchanted. They had decided that, as soon as the king left, they would make a bold stand against the rude attacks from the neighboring place or go down to a miserable death under fierce blows from the swords of their enemies.

Returning to Toury and assembling his forces, the king engaged in a risky and daring enterprise to support his host on the motte. He sent foodstuffs right through the middle of the enemy lines, sometimes secretly with a few men, sometimes openly with many. But the men of Le Puiset, too close at hand for comfort, were harassing his men unbearably and threatening to besiege the motte. So, moving camp to be within reach, he took possession of Janville, about one mile from Le Puiset, and quickly surrounded its interior courtyard with a palisade made from stakes and interwoven branches.ᵉ And while the royal host pitched its tents, the palatine count Theobald gathered the strongest possible force from his own partisans and from the Norman host, and launched a powerful attack against the king's men. He hoped to surprise them before they were entrenched and drive them back in a rout.

The king armed himself fully and went out to meet him, and both sides struggled bitterly in the field. It did not matter whether they fought with lances or swords; victory meant more to them than life, its trophy more than death. The marvelous courage displayed there was a sight to behold! The count's host was three times larger than the king's, and at first it drove the royal knights back into the village. But the king himself had a few men with him, namely his very noble relative Count Ralph of Vermandois,[8] Drogo of Mouchy, and two or three others; and he deemed retreating into the village out of fear as unworthy. Mindful of his earlier manliness,[9] he chose to stand and bear the savage onslaughts and nearly countless blows of his armed enemies, for it would dishonor his personal valor and royal excellence if he were forced to enter the village under duress.

Thinking he had victory in hand, Count Theobald rashly tried to cut down the tents of the count of Vermandois. But the count came before him with amazing speed and reviled him, saying that the men of Brie had never before presumed to do such things against the men of Vermandois. Rushing against him and exerting himself mightily, he paid Count Theobald back in kind for

e. Janville, Eure-et-Loir, is about twenty-five miles southeast of Chartres.

the wrong he had done, driving him away with great bravery. Heartened by the heroism of the count of Vermandois and the battle cry, the royal knights threw themselves against their enemies and, thirsting for blood, attacked them heartily. They struck them down, put them to shame, and pushed them, under duress, all the way back to Le Puiset, where the gate closed behind them in disgrace. Many of the enemy had been taken prisoner and even more killed; and as the outcome of battle is a changing thing, those who had earlier deemed themselves victors now blushed at being defeated. They grieved for their men who had been captured and wept for their dead.

Finally the king began to prevail against them, and Count Theobald began to plummet downward like someone moving from the top of the wheel of fortune.[10] The count and his men grew weary as time dragged on, for they were being cast down and pounded unbearably. But the power of the king and his party grew stronger from day to day as the number of leading men in the kingdom who were angry with the count grew larger. The count, chancing one day upon a pretext to pull back, namely, a wound he had received the day before, dispatched messengers to the king, commissioning them to intercede and urge humbly that the lord king allow him to return to Chartres in safety. Being more kind and gentle than people thought possible, the king deigned to grant his petition, although many men tried to talk him out of letting loose an enemy who was trapped by a lack of foodstuffs. They wanted to prevent him from suffering the same sort of trouble from the count of Chartres in the future. And so, abandoning the castle of Le Puiset and Hugh to the power of the king, the count departed. He had been deceived by a vain hope, for what he had begun happily had ended miserably when the king not only disinherited Hugh of Le Puiset but overturned and levelled the castle, wrecking its walls and filling in its wells. The place looked as if it had fallen under a divine curse.[11]

[22]
Hugh's recurring treachery

But in another encounter, a long time afterward, when he had been restored to the king's favor by the giving of many hostages and the swearing of countless oaths, Hugh again set himself to rebellion and fraud, "and taught by Sulla, he outdid his wicked master."[1] Once more he was besieged by the king, and once more he was disinherited. He continued along the path of his inborn and habitual treason by personally running his lance through the king's seneschal, Anselm of Garlande, a valiant baron. Finally Hugh took the road to Jerusalem and, like so many other wretched men, put an end to his wicked ways, polluted as they were with every kind poison, only when life was snatched from him.[a]

a. The third siege of Le Puiset occurred in 1118. This short chapter is therefore out of sequence; Suger introduces the material now in order to round off the story of Hugh. See further endnote 2.

[23]
The alliance of peace between the king of England, the king of Gaul, and Count Theobald[a]

The magnates of the kingdom and the monastic clergy worked together for an alliance of peace between the king of England, the king of Gaul,[1] and Count Theobald. And a just judgment befell those who conspired against the kingdom when they pressed the king of England and Count Theobald to arbitrate their personal quarrels.[b] Although consumed by war, they gained nothing from peace and earned fitting punishments for what they had done. Lancelin, count of Dammartin, lost his claim to safe-conduct through Beauvais without hope of getting it back. Pagan of Montjay was disappointed in his claim to the castle of Livry; one month he grieved in a heartfelt way to see the castle's enclosure destroyed, but he grieved much more the next month when it was rebuilt and made much stronger with the English king's money.[2] And Milo of Montlhéry groaned with grief when he gave up a very favorable marriage to the sister of the count because he was related to her, and from the annulment he reaped dishonor and sorrow greater than the honor and joy he had gained in taking her. That all turned out uncommonly well when these men gave judgment can be gathered from the authority of the canons where this verdict can be found: "Ties that bind men are totally null and void when undertaken against the peace."[3]

---

a. In default of anything in the text, we have supplied titles for all the remaining chapters of the book.

b. That is, they had not sought justice at the king's court.

[24]
The overthrow of Thomas of Marle's castles at Crécy and Nouvion

By their powerful right arm and by virtue of the office they have sworn to uphold, kings put down insolent tyrants whenever they see them inciting wars, taking pleasure in endless plunder, persecuting the poor, and destroying churches. Kings put a stop to their wanton behavior, which kindles even greater insanity in them if left unbridled. They become like evil spirits who prefer to slaughter those whom they fear to lose and favor by all means possible those whom they hope to keep, adding fuel to the flames which will then devour them with much greater pain.

Such a person was the most accursed Thomas of Marle. While King Louis was occupied with the wars just mentioned and many others, Thomas ravaged the countryside around Laon, Reims, and Amiens; and the devil helped him succeed, for the success of fools generally leads them to perdition. He devoured and destroyed everything like a wolf gone mad, and fear of ecclesiastical punishment did not compel him to spare the clergy, nor any feeling of humanity the people. He slaughtered all, ruined all, and even grabbed two prosperous estates from the convent of nuns of Saint John of Laon. He fortified the very formidable castles of Crécy and Nouvion with a marvelous rampart and lofty towers, as if they were his own.[a] And changing them into a lair of dragons and a den of thieves, he cruelly handed over nearly the whole land to pillaging and fires.

a. Crécy is Crécy-sur-Serre, Aisne, some eight miles north of Laon and about ninety miles northeast of Paris; Nouvion is a few miles downstream on the Serre from Crécy. This expedition will take Louis far from home.

Worn down by the unbearable trouble caused by this man, the Gallic church sat at Beauvais in a general council. It hoped to proceed with an initial judgment and publish a sentence of condemnation against the enemies of its true spouse, Jesus Christ, for the countless complaints of the churches and the miseries of the poor and the orphaned cried out for action. Cono, the venerable legate of the holy Roman church and bishop of Palestrina, took up the sword of the blessed Peter and struck down Thomas's tyranny with a general anathema. Although Thomas was not present, he stripped him of his knightly status and, in accordance with the judgment of all, deposed him from every honor as a wicked, ill-famed enemy of the Christian name.[b]

The woeful plea of this great council persuaded the king, and he quickly set his forces into motion against Thomas.[2] Accompanied by the clergy, to whom he was always humbly attached, he turned off the road toward the well-fortified castle of Crécy. Helped by his powerful band of armed men, or rather by the hand of God,[c] he abruptly seized the castle and captured its very strong tower as if it were simply the hut of a peasant. Having startled those criminals, he piously slaughtered the impious,[3] cutting them down without mercy because he found them to be merciless. What a sight! The castle was burning with such a hellish fire that everyone quickly concluded, "The whole world will fight for him against these madmen."[4]

Having won this victory, the king quickly followed up his successes, and he was heading for the other castle, called Nouvion, when a man came up and informed him: "My lord king and serene highness, be aware that the men lingering in that miser-

---

b. The Council of Beauvais met in November-December, 1114. See further endnote 1.

c. The word *manus* has been used twice in this clause; it can mean "band" or "hand," an ambiguity Suger exploits for a pun.

able castle are awful wretches. Hell is the only place they are fit
to be. The time you ordered that the commune of Laon be done
away with, they are the ones, I tell you, who set fire to the city
and the noble church of the Mother of the Lord and many others
as well. They made martyrs of nearly all the nobles of the city to
punish them for their true fealty when they tried hard to bring
help to their lord the bishop. Bishop Gaudry himself, the venerable defender of the church, they killed with great cruelty, not
fearing to lay hands on the Lord's anointed.[5] Having cut off the
finger that held his bishop's ring, they left his naked body in the
square as food for beasts and birds of prey. Then with their
wicked seducer, Thomas himself, they struggled to seize your
tower and separate you from your property."[6]

Stirred to action once again, the king attacked the evil castle
and smashed to pieces its hellish places of punishment and
sacrilege. He set free the innocent and punished the guilty severely, he alone avenging the crimes committed by many. Thirsting for justice he ordered that any of those wretched murderers
whom he ran across be fixed to a gibbet and left as common food
for the insatiable appetite of kites, crows, and vultures. In this
way he taught what those deserve who do not fear to lay hand on
the Lord's anointed.

After he had levelled those unlawful castles[d] and restored the
estates to Saint John's, he returned to the city of Amiens and laid
siege to its tower. It was held by Adam, a tyrant who was laying
waste the churches and the entire neighborhood.[7] The king
penned up the tower's defenders in a tight siege for nearly two
years before he finally forced them to surrender. He captured the
tower, and having captured it he demolished it down to its
foundations, and having demolished it he restored welcome
peace to the land. Thus he fulfilled the office of a king who "does

d. *Adulterina castella*, designated as "unlawful" because the castles had
been built without proper authorization.

not carry his sword in vain"; and he disinherited forever that most vile Thomas and his heirs from the lordship of the city.[e]

[25]
How he gained possession of the castle of Germigny and gave judgment against Haimo Vairevache

A king's power should never be thought of as being limited only to the narrow boundaries of any part of his lands, "for kings are known to have long arms."[1] This was made clear when Alard Guillebald, a skillful man with a tongue for sale, came rushing to the king from the frontiers of Berry and, with an appropriate amount of rhetoric, laid before him the complaint of his stepson. He humbly beseeched the lord king to use his royal authority and bring to court a noble baron named Haimo, surnamed Vairevache, the lord of Bourbon, who was refusing justice to Guillebald's stepson. He asked the king to curb his arrogance and insolence, for, in this case, Haimo had disinherited his own nephew, the son of his older brother Erchenbald. Guillebald wanted the judgment of the French to determine what each of them should have.[a]

The king feared that another plague of wars would spring up

e. The lordship of Amiens passed to Countess Adela of Vermandois. Suger has brought the chapter to an artistic end. It began with reflections on the *officium* of kings, and now with the help of a text from the Bible (Rom. 13:4), Suger can show that Louis had been fulfilling that *officium*.

a. These events can be dated to the summer of 1109 (Waquet, p. 180, n. 4). They are therefore badly out of chronological order.

over this matter, and that the overburdened poor would pay the penalty for someone else's pride. So, out of his love for justice and his compassion for the churches and the poor, he summoned Haimo to plead his case at court, but in vain, for Haimo defied justice and refused to come. But the king surrendered neither to lust nor to laziness.[b] He headed for the regions of Berry with a large host; and turning off the road toward Germigny, a well-fortified castle held by Haimo, he launched a vigorous attack against it.[c]

Seeing that he could not possibly hold out, Haimo abandoned hope for his own person and his castle, and found the only way to save himself. He threw himself down at the feet of the lord king, and to the amazement of many he performed the gesture repeatedly. Begging the king for merciful treatment, he surrendered his castle and entrusted himself entirely to the disposition of his royal majesty. Having learned his lesson, he delivered himself to justice with humility equal to the pride with which he had removed himself from justice. The king kept the castle and brought Haimo back into France for trial. He settled the quarrel between the uncle and the nephew fairly and conscientiously by judgment of the French or at least by mutual agreement; and, with a great deal of cost and effort, he put an end to the persecution and hardships of many.

He habitually achieved merciful results like these in those regions so that the churches and the poor might enjoy peace. But it would make dull reading if we wrote about them; so it seems best to overlook them.[d]

b. As we are dealing with events of 1109, this expression may well be directed against King Philip, who had died in the preceding year.

c. Now Germigny-sur-l'Aubois, Cher, about thirty miles southeast of Bourges and about 160 miles south of Paris.

d. The implication that Louis frequently became involved in affairs so far from Paris, particularly in areas south of the Loire, is false.

[26]
Conflict with King Henry of England

Unbridled conceit is worse than pride in this respect: a proud person believes there is no one superior to him, but a conceited person believes there is no one equal to him. To this person can be applied that saying of the poet: "Caesar could not acknowledge a superior, nor Pompey an equal"; and since "everyone who has power grows weary of a peer," Louis, king of the French, conducted himself toward Henry, king of the English and duke of the Normans, as toward a vassal, for he always kept in mind the lofty rank by which he towered over him.[1] But the king of the English, having regard for the nobility of his kingdom and the wonderful abundance of its wealth, soon grew tired of his lower standing.[2] With help from his nephew, the palatine count Theobald, and from many disaffected men of the kingdom of the French, he strove to unsettle the realm and disturb its king, for he wished to withdraw from his lordship.

The persistent plague of recurrent strife between them returned once more when the king of England joined efforts with Count Theobald and attacked the nearest border district of the king.[3] The nearness of Normandy to the countryside of Chartres made them neighbors. They sent Count Stephen of Mortain, nephew of one and brother of the other, at the head of a host to other districts, namely into Brie, for they were afraid that the king would suddenly seize that land in the absence of Count Theobald.[a] But the king chose to spare neither the Normans nor the men of Chartres and Brie. Finding himself somewhat encircled by these two foes, he laid waste the lands of one and then

a. Stephen, Henry's nephew and Theobald's brother, succeeded Henry as king of England in 1135.

the other, and with frequent fighting made known the heroic spirit of the royal majesty.

Through the excellent foresight of the kings of the English and the dukes of the Normans, the Norman border was tightly protected by an impressive line of new castles and by the channels of the unfordable rivers that flowed there. Aware of all this but still aiming to cross into Normandy, the king made his way towards the border with only a small band of knights, for he hoped to do his planning in some secrecy. He cautiously sent ahead men disguised as travellers, but they wore chainmail beneath their cloaks and carried swords at their waists. They went down the main road to a village called Gasny, an old settlement that would give the French an open and easy approach to the Normans.[b] The river Epte flowed around the middle of the village and provided safety for those inside, while no one on the outside of the village could cross the river upstream or downstream except at a distance. Suddenly the king's men cast off their cloaks and unsheathed their swords, but the villagers, seeing what was coming, surged forward vehemently with their weapons. The royal force, however, drove them back with a powerful attack of its own; and then, unexpectedly, when his men were almost worn out, the king hurried across the dangerous slope of a hill and brought them timely aid. He seized the village's churchyard and the church itself—which was fortified by a tower—but not without the loss of some men.

When he discovered that the king of England was nearby with a large host, something he generally had, he summoned his barons and urgently invited them to follow his lead. Quick to arrive were Count Baldwin of Flanders, a distinguished and courteous young man who was a true knight,[c] Count Fulk of Anjou,

b. Gasny, Eure, is on the lower Epte near its confluence with the Seine, about fifty miles northwest of Paris. See further endnote 4.

c. Count Baldwin VII of Flanders (1111–19), here shown as cooperating with Louis for the first time.

and many other leading men of the kingdom. Having broken through the defensive barrier of Normandy, some of them fortified the village while others opened up to pillage and fires a land that long peace had made rich. They wreaked unbearable havoc in every direction with their raiding, something that usually did not happen when the king of the English was present.[5]

Meanwhile, the king of England quickly made preparations for the building of a castle and urged on the workmen. While King Louis left his own stronghold protected by a guard of knights, King Henry erected his castle on the hill nearest to it. From there he used his many knights and the arrows fired by his crossbowmen and archers to drive back his enemies. He planned to cut the French off from the foodstuffs the land produced and force them to plunder their own land out of a dire need to support themselves. But the king of the French let fire his own arrows and immediately paid him back in kind, just as if he were throwing dice with him. He hastily assembled his host, returned at dawn, and forcefully attacked that new castle, commonly called Malassis, expending much effort while giving and receiving many heavy blows.[d] This is the kind of toll generally paid in this kind of marketplace, and he paid it like a man. He plundered and destroyed, and with true valor brought to nought whatever had been plotted there, adding to the excellence of his kingdom and the shame of his opponent.

Fortune is a powerful force that no one can escape, for as the saying goes: "You will rise from teaching rhetoric to become a consul if fortune wishes; and if it wishes, you will fall from being a consul back to teaching rhetoric."[e] The king of England had been enjoying very good luck after a long and wonderful run of successes, but he now found himself disturbed by a different and luckless turn of events, like someone falling from the top of the

---

d. Malassis means "badly located." See further endnote 6.

e. Juvenal, *Sat.* 7:197f. Teachers of rhetoric were sophists who were held in very low esteem in ancient times.

wheel of fortune.[7] From this region the king of France strove with all his power to make endless trouble and countless attacks upon him, as did the count of Flanders from the neighboring region of Ponthieu and Count Fulk of Anjou from the region of Maine.[8] The king of England suffered war damage inflicted on him not only by these men from outside his lands but also by his own vassals inside them, namely Hugh of Gournay, the count of Eu, the count of Aumale, and many others.[9]

To crown his misfortune, he was even troubled by a piece of wickedness inside his very own household. Frightened thoroughly by a clandestine conspiracy of stewards and chamberlains, he changed beds often and, dreading night's terrors, regularly increased his armed guards. He also ordered that a shield and sword be placed before him every night while he slept. One member of the cabal, named H.,[f] was an intimate counsellor who had been enriched by the king's generosity; but having become powerful and renowned, he became even more renowned as a traitor. Caught taking part in this terrible plot, he was mercifully condemned to losing his eyes and genitals when he deserved to be choked to death by a noose. Living under conditions like these, the king never felt safe; and despite his reputation for valor and greatness of spirit, he took the precaution of wearing his sword even in his own house. And he also punished those whom he considered his most faithful men if they went out of their homes without swords at their sides, making them pay a large sum as if it were a trifle.

During those days Enguerrand of Chaumont, a valiant and courageous man, boldly went forth with a band of knights and gallantly took hold of the castle called Andelys.[g] Its ramparts

---

f. The name of Henry's attacker is not given by Suger, but the sources indicate that he was from lowborn ranks. See further endnote 10.

g. Enguerrand possessed territories in the French Vexin. Andelys, Eure, is in the Norman Vexin, about sixty-five miles northwest of Paris.

were being guarded by men who were secretly on his side. Relying on help from King Louis, he seized and fortified it with
supreme confidence; and from there he brought under his full
control all the land up to the river Andelle—everything from the
river Epte all the way up to Pont-Saint-Pierre.[h] Then, supported
by a large company of knights who outranked him in nobility,
Enguerrand went out onto the plain to confront the king of
England. And in turning him back he mocked the king rudely
and made use of the land within the above limits as his own.
After a long delay the king of England decided to accompany
Count Theobald and bring help from the region of Maine to
those besieged in the tower of the castle of Alençon. But he
suffered a setback at the hands of Count Fulk, losing many of his
men, the castle, and, what made his loss the more inglorious,
even the tower.[11]

King Henry was troubled for a long time by losses like these,
and his fortunes had sunk almost to the very bottom. But although a wanton man, he was a generous donor to churches and
a liberal giver of alms. So, after he had been harshly whipped and
chastised for some time, the divine mercy decreed that he be
spared and mercifully lifted him up from the depths to which he
had sunk. The wheel suddenly brought him back from the pit of
misfortune to the summit of success, for the divine hand rather
than his own abruptly pushed his antagonists who were higher
up, and they began to plummet downward, plunging all the way
to the very bottom. But this is the customary way of the Divinity, which mercifully extends the right hand of its clemency
to men who have been abandoned by human help and are at the
very brink of despair.[i]

h. Pont-Saint-Pierre, Eure, is on the west bank of the Andelle in Normandy, just upstream from its junction with the Seine, about ten miles
northwest of Andelys and a similar distance southeast of Rouen.

i. Suger again uses the metaphor of a wheel to describe fluctations of

Count Baldwin of Flanders had been severely harassing King Henry with bitter attacks and frequent invasions of Normandy. On one occasion, when the count was making war with unrestrained knightly spirit on the castle of Eu and the neighboring coast, a sudden glancing blow from a lance struck him in the face. He disdained to take care of so small a wound, but did not disdain to die; and in coming to such an end, he saw fit to do a favor not only to the present king of England but all later ones as well.ʲ

And then there was Enguerrand of Chaumont, a very daring man who had become overconfident in his attacks on King Henry. He did not flinch when he brought about the destruction of some land in the archdiocese of Rouen which belonged to the blessed Mary, Mother of the Lord, but a very serious illness laid him low. Having been tormented for a long time by continual bodily pain, which he deserved but could not bear, he departed this life, having learned too late what was due to the Queen of Heaven.[13] There was also the case of Count Fulk of Anjou, who had earlier allied himself to King Louis by personal homage, many oaths, and even a large number of hostages. But Count Fulk now put greed before fealty, and inflamed by treachery gave his daughter in wedlock to William, son of the English king, without consulting King Louis. He falsely betrayed his sworn word to be an enemy of King Henry and joined himself to the English king by ties of friendship of this kind.[14]

Campaigning from his own region, King Louis forced the land of Normandy to grow silent in his sight.[15] Sometimes large, sometimes small, the size of his band of men did not matter when he delivered the land over to plundering. After some time

---

success, but this time its operation is linked with God. He sustains the image throughout the paragraph.

j. Count Baldwin VII of Flanders was wounded in battle in September 1118 and died the following June. Eu is about fifty-five miles north of Rouen. See further endnote 12.

his continual ability to harass the English king made him despise him and his men, and pay no attention to them. But the king of England took note of the reckless and daring behavior of the king of the French and, gathering together many of his strongest men, one day suddenly sent out from their hiding place a force of knights in battle order against him. Setting fires that would leap up and throw him into disarray, King Henry made his armed knights dismount so that they might fight more bravely on foot, and wisely busied himself taking whatever military precautions he could.

King Louis and his men, however, deemed it unworthy to plan carefully for battle and rushed against their enemy in a bold but careless attack. The men of the Vexin, along with Burchard of Montmorency and Guy of Clermont, were the first to set their right arms to work.[16] This brave band cut down the first battle line of Normans and chased their foes from the glorious field of combat, and with a powerful hand drove the first line of knights back on top of the armed foot soldiers. The French then decided to pursue the enemy but fell into disorder when they pressed against the Normans' surprisingly well-aligned and positioned ranks. And as happens in these cases, they gave ground when they could not withstand the pressure from their foe's ordered row.[17]

The sight of his host falling back astonished the king; but as he usually did in bad times, he relied on his own hardy fighting spirit to help himself and his men. He returned to Andelys as decently as possible, but not without his wandering host sustaining great harm, and he suffered for a while from the misfortune which his own foolishness had suddenly brought upon him.[k] But he became more courageous than he usually was in

k. The statement that Louis returned to Andelys "as decently as possible," while strictly true, conceals the harsh reality. In his flight there from Brémule in defeat, Louis became lost in a wood and had to be escorted back to Andelys by a peasant (OV 4:361f).

hard times and, as befits true men, more steadfast. To avoid
being taunted any further by his enemies for not daring to enter
Normandy, he called back his host, summoned those who were
absent, and invited the leading men of the kingdom to join him.
He then notified the king of the English on what day he would
enter his land to engage him in a very great battle, and hurried to
fulfill his promise as if it were a sworn agreement. Leading a
marvelous host he rushed into Normandy, ravaged the land and,
penetrating as far as Breteuil, captured the well-fortified castle of
Ivry with fierce fighting and burned it with fire.[18]

He lingered in the land for a little while but found neither the
king of the English nor anyone else on whom he might take
adequate revenge for the insult he had suffered. So he turned
his attention to Count Theobald, withdrew to Chartres, and
launched a powerful attack against the city, striving to burn it
with fire. Then, all of a sudden, the clergy and townspeople
came up to him bearing the tunic of the blessed Mother of God
before them.[19] They devoutly begged that he be merciful and, as
chief protector of her church, spare them out of love for her,
imploring that he not take revenge on them for a wrong committed by others. The king made the loftiness of his royal majesty bow down before their pleas; and to prevent the noble
church of the blessed Mary and the city from being burned
down, he ordered Count Charles of Flanders to call back the host
and spare the city out of the love and reverence he bore the
church. But when they had gone home, they did not stop punishing the misfortune of a moment with a long, constant, and very
heavy revenge.[20]

The pontificate of Calixtus and the
abbacy of St. Denis

At that time Paschal, the supreme pontiff of venerable memory, passed from the light of this world into that of eternity; and he was succeeded by Gelasius, the former chancellor, John of Gaeta, who had been appointed pope by canonical election.ᵃ But he found himself unbearably burdened by trouble from Burdinus, the deposed archbishop of Braga, who had been thrust upon the apostolic see by the violent actions of the emperor Henry, and by disturbances the Roman people had been bribed to create. Kept away from the holy see by their tyranny, he followed the custom of popes of old and fled to the care and protection of the most serene King Louis and to the sympathy of the Gallic church.ᵇ

Prompted by the torment of great poverty, the lord pope Gelasius came by boat and landed at Maguelonne, a narrow island in the sea, on which sat a single isolated town.ᶜ Only a few clergy and a small number of servants assisted its bishop, but a strong wall fortified the settlement against attacks from the Saracens who roam the seas. The lord king sent us there after he had received word of his arrival. We carried out our commission, received his benediction for presenting him the first fruits of the realm,³ and joyfully carried back news of the day that had been

---

a. Paschal II died on January 21, 1118; his successor, John of Gaeta, took the name Gelasius II.

b. The emperor Henry V arrived in Rome on March 1, 1118, and set up a rival pope, Burdinus, who had been deposed from the see of Braga in 1114. He took the name Gregory VIII. See further endnote 1.

c. The island of Maguelonne is seven miles south of Montpellier. See further endnote 2.

decided on for a discussion between them, and of the place, namely Vézelay.

While the lord king was hurrying to meet him, he learned that the same supreme pontiff who had long suffered from gout had solved a problem for both the Romans and the French by losing his life.[4] Many monastic clergy and prelates of the church rushed to attend his apostolic funeral; among them was Guy, the venerable archbishop of Vienne. Already noble because of his kinship to their imperial and royal highnesses, he had become even more noble by his way of life. In his dreams the night before the funeral he had seen the moon, which had been placed under a cloak, entrusted to him by a very powerful person. It was an apt portent of what would soon happen, although at the time he did not know what it meant. The representatives of the Roman church present at the funeral became afraid that a vacancy in the papal office would threaten the interests of the church. They elected him supreme pontiff, and he now understood quite clearly the truth of the vision.[d]

Raised up to so lofty a dignity, he safeguarded the rights of the church splendidly, humbly, and bravely; and helped by the love and service of the lord king Louis and of his own niece, the noble queen Adelaide, he was better able to take care of the church. During a well-attended council that he celebrated at Reims, he postponed a session in the interests of peace for the church and went out to the border toward Mouzon to meet the legates of the emperor Henry.[e] He gained nothing; but, just as his predecessors had done, he bound Henry with the chain of anathema in a full council attended by the French and the Lotharingians. And

d. Archbishop Guy of Vienne, the uncle of Louis's wife Adelaide, was elected pope at Cluny on February 21, 1119. He took the papal name Calixtus II. See further endnote 5.

e. Mouzon, Ardennes, is just south of the present French border with Belgium, about sixty miles northeast of Reims. See further endnote 6.

when he had gloriously arrived at Rome enriched with donations that the churches had pledged, he received a wonderful welcome from the clergy and the Roman people, and happily saw to the administration of the church in a manner superior to that of many of his predecessors.

He had not held the holy see for long before the Romans came to prefer him to Burdinus because of his nobility and generosity. The schismatic Burdinus had been thrust upon them by the emperor; and, while sitting at Sutri, he had even made the clergy genuflect before him as they crossed to the thresholds of the apostles. The Romans therefore captured him, held him in prison and, dressing him in a cloak of undressed goatskins reeking with blood, placed this devious antipope,[f] nay antichrist, across the back of that devious animal, the camel. Taking revenge for the shame suffered by the church of God, they led him forth on the royal road through the middle of the city to make the events more widely known. And at the command of the lord pope Calixtus, they condemned him to perpetual imprisonment in the mountains of Campania near St. Benedict. Then, wanting to keep fresh the memory of their superb revenge, they painted a scene in a room of the papal palace, showing Burdinus being trampled under the feet of the lord pope.[8]

With the lord Calixtus presiding in splendor and subduing the robbers in Italy and Apulia, the light of the pontifical throne was placed not under a bushel but high on a mountain top.[9] The church of the blessed Peter shone forth brightly as did the other churches of the City and even those beyond, for they recovered what they had lost and enjoyed the most welcome patronage of a great lord. Having been sent by the lord king Louis on some affairs of the kingdom, I met the pope in Apulia at the city of

---

f. An early use of the word "antipope," which perhaps owes something to Suger's penchant for punning (*antipapam, immo antichristum*). See further endnote 7.

Bitonto. Moved by reverence for the lord king and our monastery, this apostolic man received us with honor and wished to retain us longer; but we were called away by love for our church and by the persuasion of our companions, among others the abbot of St. Germain, our associate who had grown up with us.[10]

Having concluded the business of the kingdom we had undertaken, we were in a hurry to return home safely as travellers usually are, and were enjoying the hospitality of a villa when I went back to bed at the end of Matins fully clothed to await the dawn. Half asleep, I seemed to see myself on the wide expanse of the sea, all alone in a flimsy boat. Left drifting without any oars, the boat was being precariously tossed about, sometimes rising, sometimes falling with the unending motion of the waves. A horrible fear of shipwreck overwhelmed me, and I wore out the ears of the Divinity with my loud shouting. Then suddenly, by the divine mercy, a gentle and calm breeze somehow came up out of a cloudless sky and turned the tremulous, nay perilous prow of my miserable boat in the right direction. It made its way more quickly than anyone would have thought possible and reached a safe harbor.

Aroused by the dawn[11] I set out on the road I had taken and travelled along lost in deep thought as I tried to recall the vision and discern its meaning, for I feared those turbulent waves meant that I would suffer some severe misfortune. Suddenly, a servant from our household encountered us on the road; and after he recognized my companions and me, he was both happy and sad as he led me to one side. He reported the death of my predecessor, our lord abbot Adam of good memory, and the election of our own person, which had been carried out in full assembly with the assent of those present, but without the king being consulted in the matter. So, when the preeminent and most religious of the brothers, and also the noblest knights, had brought word of the election to the lord king for his approval, they found themselves locked up in the castle of Orléans, the victims of much abuse.[g] Tears welled up in me as I was moved by an emotion of human feeling and filial piety for the spiritual father who had raised me. I grieved deeply over his temporal death and most devoutly implored the divine mercy to deliver him from eternal death.

Having been consoled by my companions, I relied on my own sense of propriety and regained my composure. But I was worried about three possible losses if I followed the strict position of the Roman church and the guidance of the lord pope Calixtus who esteemed me highly, and accepted the election against the will of the lord king. I would permit my mother church, which had fostered me lovingly from infancy in the sweet bosom of her generosity, to be ruined and damaged on my account by each destroyer when it had never been a cause of dispute between them before.[13] Secondly, I would allow my brothers and friends to suffer humiliation and shame in the royal prison out of love for me. And finally, if I rejected the election for these and like reasons, I would disgrace myself for having been a failure in such an important matter. While I was trying to decide whether to send one of my own party back to the lord pope to seek his advice, a noble Roman cleric who was a close friend of mine unexpectedly came upon us. He promised to undertake at his own expense the same costly task we wished to do through our own men. In addition, we sent ahead to the king one of our servants along with the one who had found us, and they were to bring back news of the outcome of this bothersome and perplexing business. We did not wish to subject ourselves needlessly to troubles from the king.

And as we followed after them, it seemed as if we were being

g. Orléans is a considerable distance from St. Denis, about eighty-five miles to the south. Presumably the monks and knights were imprisoned there because it was there that they broke the news of Suger's election to Louis. See further endnote 12.

tossed about on a wide sea without any oar. Unsure as to what would happen, we were indeed worried and very deeply disturbed.[h] However, the abundant mercy of almighty God steered our nearly shipwrecked vessel with a gentle breeze, for our messengers suddenly returned and reported that the lord king was peaceably disposed. The prisoners had been freed, and the election had been confirmed. We interpreted all this as proof that God had willed it, for only the will of God could have brought about so swiftly what we had wished. After we returned to our mother church with the help of God, it welcomed home its prodigal son sweetly, filially, and nobly; and we even had the pleasure to find there our lord the king coming to meet us, with his face once so severe, now so serene. Also awaiting our arrival were the archbishop of Bourges, the bishop of Senlis, and many other churchmen who greeted us with high respect, much to the joy of the great crowd of assembled brothers.[14] On the next day, namely the day before Passion Sunday, I was ordained a priest, unworthy as I was. And on the Sunday following, the day of *Isti sunt dies*, even though undeserving I was consecrated abbot in the presence of the very holy body of the most blessed Dionysius.[i]

As usually happens when almighty God elevates someone from the depths to the heights, he "lifts the poor man up from the dunghill, so that he might make him sit with princes."[15] In a similar way, his most benign and powerful hand made me more humble and more devout in all things, to the extent that fragile human nature allowed. And his mercy brought success in every endeavor to such a little person as me, for he knew the imperfec-

---

h. Louis's actions had created a tense and awkward situation for Suger, given the attempts being made by churchmen to free monasteries from lay influence on the elections of abbots.

i. Suger was ordained priest on Saturday, March 11, 1122, and consecrated abbot on the next day (Cartellieri, no. 23f). *Isti sunt dies* is from the responsory for Passion Sunday, which occurred two weeks before Easter Day.

tions of my birth and skill.[j] These successes included the recovery of old estates belonging to the church and the gaining of new ones, the enlargement of the church on each of its sides, and the restoration or construction of buildings.[16] But the most important and welcome thing, indeed the highest privilege he mercifully granted me, was that he fully reformed the holy order of his holy church in that place, to the honor of his saints and of himself. And he peacefully brought about this reform of holy religion that enables one to enjoy God, without scandal and without any disturbance among the brothers, something to which they were quite unaccustomed.[17]

An abundance of freedom, good repute, and worldly wealth followed this moving display of the divine will; and even in present times our faint heart has begun to beat somewhat faster. One can see that somehow we ourselves have been rewarded with worldly goods as well. Popes,[18] kings, and princes love to show their appreciation to the church by giving it presents; and thus they have poured down on it a deluge of precious gems, gold and silver, rich coverings, and other ecclesiastical ornaments. And we too can truly say: "All good things have come to me together with that."[19] By this experience of God's glory to come, we charge and implore through the mercy of God and his terrible judgment that the brothers who come after us never allow holy religion to grow cold. For it reconciles men with God, makes whole what is broken, restores what is lost, and makes rich what is poor. And just as those who fear God need nothing, those who do not fear him, even kings, will be found deficient in all things, themselves included.

During the year following our ordination, we lost no time in visiting Rome to prevent being charged with ingratitude, for the holy Roman church had welcomed us cordially at Rome and

j. The reference to Suger's size is probably to be taken literally, as well as an expression of humility.

elsewhere in many different councils before our promotion when we were acting on behalf of our own church and others.[20] It had also joyfully given ear to our pleadings and dealt with our affairs more favorably than we deserved. We were again welcomed with great honor by the lord pope Calixtus and the whole curia; and for six months we stayed there with him, attending a great council of 300 or more bishops at the Lateran; it had been called to bring the quarrel of investitures to a peaceful conclusion.[k] We visited different places associated with the saints where we might pray, namely St. Benedict of Monte Cassino, St. Bartholomew of Benevento, St. Matthew of Salerno, St. Nicholas of Bari, and the Holy Angels of Gargano.[21] Then, with the help of God, we returned home safely after we had gained the favor and love of the lord pope along with letters of recommendation.

On another occasion some years later, the pope cordially called us back to the curia to honor us even further and joyfully raise us to a higher position, as he explained in his letters.[22] But having received sure word at the city of Lucca in Tuscany that he had died, we turned back to avoid a fresh encounter with that old avarice of the Romans. He was succeeded by the bishop of Ostia, a person of proven ability but a serious and strict man who took the name Honorius when he became pope.[l] He recognized the justice of our claim over the monastery of Argenteuil which had been disgraced by the very wretched behavior of its young women. He examined the evidence presented by his own legate, Matthew, bishop of Albano, and by the lord bishops of Chartres, Paris, and Soissons in addition to archbishop Rainald of Reims

k. In March 1123 the First Lateran Council, the ninth ecumenical council according to the Roman reckoning, ratified the compromise on investitures that Emperor Henry V and Pope Calixtus II had agreed to at Wörms in the preceding year.

l. Following the death of Calixtus II on December 13, 1124, Lambert of Fagnano, the cardinal-bishop of Ostia, was elected pope under the name Honorius II.

and many other men. He also read through the charters of kings of old—Pepin, Charles the Great, Louis the Pious, and others— concerning our right over the place, which our messengers had presented to him. Then, aware of the justice of our cause and the enormously bad conduct of those women, he confirmed and restored the monastery to St. Denis on the advice of his entire curia.[23]

[28]
How he assembled the host of the kingdom, warded off the German threat, and rendered thanks to the blessed Dionysius

But let us now return to the task of commemorating the history of the king. Before the lord pope Calixtus had died, the emperor Henry had come to harbor enduring ill will against the lord king Louis, for he had been bound with anathema in a council held by the lord Calixtus at Reims, in the kingdom of the French.[1] The emperor assembled the greatest possible host of Lotharingians, Germans, Bavarians, Sueves, and, even though he was being troubled by them, Saxons. Feigning a movement elsewhere, he was plotting a surprise attack against the city of Reims, on the advice of the English king Henry, whose daughter he had married and made his queen, and who was also waging war against the king.[a] The emperor intended to destroy the city

a. King Henry I's daughter Matilda had married Emperor Henry V in 1114; following her husband's death in 1125, she married Geoffrey V Plantagenet, count of Anjou, in 1128. The events of this chapter occurred in the summer of 1124.

suddenly or besiege it, and thereby subject it to as much suffering and shame as the lord pope presiding there had inflicted on him.

Having learned of the plot from his close advisors, the lord king Louis bravely and boldly called up a levy which he did not await, summoned his nobles, and explained to them what was happening. Then he hurried to the blessed Dionysius, for common report and frequent experience had taught him that he was the particular patron and, after God, the foremost protector of the realm.[2] Offering prayers and gifts, he begged him from the bottom of his heart to defend the kingdom, to keep safe his person, and to resist the enemy in his customary way. For the French have a special privilege from him: if another kingdom should dare invade theirs, the relics of that blessed and wonderful defender himself, together with those of his companions, are placed on the altar in order to defend the kingdom; and the king had this done with solemnity and devotion in his presence.[b] He then took from the altar the standard belonging to the county of Vexin, which he held as a fief from the church, and gazed upon it. Taking it up as he had vowed, as if from his lord, so to speak, he rushed out against the enemy with a small band to protect his person, and sent forth a mighty call for all France to follow him.[3] The customary fighting spirit of France became angry at this unaccustomed brazenness of its enemies. Stirring itself on all sides, it sent forward select forces of knights, the very strongest men, who were mindful of the manliness of an earlier age and the victories of old.[c]

From all directions we gathered together in great strength at Reims. Numerous hosts of knights and foot soldiers came into

b. Here and later, Dionysius's companions are SS Rusticus and Eleutherius.

c. Suger here suggests historical comparisons for the events of this chapter.

view, and they seemed to devour the surface of the earth like locusts, not only along the courses of the rivers but also over the mountains and the plain. For a full week the king stayed there awaiting the invasion of the Germans, while the magnates of the kingdom drew up plans along these lines: "Why don't we make a bold move against them," they said, "in case they retreat and get away unpunished for doing whatever they arrogantly dare against France, the mistress of these lands? Let them face what they deserve for their insolence, not in our land but theirs, which by royal right of the French, belongs to the French who have often subdued it. We shall turn the tables by doing to them in public what they had plotted to do to us in secret."[d]

But others, hardened by experience, persuaded the magnates to wait longer until the enemy crossed the borders of the march. Then, when the Germans were cut off and unable to flee, the French could attack, overthrow, and slaughter them without mercy as if they were Saracens. The unburied bodies of the barbarians would be abandoned to wolves and ravens, to their everlasting shame; and such great slaughter and cruelty would be justified because the land was being defended.[5]

With the king present, the magnates of the kingdom made arrangements in the palace for their battle lines of warriors to be brought together for mutual assistance. One, over 60,000 strong, was made up of knights and foot soldiers from Reims and Châlons.[e] The second, comprising the men of Laon and Soissons, was no smaller; and the third included the men of Orléans, Etampes, and Paris together with a large host from St. Denis

---

d. Louis's call met with a good response, attracting a number of powerful vassals including his old enemy Theobald. Such a gathering of vassals was the first for centuries, and in this respect the events of 1124 anticipate the battle of Bouvines in 1214. See further endnote 4.

e. As did their ancient counterparts, medieval historians habitually overestimated the size of armies. See further endnote 6.

which was especially devoted to the crown. Hoping for the aid of his protector, the king decided to place himself amid the men of St. Denis. "In this battle line," he said, "I will fight safely and valiantly. The saints our lords will protect me, and these men raised me as a compatriot and a friend. They will help me while I live; or if I die they will keep my body safe and carry it home."[f]

The palatine count Theobald replied to the earnest request of France, and arrived there in the company of his uncle Hugh, the noble count of Troyes, even though he was waging war on the king with another uncle, the English king.[7] They constituted a fourth contingent while the fifth, formed by the duke of Burgundy and the count of Nevers, led the way. The distinguished Count Ralph of Vermandois, noteworthy for being the first cousin of the king, came supported by his best knights and a large host, equipped with hauberks and helmets, from St. Quentin and all his land. The count, chosen to protect the right wing, approved the assignment of the men of Ponthieu, Amiens, and Beauvais to the left while the most noble count of Flanders was appointed to guard the rear. He had with him ten thousand knights anxious for a fight, and would have tripled the size of his host had he had sufficient warning. Duke William of Aquitaine, the distinguished count of Brittany, and the warlike Count Fulk of Anjou did their best to rival these barons who had come from lands bordering the region; but the length of the journey and the short notice did not allow them time to gather their forces in order to punish severely this insult to the French.

Other arrangements were also made. Everywhere the hosts engaged in battle, wagons and carts would carry water and wine to the tired and wounded if the site were suitable. Then, with the wagons circled like the defenses of a castle, those whose wounds made them too weak for combat might there regain

f. Note how Suger stresses the links between the crown and St. Denis, a burial place of former kings and the abbey where Louis VI had been educated.

their strength. They could drink while their wounds were being bandaged; and, toughened in spirit, they would return to the clash of arms in order to win the palm of victory.

The plans for this huge and awesome undertaking became well known, and the news that a powerful levy of men had appeared reached the ears of the emperor. With feint and fraud, he veiled his true motive for flight and headed for other parts. He preferred to bear the shame of failure rather than risk his life and the ruin of his empire by facing the most dire revenge of the French. When the French learned of all this, the pleadings of the archbishops, bishops, and the monastic clergy just barely kept them from devastating his kingdom and harassing the poor.[8]

The French went home, having won a grand and prestigious victory, which was just the same as or even superior to an actual triumph in the field. Overjoyed and by no means ungrateful, the king came humbly before his protectors, the most holy martyrs. Giving them the greatest thanks after God, he devoutly restored the crown of his father, which he had unjustly retained, for by right all crowns belong to them.[9] He freely surrendered to them the Lendit fair held outside in the square, for the one inside already belonged to the saints.[10] He also confirmed by royal charter their complete jurisdiction as *viquier* within the area marked by crosses and marble columns, which stand and face all our enemies like the Pillars of Hercules at Cadiz.[11] The sacred and revered silver reliquaries containing the most holy bodies rested atop the high altar during the entire period that the forces had been assembled for war. Day and night the brothers venerated them while they continually celebrated a most solemn office, and the very devout people and nuns crowded around to offer many different prayers in support of our host. Shedding tears like a son, the king himself placed his lords and patrons on his shoulders[12] and carried them back to their usual place; and for these and other favors received he awarded them numerous gifts of land and other goods.

But the German emperor, debased by this deed, went downhill

from day to day and lived his last within the circle of a year. He proved true a judgment of the ancients that anyone, noble or base, who disturbed the kingdom or the church and because of some quarrel caused the bodies of the saints to be raised up, would not live a year but perish right away or within that period of time.g

The king of England, for his part, had been an accomplice to the German scheme. Waging war with Count Theobald against King Louis, he planned to lay waste or seize the neighboring borderland while the king was away. But one baron alone, namely Amalric of Montfort, a man most keen in the art of war, drove him back with support from the valiant host of the Vexin. Finding little or no profit, he went home, having been deceived by a vain hope.13

France has done nothing more renowned than this deed, either in modern times or in the distant past. And she has never displayed the splendor of her power more gloriously than when she united the strength of her members and triumphed at the very same time over the Roman emperor and, although King Louis was absent, the English king. Indeed, from that time the pride of his enemies was stifled, "the earth grew silent in his sight," and all enemies within his reach stretched out their hands in alliance and returned once more into his favor. Thus, "he who denies what an armed man justly seeks, yields all."14

g. Henry V died on May 23, 1125. Suger has earlier expressed similar feelings of righteous approval over the death of Henry (above, cap. 10).

[29]
His expeditions into the Auvergne

At that happy time, the bishop of Clermont in the Auvergne, a man of upright life and a splendid defender of the church, was hounded and put to flight by a fresh flare-up of that old pride of the men of the Auvergne. Once again it could be said of them: "The men of the Auvergne dared to portray themselves as brothers of the Latins."[1] Taking refuge with the lord king, the bishop tearfully placed before him the complaint of his church. The count of the Auvergne had seized his city and, helped by great fraud on the part of his dean, had fortified the cathedral church of the blessed Mary like a tyrant. The bishop threw himself at the feet of the king, who tried to prevent him from doing so, and begged him as a suppliant to free the enslaved church from its bondage and curb that unfettered tyrant with the sword of his royal majesty.

Ever prompt to aid churches, the king joyfully made the cause of God his own; but it cost him dearly when verbal threats and letters sent under his majesty's seal were not enough to make the tyrant reform. Springing into action, the king assembled a force of knights and set a huge host of the French into motion against the disobedient Auvergne.[a] When he came to Bourges, the leading men of the land—the warlike Count Fulk of Anjou, the very powerful Count Conan of Brittany, the distinguished count of Nevers, and many other magnates of the kingdom, who had come with a large band of knights—fulfilled their obligations to the realm and joined him. They were rushing to take

a. This expedition against Count William VI of the Auvergne (1096–1136) is treated out of chronological order, for it occurred in 1122 (Luchaire, no. 318). It took Louis far from Paris, about 230 miles south to Clermont-Ferrand.

revenge on the men of the Auvergne for this insult against the church and the kingdom.[b] And so, after the royal forces had laid waste the land of their enemies and drawn near to the city of Clermont, the men of the Auvergne abandoned their castles perched high in the mountains and entrusted themselves to the safety provided by the well-fortified city.

Laughing at the foolishness of their enemies, the French met and decided to postpone their march on Clermont, for the men of the Auvergne must now abandon the city to prevent losing their castles, or stay there for the time being and eat up all their foodstuffs. The French turned aside to a very excellent castle called the Bridge, sited on the river Allier; having pitched their tents all about the place, they wreaked equal havoc upon the plains and the peaks.[c] Their boldness was worthy of giants and seemed to reach the sky itself as they took hold of the strongly fortified pinnacles of the mountains; they carried off as booty not only the flocks but their shepherds, too, for good measure. They brought up siege engines next to the tower of that fortress and, amid much slaughter, forced its surrender under a hail of millstones and a rain of arrows. News of all this sent terror through the men who held Clermont, for they expected the same or worse for themselves. Having prepared themselves for flight, they went out of the town and abandoned it to the judgment of the king. Victorious in all things, the king restored the church to God, the towers to the clergy, and the city to the bishop, after he had confirmed peace between them and the count by the taking of oaths and the exchange of many hostages.[3]

b. Note how Suger assimilates the wrong done to a church with a wrong done to the kingdom. See further endnote 2.

c. The Bridge is Pont-du-Château, Puy-de-Dôme, some eight miles east of Clermont-Ferrand. This is the southernmost point that Suger describes Louis as having gone.

But five years had hardly passed before peace was again broken by the capricious treachery of the counts of the Auvergne, and a repetition of that disaster suffered by the bishop and the church led to a repeated complaint to the king.[d] Refusing to wear himself out in a futile effort, the king assembled an even greater host than the first one and once more headed for the land of the Auvergne. By now his body was heavy, weighed down as it was by burdensome folds of flesh; no one else, not even a beggar, would have wanted or been able to ride a horse when hampered by such a dangerously large body.[5] But despite the protests of many of his friends he let himself be carried away by his amazing fervor of spirit. He endured the summer heat of June and August, something even young men shrank from, and poked fun at those who could not bear it. But he often had to be carried through narrow passages in the swamps on the sturdy arms of his men. Travelling with him on this expedition were the very powerful Count Charles of Flanders, Count Fulk of Anjou, the count of Brittany, a host from Normandy that owed tribute to the English King Henry, some barons, and enough of the magnates of the kingdom to have conquered even Spain.

And so, crossing the difficult passages into the Auvergne and skirting the castles that blocked the way, the king came to Clermont. He brought up the host against the unfinished castle of Montferrand, which stood facing the city; the knights who had to defend the castle found themselves in dread of this awesome army of the French, which was so different from theirs. They marveled at the splendor of hauberks and helmets gleaming in the sun. Taken aback by this sight alone, they gave up the outer defenses and took themselves just in time into the tower and the area around it. A fire that spewed forth great flames was put to the houses in the abandoned zone, and it reduced to ashes

d. This second expedition probably occurred in 1126. See further endnote 4.

everything except the tower and its precinct. On that first day we pitched our tents outside to avoid the heat arising from the rapid burning of the village, and on the following day, when the flames had died down, we carried them inside.

Very early in the morning the king did something that saddened them but delighted us. Our tents had been pitched on the side nearer the tower; even with armed guards stationed between us and them, the enemy harassed us all night long with constant attacks and unending showers of arrows and missiles, so that we had to cover ourselves with our shields. But the king selected that superb knight and distinguished baron, Amalric of Montfort, to lay ambushes on their flanks and make sure that our foes did not return to the precinct of the tower unhurt. Amalric knew well what to do. Taking up his weapons amid the tents, he rode swiftly abreast of the enemy while our men blocked their path. He surprised some of them and, having seized them, quickly dispatched them to the king. When they begged that he allow them to be ransomed, he ordered that they each lose a hand; so maimed, they were sent back to their companions in the tower, carrying their fists in their fists.

The others, terrified at these events, left us in peace after that. Military machines and engines were built and standing by, and all the Auvergne lay open to the will and pleasure of the host when Duke William of Aquitaine arrived there supported by a levy of Aquitainians.[e] He pitched camp in the mountains and gazed down upon the columns of the French glittering on the plain. Startled by the size of this huge host, he gave thought to his lack of power and regretted that he had come to confront the king. Having sent messengers of peace, the duke stood before him and addressed him as his lord, pleading as follows: "Your

e. Duke William X of Aquitaine (1126–37). He is generally overshadowed in the popular imagination by his father, Duke William IX, the Provençal lyricist, and by his daughter Eleanor.

duke of Aquitaine, lord king, salutes you with great respect and wishes you every honor. May your royal highness see fit to receive the service of the duke of Aquitaine and preserve him in his right. For even as justice demands the service of a vassal, so it also demands a just lordship. The count holds the Auvergne from me, which I in turn hold from you. And if he has done anything wrong, I must deliver him to your court for trial when you command it. We have never stood in the way of this, and indeed we offer to deliver him now and implore you as a suppliant to accept what we offer. Should your highness have any doubt in this regard, we are prepared to give you a large and sufficient number of hostages. If the leading men of the kingdom so judge, let it be done; if they judge otherwise, so be it."[f]

The king took counsel with the leading men of the kingdom on these issues and, as justice dictated, accepted the duke's fealty, his sworn oath, and a sufficient number of hostages. Having restored peace to the land and the churches, he set a date when those concerned would attend to these affairs at Orleáns in the presence of the duke of Aquitaine, something they had refused to do up to that time. Then he gloriously led back his host and returned home into France a victor.

f. The duke's words, as reported by Suger, enunciate an important principle: the count of the Auvergne is a vassal of the duke of Aquitaine; but because the duke himself is a vassal of the king, the count is ultimately answerable to the king. The concept was important in the recovery of royal power by the Capetians, and such a clear acceptance of it by a major vassal far from Paris is significant. See further endnote 6.

The murder of Count Charles of Flanders

We intend now to record a distinguished deed, the most noble that the king accomplished from the time he was a youth up to the very end of his life. The full telling of it would need much detail, but we shall narrate it briefly to avoid being tedious, showing what he did, but not how he did it.

Count Charles, the son of the king of the Danes by the aunt of the lord king Louis, was a renowned and very powerful man.[a] By right of kinship he succeeded the very courageous Count Baldwin, son of Robert the Jerusalemite, and governed the well-populated land of Flanders with valor and care.[b] Besides being a splendid defender of God's church, he was prominent for generous almsgiving and a noteworthy guardian of justice. Citing obligations arising from the holding of fiefs, the count followed procedure and summoned to the judgment of his court several powerful men of low birth whom riches had lifted up to a higher rank. They were arrogantly trying to remove their branch of the family from under his lordship, even though they all had risen up from the scum of servile status. These self-important and well-

a. Charles the Good, count of Flanders (1119–27), was the son of King Canute of Denmark and Adele, the daughter of Count Robert "the Frisian" of Flanders (1071–93) and uterine sister of Queen Bertha, the mother of Louis VI.

b. Charles's immediate predecessor, Count Baldwin VII (1111–19) was the son of Count Robert II (1093–1111), commonly called "the Jerusalemite" because of his participation in the First Crusade. Louis's mother Bertha was also the uterine sister of Robert II. The high degree of urbanization in twelfth-century Flanders and the great number of its citizens who went on crusades against Saracens and pagans east of Germany point to a large population and support Suger's observation that Flanders was well populated.

known traitors, namely the provost of the church of Bruges and his party, most cruelly plotted his downfall.[1]

Having come to Bruges, the count attended the church of God early one morning and, holding a service book in his hand, was saying his prayers as he lay prostrate on the stone floor. Then suddenly Burchard, the nephew of the provost and his brutal accomplice, joined company with some members of his same wicked stock and other partners in this most vile treachery. Silently sneaking up behind the man who was praying, or rather talking with God, he carefully unsheathed his sword and lightly touched the neck of the count as he lay on the floor. Somewhat startled, the count raised himself up a little, to the advantage of the man carrying the weapon. Turning it on him, an impious man struck one blow and wickedly beheaded a pious one, and a serf his lord.[c]

His accomplices in this evil murder were standing nearby, thirsting for his blood like mad dogs raging over abandoned bodies. Taking delight in butchering the innocent, they boasted mightily that they had completed the sad work they had conceived, the iniquity they had brought to birth.[2] Blinded as they were by malice, they piled iniquity on iniquity when they slaughtered every member of the garrison and every one of the count's noble barons whom they could find in the church or outside of the castle. They sent them unprepared to an unfortunate and wretched kind of death without benefit of confession, but we firmly believe that they found death profitable. Sacrificed like this out of fealty to their lord, they were found praying in

c. The murder of Count Charles occurred while he was praying in the church of St. Donatian in Bruges on March 2, 1127 (Galbert, p. 111f). The murder of a man on consecrated ground was particularly heinous, and the murder of a nobleman by someone from low social origins furnishes Suger with another reminder of the danger posed by such people when they rise in status. See cap. 26 at n. f for an earlier reminder.

church; and as is written: "Where I find you, there I shall judge you."[3]

Those beasts buried the count in the church itself, for they feared that a mournful and honorable burial for him outside would arouse his devoted people to take revenge for his glorious life and even more glorious death. They converted the church into a den of robbers,[4] turning it and the count's adjoining residence into a fortress. Having stored up every kind of foodstuff and provision, they gave thought to defending themselves there and very arrogantly made plans to win the land over to their side.

The horror of this extremely wicked deed shocked the barons of Flanders, who had no part in the plot. Holding tearful funeral rites, they avoided any suspicion of bad faith when they reported to the lord king Louis what had happened, and not only to him, for news of it flew through the whole world. The king's love of justice and affection for a kinsman aroused him to avenge such great treachery, and warfare with the English king and Count Theobald did not hold him back.[5] He eagerly entered Flanders, burning with a desire to carry out the work of brutally destroying those miserable wretches, and installed as count of Flanders William the Norman, the son of Count Robert the Jerusalemite of Normandy, for the office belonged to him by right of kinship.[d] The king came down to Bruges without fearing the barbarity of the land or the family defiled by treason. Besieging those traitors, he confined them to the church and tower, denying them any foodstuffs other than what they had, and those, by divine will, were already spoiled and unfit for use. After he had worn them down for some time with hunger, disease, and the sword, they abandoned the church and kept only the tower, so that the tower might keep them.[7]

d. William the Norman, better known as William Clito, was the son of Robert Curthose, duke of Normandy, also called "the Jerusalemite" for his participation in the First Crusade. See further endnote 6.

They soon lost all hope for their lives, for their lute had already changed its tune to mourning and their organ to the voice of those who weep.[8] That wretched Burchard, having gained the consent of his companions, slipped away in flight. He wanted to leave the land but found no way, for his evil deed alone was enough to block him. Stopped by order of the king while he was returning to the stronghold of a friend and counsellor, he was tied to the top of a tall wheel and delivered over to the greedy appetite of ravens and winged creatures, a miserable death of a choice kind. His eyes were pecked out and his whole face torn to shreds by the birds from above, and his body was pierced a thousand times by arrows, lances, and javelins from below. He died a very vile death, and his remains were thrown into a sewer.[9]

Berthold, the ringleader in this wicked behavior, likewise decided to flee. He roamed about here and there somewhat freely; but his arrogance alone defeated him, for he used to say: "Who, me?" or "What, me?" His own men seized and delivered him over to the judgment of the king, who condemned him to a well deserved and very demeaning death. He was hung from a gallows next to a dog; and whenever someone struck the dog, the animal turned its anger on the man, eating up his whole face with its biting. Sometimes, horrible to say, it even befouled him with excrement. And in this way, more wretched than the most wretched, he ended his wretched life with eternal death.[10]

The king inflicted many hardships on those whom he had confined in the tower and made them surrender. He had them thrown down from its top one after the other in the presence of their people, and all their necks were broken.[11] But one of the traitors, named Isaac, whom fear of death had led to a monastery for the tonsure, he had defrocked and fixed to a gibbet.[12] Then, having won a victory at Bruges, the king and his forces moved in haste against the very fine castle of Ypres to take vengeance on William the Bastard, who had given his support to this treachery.^e The king sent messengers to the men of Bruges[13] and won their support by threats and flattery. When William came out with three hundred knights to encounter the king, one part of the royal host rushed against him and the other boldly took control of the castle, entering from the side at another gate. The king kept the castle and banished William after he had dispossessed him throughout Flanders; and since William had hoped to possess Flanders through treachery, he deserved to gain nothing at all in Flanders.[14]

By these and other kinds of vengeance and the shedding of much blood, Flanders was washed and, as it were, rebaptized. Then, after the investiture of William the Norman as count, the king returned home into France with the help of God, a victor.[15]

[31]
The death of Thomas of Marle

In another instance the king took a very similar revenge, pleasing to God and renowned among men. He made use of his swift and mighty hand and, like someone putting out a smoking firebrand, snuffed out the life of a most accursed man, Thomas of Marle, who had been harassing the church of God with no respect for God or man.

Driven by the lamentations of the churches, the king arrived at Laon to take his vengeance, and then decided to lead his host directly to Coucy against Thomas.^a The bishops and notables of

e. William derived his title "the Bastard" from being the illegitimate son of Philip of Loo, the second son of Count Robert the Frisian.

---

a. Thomas of Marle, again described as *perditissimus* ("most accursed") in the preceding paragraph, is making a third and final appearance. This expedi-

the kingdom had urged such action; but above all the distinguished Count Ralph of Vermandois, who had more power than anyone besides the king in those districts, had advised it. The king pressed on toward the castle, but his vanguard, which had gone ahead to find a good approach, reported back that they had found no suitable access at all. This news made many of his men urge a change of plans, but the spirited king angrily replied: "We made this plan at Laon, and we shall not change what was decided there, no matter whether we live or die. People would rightly belittle the grandeur of our royal majesty and make fun of us if we turned tail and ran in fear of a scoundrel."

After these words, he summoned amazing zeal and, despite the weight of his body, led his host across steep slopes and along paths blocked by woods, paying no regard to the danger. When the king had come close to the castle, the very valiant Count Ralph, who was maneuvering on another side, learned that ambushes had been set for the host and were just about to seal its doom. He took up arms on the spot and headed there with a few companions by a hidden path. Seeing that some knights whom he had sent ahead had already struck Thomas and that he had fallen, Ralph spurred on his horse, charged forward, and struck him ardently with his sword. He delivered a deadly wound and, if no one had stopped him, he would have done it again. Mortally wounded and taken captive, Thomas was delivered to King Louis, who commanded that he be carried off to Laon, much to the approval of nearly everyone, both his men and ours.

On the following day, the lord king Louis confiscated his estates in the plain and tore down his enclosures; sparing the land, because he possessed it now as lord, he returned to Laon. But neither wounds, nor prison, nor threats, nor petition could

---

tion against him in the fall of 1130 is also prompted by ecclesiastical complaints. Coucy is about fifteen miles southwest of Laon, which in turn is about eighty miles northeast of Paris.

force that most accursed Thomas to set free the merchants whom he was holding in his prison. He had robbed them with unbelievable treachery despite their right of safe-conduct.[b] Thomas received the king's permission to summon his wife to his side, but he seemed more upset about the loss of the merchants who were demanded of him than over the loss of his life. The very severe pain of his wounds had plunged him to the point of death, and many urged him to make his confession and receive the viaticum. He yielded reluctantly; but when the hand of the priest carried the body of the Lord into that room where the wretch was living, it seemed that the Lord Jesus would in no way allow himself to enter the most contaminated vessel of a man who was thoroughly impenitent. Just as soon as the scoundrel lifted up his neck, it twisted back and broke on the spot; bereft of the Eucharist, he breathed forth his utterly foul spirit.[1] The king, however, did not stoop to take further vengeance on a dead man or a dead man's land. He extracted the release of the merchants and the greatest part of Thomas's treasures from his wife and sons.[c] And having restored peace to the churches by the death of the tyrant, he returned home to Paris a victor.

On another occasion, at the instigation of Stephen of Garlande, a great quarrel over the office of seneschal arose between the lord king and Amalric of Montfort, an eminent man whose position had been strengthened by aid from the English king and Count Theobald. The king marched his host quickly and laid siege to the castle of Livry.[d] Setting up siege engines and rushing

b. Another reminder that the activities of such marauders as Thomas were detrimental to the interests of merchants.

c. Thomas was survived by his third wife, Milesende, and one known son, Enguerrand. Milesende was the daughter of Guy of Crécy, and so related to Louis's enemy Hugh of Crécy. Enguerrand succeeded to his father's property, and was attacked by Louis in 1132. He reached an accord with the king when he agreed to marry a niece of Louis's cousin and ally, Count Ralph of Vermandois (Luchaire, no. 491).

d. About seven miles northeast of Paris, Livry was a Garlande fortress in

against it repeatedly, he assaulted it with constant blows and captured it with great force. But his first cousin, the distinguished Count Ralph of Vermandois, lost an eye when he leapt to the attack and was hit by a tile from a catapult. So the king demolished that mighty castle down to its foundations and burdened his foes with such heavy and violent warfare that they departed in firm peace, renouncing both the office of seneschal and their claim to its inheritance. In this fighting the king himself was ever swift against his enemies as becomes a true knight. He had a leg cut open by a tile thrown from a catapult, but he boldly shrugged off a severe injury as if the throne of his royal majesty considered the pain of a wound as something unworthy; and with a stiff upper lip he endured his suffering as if he had nothing to endure.

[32]
The visit of Pope Innocent to France

At that time a dangerous schism dealt the Roman church a grave wound that nearly struck its very heart. After the supreme pontiff and universal pope Honorius of venerable memory had gone the way of all flesh, the senior and wiser among the members of the Roman church reached an agreement to prevent it from being thrown into turmoil. A solemn election would be held according to Roman practice at St. Mark's and nowhere else, and only if all participated.[a] But those who had been close

1128 when this expedition occurred. These events are out of chronological order. See further endnote 2.

---

a. Pope Honorius II died on February 13, 1130. The church of St. Mark's is near the ancient Capitol in Rome.

to the pope from continual service and companionship feared a possible riot among the Romans and dared not meet at St. Mark's. So, before making public the death of the lord pope, they elected as supreme pontiff the venerable Gregory, cardinal deacon of St. Angelo. But those who supported the party of Peter Leo summoned others and assembled at St. Mark's, as they had agreed. Having learned of the death of the lord pope, they honored their pledges and elected the very same cardinal priest Peter Leo, with the approval of many bishops, cardinals, clergy, and Roman nobles. Starting in this way a dangerous schism, they ripped apart the seamless robe of Christ the Lord and divided the church of God.[b] And while "each side defended itself with high authority," they enticed each other over to their respective factions, bound each other with anathema, and paid no heed to any judgment but their own.[2]

But after the party of Peter Leo won control, with help from his relatives and support from the Roman nobility, the lord pope Innocent decided to leave the City with his followers in order to win the whole world over to his cause. He came down by sea to the regions of the Gauls, for he had chosen the very noble kingdom of the French as the most reliable and safe refuge after God for the defense of himself and the church. Having sent messengers to King Louis, he implored him to bring help to his own person and to the church.

Being a very devout defender of the church and deeply moved by this plea, the king quickly convened a council of archbishops, bishops, abbots, and monastic clergy at Etampes.[c] He followed their advice and paid more attention to personal character than

b. The soldiers who crucified Christ found that his robe had no seam (John 19:23), a circumstance that was taken to prefigure the unity of the church. Gregory claimed to be pope under the name Innocent II, and Peter Leo under the title Anacletus II. See further endnote 1.

c. Etampes, some thirty miles south of Paris, was in Louis's patrimony. See further endnote 3.

to the election itself, for it often happens that a less than regular election takes place when the riotous Romans cause trouble for the church.[4] The king gave his assent to Innocent's election on the recommendation of his men, promised to support him in the future, and delegated us to bring the first fruits of welcome and service to him at Cluny. Overjoyed by such great support, the pope sent us back home with his grace and benediction, to return his thanks to the lord king.

While the lord pope was travelling down to St. Benedict on the Loire, the lord king went with his queen and his sons to meet him. He bowed his noble head, so often crowned with a diadem, as if to the tomb of Peter, and cast himself at his feet, promising him and the church love befitting a catholic and the fruits of devout service.[5] King Henry of England followed his example and came to meet the lord pope at Chartres. He also threw himself very devoutly at his feet, pledged total filial obedience, and promised that he and his people would honor their word and welcome him as if the land were his own.[6]

While visiting the Gallic church as the circumstances required, the lord pope crossed over to the regions of the Lotharingians. The emperor Lothar came in great style amid a large company of archbishops, bishops, and magnates of the German kingdom to meet him at the city of Liège. In the square before the episcopal church, the emperor very humbly offered himself as a squire and hurried over to him on foot through the middle of the holy procession. In one hand he held the sceptre to defend the supreme pontiff, and in the other the reins of his white horse, and led him about as if he were his lord. Then, when the whole procession dismounted, the emperor lifted him up and carried him along, making clear the loftiness of his paternity to all assembled, the famous as well as the common crowd.[7]

With peace ratified between the empire and the church, the lord pope desired to celebrate the approaching feast of Easter with us in the church of the blessed Dionysius, which he regarded as a favorite daughter. And so, revering God, our mother the church, and her daughter abbey, we received him joyfully on the day before the Lord's Supper. We conducted a procession splendid in the eyes of God and men, assembled amid hymns of jubilation, and embraced him on his arrival.

He celebrated the Lord's Supper with us in the Roman way, giving us an expensive gift, called the *presbiterium*.[d] He then observed the venerable Crucifixion of the Lord and passed the whole night keeping the vigil of the most holy Resurrection with proper honor. Very early the next morning he travelled somewhat secretly along an outside road, amid a large company of attendants, to the church of the Martyrs on the Highway.[8] His assistants had made their preparations following the Roman custom and clothed him there with many wonderful vestments. They placed on his head the Phrygian mitre, an imperial adornment ringed with a crown of gold and shaped like a helmet, and led him forth on a white horse covered with trimmings. They themselves wore fine cloaks and rode an assortment of horses draped with white cloths, and went forth in pairs joyfully chanting hymns. The barons who held fiefs of our church and the noble castellans escorted the mounted pope on foot, leading his horse by the reins as they fulfilled the office of squires with great humility. Some people went ahead of the procession and tossed out handfuls of coins, so they could move back the crowd, which was getting in the way. The royal road was a brilliant sight to behold, with branches spread about and rich cloths hanging from the trees. A troop of knights and a large body of people respectfully gathered about him, and even members of that blind synagogue of the Jews of Paris came forward and offered him the scroll of the Law beneath a veil. They received this merciful and

d. "Wages paid by the bishop (especially the pope) to the priests" (Niermeyer, *Lexicon*, p. 838, meaning 6).

pious prayer from his mouth: "May almighty God take away the veil from your hearts."[e]

He soon arrived at the basilica of the saints. Its golden crowns glistened, and the radiance of its precious gems and pearls shined a hundred times more brightly than silver or gold. He celebrated the divine services in a divine manner and, with us assisting, sacrificed the most sacred Victim of the true Paschal Lamb. When mass had ended, his party retired to the cloister where tables had been set up and fine carpets strewn about. Then reclining as if in bed, they consumed a corporeal lamb and partook of the other dishes of a noble table in the customary way. On the following day, they repeated their procession and moved from the church of St. Remigius to the main church.[f] And so when three days after Easter had passed, he thanked us, promised us aid and counsel, and made his way to Paris. He then spent some time travelling about the land, visiting the churches of the Gauls, supplying his wants from their wealth, and finally decided to stay awhile at Compiègne.

About that time, an unparalleled and unprecedented misfortune befell the kingdom of France. Philip, the son of King Louis and a radiant and charming boy, was the hope of good men and a terrifying prospect for evildoers.[g] But he was riding through a suburb of the city of Paris one day when his horse stumbled over a diabolical pig that it bumped into on the road. Taking a very bad fall, the horse threw the noble youth riding it against a stone and crushed him underfoot with all its weight. At this sad news

e. The Jews of Rome customarily held out copies of the Torah before new popes; Suger seems to describe a similar practice. See further endnote 9.

f. The church of St. Remigius was some 500 yards east of the abbey church.

g. Reminiscent of Romans 13:3. Philip, the eldest son of King Louis and Adelaide of Maurienne, had been born in August 1116. These events occurred in October 1131.

the city was horrified, as were the many who heard of it, for on that very day the king had summoned the host for an expedition. They cried out, they wept, and they wailed. They picked up the tender young boy who was nearly dead, and carried him to the nearest house; but, sad to say, he breathed his last as the darkness of night fell. So great, so astounding were the grief and sorrow that struck his father, his mother, and the leading men of the kingdom that Homer himself would have lacked the skill to express it.[10]

With many bishops and leading men of the kingdom gathered about, he was buried in accordance with royal custom in the church of St. Denis, in the tomb of the kings on the left side of the altar of the Holy Trinity.[h] His wise father grieved mournfully and cursed his wretched life because he was the one who survived, but he then allowed himself to be consoled by the counsel of religious and wise men. We, his intimates and close associates, feared that the continual torment of a weakened body would lead to his sudden death. So, in order to forestall insurrection from rivals, we advised him to have his son Louis, a very handsome youth, crowned with the royal diadem and made king with him by anointing with holy oil.[i] Accepting our advice, he came with his wife, his son, and the magnates of the kingdom to Reims; and in a plenary and solemn council convened there by the lord pope Innocent, he provided a happy successor for the realm when he had his son elevated to the kingship by anointing him with holy oil and conferring on him the crown of the kingdom. Many saw in this a portent that his power would expand, for he received the abundant blessings of so many and such

h. The burial of Philip at St. Denis is a sign of the close relations existing at this time between Louis and the abbey. King Philip I, it will be recalled, was buried at the abbey of Saint Benedict on the Loire (above, cap. 13).

i. Louis, the second son of King Louis and Adelaide of Maurienne, had been born about 1120–21. See further endnote 11.

powerful archbishops and bishops from such different regions—France, Germany, Aquitaine, England, and Spain.[12]

The father lightened his sorrow for his dead son by the joy he took in his living one, and returned to Paris while the lord pope closed the council and chose to take up residence in Auxerre. But he found an opportunity to return to his native land in the company of the emperor Louis,[j] who had promised to take him to Rome amid a strong force to depose Peter Leo. And so he went there with him and installed him as emperor Augustus; but the Romans rebuffed him, and the lord pope was not able to have any peace while Peter Leo lived. When Peter Leo departed from this world, however, peace was restored to the church with the help of God, but only after much wavering and a lengthy period of almost fatal stagnation. And then finally the lord pope, with a happy outcome, ennobled his most holy see by the meritorious conduct of his life and office.

[33]
How he prepared for death

By this time the weight of his fleshy body and the toil of endless tasks had quite beaten down the lord king Louis.[a] He was failing in his body, something which is the lot of the human condition, but not in his spirit. If anything prejudicial to his royal majesty took place anywhere in his kingdom, he never

j. Suger slipped and named the emperor "Louis" rather than "Lothar."

a. Here we rejoin the lessons composed by Suger for liturgical use at St. Denis on the anniversary of Louis's death (above, Introduction). The rest of the book reproduces this text.

allowed it to go unpunished. At the age of sixty he had great experience and determination; and if the constant torment of an overly fat body had not stopped him, he would have overcome and crushed his enemies everywhere.[1] For this reason he often groaned and complained to his intimates: "Alas! What a wretched fix! Rarely, if ever, does one have experience and strength at the same time! If I had possessed experience in my youth, or at any rate if I possessed strength in my old age, I would have mastered many kingdoms with the greatest of ease."

The weight of his body weakened him to the point where he had become very stiff in bed; but he did not slacken his struggle against the king of England, Count Theobald, and all others. Whoever saw or heard of his outstanding deeds sang praises for his noble spirit but shed tears for his weakened body. Despite being hindered by this hardship and so wounded in a leg that he could hardly drag it about, he maneuvered against Count Theobald and set fire to all of Bonneval, except the cloisters of the monks, which were under his protection. On another occasion, although he himself was elsewhere, he sent his men to destroy Château-Renard, part of the fief of Count Theobald.[b] And then he made his last expedition when he led a very noble host and burned down the castle of Saint Brisson on the river Loire, forcing the surrender of both the tower and its lord, who had been greedily plundering merchants.[c]

While at the new castle of Montraër on his return from this campaign, he began to be sorely troubled by a bad attack of the diarrhea and dysentery from which he sometimes suffered.[d]

b. Louis's leg was wounded at Livry in 1128. Bonneval, Eure-et-Loir, is on the upper Loir about eighteen miles south of Chartres. Château-Renard, Loiret, is about fifty miles east of Orléans. The expeditions against Bonneval and Château-Renard are dated 1132–33 (Luchaire, no. 530).

c. Saint Brisson, Loiret, is upstream on the Loire about forty-five miles southeast of Orléans. This expedition took place in the fall of 1135.

d. Montraër is the modern Châteauneuf-sur-Loire, Loiret, upstream about

Being farsighted in counsel, he took care and had pity on his own soul, and provided for himself in a manner pleasing to God. He made his confession frequently, said devout prayers, and had his whole heart set on one wish. He wanted to be carried by any means possible into the presence of his protectors, the holy Martyrs Dionysius and his companions. Before their most holy bodies, he would lay down the crown and the kingdom, and profess the monastic way of life. He would exchange crown for crown and put on the humble habit of the blessed Benedict in place of his royal regalia and imperial trappings. Let those who belittle monastic poverty behold how not only archbishops but even kings themselves place eternal life before that which is passing. They too seek the firm protection that is provided only by the monastic way of life.[2]

However, his diarrhea tortured him from day to day with heavy discharges. To stop them, the doctors gave him extremely bothersome medicines to drink and all kinds of terribly bitter powders to take. Not even the hale and hearty could have endured them, and as a result he felt really wretched. But amid these and similar torments, he retained his good will and innate charm, treated everyone in a kindly way, and let them come into his presence. He was pleasant to all those around him, as if he were suffering no distress.

Despite his very severe dysentery and the slow decline of his tormented body, he shuddered at the thought of dying shamefully or unready. He called together the monastic clergy, bishops, abbots, and many priests of the church and, casting aside all shame out of reverence for the Divinity and the holy angels, asked to make a very devout confession in their presence and to be strengthened for death by the most sustaining viaticum of the body and blood of the Lord. And while they were hurriedly

---

fifteen miles east of Orléans. Louis fell ill there in November 1135 (Luchaire, no. 559).

making preparations, the king himself unexpectedly rose up, arranged himself, and to the astonishment of all went out of his bedroom fully dressed to meet and come reverently into the presence of the body of the Lord Jesus Christ. With all the clergy and laity looking on, he divested himself of the kingship, laid aside the kingdom, and confessed that he had administered it sinfully. He invested his son Louis with the ring and bound him by his sworn word to protect the church of God, the poor, and the orphans, to preserve his law for each person, and to arrest no one in his court if he had not committed a crime while present in the court itself.

Out of love of God he there bestowed on the churches, the poor, and the destitute his gold, silver, attractive vases, tapestries, quilts lined with silk, and all the movable goods he possessed and found useful. He kept neither his cloaks, his royal garments, nor even his shirt. He sent through us to the holy Martyrs his valuable cape, his very costly gospel book encased with gold and gems, his golden censer weighing forty ounces, his candelabra of one hundred and sixty ounces of gold, his very expensive chalice with its gold and most precious gems, his ten valuable copes made of silk, and the very costly hyacinth that had belonged to his grandmother, the daughter of the king of the Russians. This jewel he delivered from his hand into ours, ordering that it be set in the crown of thorns of the Lord, and devoutly promised that he would follow close behind us if he possibly could.[e]

Unburdened of these possessions and bathed in the mercy of God, he knelt with great humility before the most sacred body and blood of our Lord Jesus Christ, for those who had just celebrated mass brought communion to him there in a devout pro-

e. Anna, the daughter of Prince Iaroslav the Wise of Kiev, married Henry I of France in 1051. In the following year she gave birth to Philip, the father of Louis. See further endnote 3.

cession. With a sincere heart and mouth, he broke forth into a profession of catholic faith and spoke not as an unlearned man but as a most learned theologian: "I, Louis a sinner, profess the one and true God, Father, Son, and Holy Spirit. I profess that one person of this holy Trinity, namely the only-begotten, consubstantial and co-eternal Son of God the Father, was incarnate of the most holy virgin Mary, that he suffered, died, and was buried, that he arose on the third day, ascended into heaven and is seated on the right hand of the Father, and that he judges the living and the dead at the last and great judgment. We believe that this Eucharist of his most holy body is that same body that was taken from the Virgin and that he delivered to his disciples, so that they would be joined together, remain together, and constantly dwell in him. We also most firmly believe and profess with our heart and mouth that this most holy blood is that very same that flowed from his side when he hung from the cross, and we ardently desire that our death be strengthened by this most sustaining viaticum and be defended by its most firm protection against every power of the air."[4]

But he surprised everyone, for after he had made a confession of his sins and devoutly received the body and blood of Jesus Christ in communion, he almost immediately began to get stronger. He went back to his bedroom and, casting aside all pomp and worldly pride, lay down with only a simple linen coverlet. And when he saw that I was weeping as any man would for one who had been so great but was now so small, for one who had been so lofty but was now so lowly, he said: "Dearest friend, do not weep for me, but rather celebrate with great joy. For, as you see, the mercy of God has allowed me to prepare myself before meeting him."

[34]
His pious death and burial

While his health slowly recovered, he came down to the river Seine near Melun by whatever means of transport he could endure. His very devoted people, for whom he had preserved the peace, rushed out to meet him from fortresses, villages, and fields they abandoned, flocking together along the road and commending his person to God. He travelled very swiftly and, as God granted, made his way on horseback to visit and give thanks to the holy Martyrs whom he loved.[a]

The brothers and nearly the whole countryside solemnly and devotedly welcomed this pious father and noble defender of the church. With great modesty he prostrated himself before the most holy Martyrs, tearfully fulfilling his vow to give them devout thanks for the benefits he had received and imploring them very humbly to continue watching over him.

When he had come to the castle of Béthizy, messengers from Duke William of Aquitaine caught up with him and announced that the duke, who had set out on a pilgrimage to Santiago, had died on the way.[b] But before he had departed on the expedition and again on the journey as he lay dying, the duke had decided to deliver to the king for the purpose of marriage his daughter, a very noble girl named Eleanor, and all his land, so that he could hold it for her. Having taken counsel with his close advisors, he happily accepted the offer with his usual greatness of soul and promised her in marriage to his dear son Louis.[c] In putting

a. Suger has touchingly described the warm reception Louis received during his last progress through the royal domain. He had kept the peace.

b. In early June 1137 messengers arrived from Duke William X of Aquitaine, who had died on a pilgrimage to the shrine of St. James at Compostella (Santiago, Spain). Béthizy, Oise, is about forty miles northeast of Paris.

c. Suger was writing before the disastrous falling out between Louis VII

together a stately escort to send him to Aquitaine, he assembled a very noble host of five hundred or more knights from among the best men of the kingdom, and placed it under the command of the palatine count Theobald and Count Ralph of Vermandois, his distinguished relative. To their company he added me, his intimate friend, and any others of sound counsel whom he could find, and said farewell to his departing son as follows: "May the most powerful right arm of almighty God, through whom kings reign,[2] protect you and your companions, my dearest son. For if by some misfortune I were to lose you and those whom I send with you, I would no longer care for myself and the kingdom." He entrusted them with ample treasure and enough money for their needs, and warned them with his royal authority not to plunder anything in the entire duchy of Aquitaine, not to harm the land or the poor of the land, and not to turn friends into enemies, promptly ordering that each day the host be paid a fitting wage from his own treasury.[d]

When we had come through the regions of the Limousin to the district of Bordeaux, we pitched our tents facing the city but on the other side of the great river Garonne, and waited there until Sunday before crossing over to the city in boats. Then, with the leading men of Gascony, Saintonge, and Poitou assembled, the prince joined himself in marriage to the previously mentioned girl and had her crowned with the diadem of the kingdom. We returned through the district of Saintonge ready to put down any enemies we might encounter, but we came to the city of Poitiers after receiving a warm welcome throughout the whole land.

That summer was very hot, even more punishing than usual,

---

and Eleanor; doubtless he would have told the tale differently had he known what was to happen. See further endnote 1.

d. The generous grant of treasure to a host of over 500 knights was, as Suger implies, a precaution against their helping themselves to what they needed on their journey.

and we found ourselves exhausted, weakened, and completely worn out by its all-consuming heat. The lord king Louis himself suffered another severe attack of dysentery and diarrhea in Paris, and the summer's unbearable misery totally wasted him away. Never lacking prudence at these moments, he summoned the venerable Bishop Stephen of Paris and the pious Abbot Gilduin of St. Victor to his side; and he made his confession to Abbot Gilduin with great intimacy, for he had built his monastery from its foundations.ᵉ He recited his confession, and devoutly sought to be fortified for death by the viaticum of the Lord's body. He also wished to be carried to the church of the holy Martyrs to discharge with great humility a vow he had often made. But, overcome by the agonies of his illness, he fulfilled with his heart, mind, and will what he could not carry out in deed. He ordered that a carpet be spread on the ground and ashes be shaped on the carpet in the form of a cross. Having been laid upon it by the hands of his attendants, he made himself ready by the sign of the holy cross and sent forth his spirit on the calends of August, in the thirtieth year of his administration of the kingdom and nearly the sixtieth year of his life.

At the very same hour his body was wrapped in a precious cloth and carried for burial to the church of the holy Martyrs.ᶠ But something happened when his men went ahead to prepare his burial site; it does not seem proper to pass over it in silence. The king had talked with us on occasion, nay many times, about the tombs of the kings, showing pleasure at the thought of meriting burial between the sacred altars of the holy Trinity and the holy Martyrs. There he would obtain forgiveness for his sins

e. Bishop Stephen of Paris (1124–42) was the brother of Louis's butler Guy of Senlis, while Gilduin was abbot of St. Victor, a house of canons regular established in Paris with Louis's help in 1113.

f. When Louis died on August 1, 1137, no time was lost in transporting his body to the abbey of St. Denis. Perhaps there were fears that he would be buried elsewhere. See further endnote 3.

by the help of the saints and the prayers of visitors; and in this way, he quietly made his will known.

Before departing with his son, we had made plans with Herveus, the venerable prior of the church, for him to be buried before the altar of the holy Trinity, on the side opposite the tomb of the emperor Charles, with the altar between them. But this place was already taken by Carloman, king of the French; and what we had proposed could not be done, for it is neither right nor customary for kings to be exhumed.[g] Nevertheless, they defied the belief of nearly everyone that the site had been taken, and examined the location where, as if by some premonition, he had ardently desired to be buried. And they found a space unoccupied that was neither too large nor too small but fit the length and width of his body perfectly. So, in accordance with royal custom, he was buried there amid a multitude of prayers and hymns, with very solemn and devoutly conducted funeral rites.[5] Now he awaits his part in the future Resurrection, as near in spirit to the company of the holy spirits as in body to the holy Martyrs, for he lies buried very near them so that he may obtain their aid. "Happy the man who knows in advance the exact place where he will lie when the whole world totters into ruins."[6]

May the Redeemer heed the intercession of the holy Martyrs and raise up again a soul so devoted to them, and may he deign to give him a place in the company of the saints, he who laid down his life for the salvation of the world, our Lord Jesus Christ, who lives and reigns, King of kings and Lord of lords, world without end. Amen.

g. The emperor Charles was Charles the Bald (emperor 875–77); Carloman was king from 879 to 884. See further endnote 4.

Endnotes

INTRODUCTION

1. For the biography of Suger, Cartellieri remains fundamental; see too *Abbot Suger*. Among narratives, Marcel Aubert, *Suger* (Rouen, 1950) is readable if somewhat benevolent. From the point of view of art and architectural history, see von Simson and Panofsky as well as E. Male, *Religious Art in France, the Twelfth-Century*, trans. Marthiel Mathews, ed. Henry Bober (Princeton, 1978), pp. 359–80, and William W. Clark, "Suger's Church at Saint-Denis; The State of Research," in *Abbot Suger*, pp. 105–30. See too E. R. Labande, "Memoria Sugerii abbatis," *Cahiers de civilisation médiévale* 25 (1982), pp. 121–27.

2. A. Luchaire, *Les Premiers Capétiens* (Paris, 1901), p. 311 (=Ernest Lavisse, ed., *Histoire de France* 2.2). Similarly, Marc Bloch saw Louis's reign as a "decisive turning point" in *Feudal Society*, trans. L. A. Manyon (London, 1962), p. 69; so too G. Barraclough, *The Crucible of Europe* (London, 1976), p. 84. This perception may go back to the twelfth century, for in his *De nugis curialium*, written toward the end of the century, Walter Map saw the reign of Louis as marking the completion of a long period of warfare: "From the decease of that Louis ['the Pious,' son of Charlemagne] the sword did not depart from France until the Lord in his pity sent this Louis [VI]," p. 443; see the sentences following this quote for a quaint view of Louis's recovery of power in the royal domain.

3. For the twelfth-century evidence on Suger's birth, see his own statement (below, cap. 27) and charters of 1130 and 1137 (Lecoy, pp. 326, 334) as well as a passage in the life of Suger written by William (Lecoy, p. 380). For recent information, see above all John F. Benton, "Introduction: Suger's Life and Personality," in *Abbot Suger*, pp. 3–15, esp. 3f, 11–15. The question is also discussed by Charles Higounet, *La Grange de Vaulerent* (Paris, 1965), p. 126, by Bournazel, p. 72, and by Spiegel, p. 34, n. 89. For brief remarks about Suger's entrance into monastic life, see William, *Vita* (Lecoy, p. 408) and *De admin.* 33, 34A (Panofsky, pp. 61, 81).

4. On the early history of St. Denis, consult J. M. Wallace-Hadrill, *The Frankish Church* (Oxford, 1983), pp. 126ff, and Spiegel, pp. 14ff.

5. The quote is from Abelard, p. 86. On linkage between the abbey of St. Denis and the French monarchy, see in general Sumner Mc-Knight Crosby, *The Royal Abbey of St. Denis: From Its Beginnings to the Death of Suger, 475–1151*, edited and completed by Pamela Z. Blum (New Haven, 1987); Gabrielle M. Spiegel, "The Cult of Saint Denis and Capetian Kingship," *Journal of Medieval History* 1 (1975), pp. 43–70; and Alexander Patschovsky, "Der Heilige Dionysius, Die Universität Paris und Der Französische Staat," *Innsbrucker Historische Studien* 1 (1978), pp. 9–31. See most recently on the cult of the blessed Dionysius prior to Suger, Colette Beaune, *Naissance de la nation France* (Paris, 1985), pp. 83–90.

6. On Suger's filial sentiments toward the abbey of St. Denis, see below, cap. 27, and *De admin.* 28 (Panofsky, p. 51) and 27 (p. 47). On his interests in old charters, see *De admin.* 3 (Lecoy, p. 160) and cap. 27, n. 23, below.

7. For Suger at Berneval (near Fécamp about forty miles northwest of Rouen), see Catellieri, no. 9f. And for his activities at Toury, see below, cap. 19, and *De admin.* 12 (Lecoy, pp. 170ff), with a charter of 1111 (p. 365).

8. See 1 Samuel 2:8 for the quote used by Suger in *De admin.* 28 (Panofsky, p. 50) as well as in a charter of 1137 (Lecoy, p. 334). On the matter of Louis and Suger being associates at St. Denis, Suger refers to Louis as having been at St. Denis *ab infantia* (*De admin.* 33A, Panofsky, p. 67) and, more generally, to Louis as having loved the holy Martyrs *ab puero* (below, cap. 1). Being about the same age, they were probably both at the abbey at some point in time during their youthful years; on the date of Louis's birth, probably 1081 but perhaps 1082, consult Joseph Calmette, "L'âge de Louis VI," *Orientalia Christiana periodica* 13 (1947), pp. 36–39. Almost all the sources for Louis's life are collected in Luchaire. There is little of value in Jacques Delperrié de Bayac, *Louis VI: La Naissance de la France* (Paris, 1983).

9. On Louis's association on the throne with his father Philip, see Luchaire, no. 8, and Lewis, p. 51. King Philip's union with Bertrada of Montfort, the source of tension over the succession, is discussed by Georges Duby, *Medieval Marriage: Two Models from Twelfth-Century France* (Baltimore, 1973), pp. 29–45; Duby, *The Knight, the Lady and the Priest* (New York, 1983), pp. 3–21.

10. For the confirmation of the monastery's privileges, see Luchaire, no. 315.

11. Tardif, no. 391.

12. *Chron. Mor.*, p. 47. Luchaire's index of personal names, with its references to Suger (p. 364), allows his activity at court during the later years of Louis's reign to be conveniently documented. On Stephen of Garlande's departure from court in 1127, see cap. 31, n. 2, below.

13. On the word *familiaris*, "a term used for both clerks and laymen who were on intimate terms with the king," see Judith A. Green, *The Government of England under Henry I* (Cambridge, 1986), p. 20, with pp. 24–26 and 36f, where contemporary English evidence is considered.

14. *De admin.* 3 (Lecoy, p. 161).

15. It may well be that, as F. Hugenholtz and H. Teunis suggest in "Suger's Advice," *Journal of Medieval History* 12 (1986), pp. 191–205, at 202f, Suger's telling of the *Deeds* was influenced by events that occurred early in the reign of Louis VII; but this issue deserves further discussion. The date at which Suger wrote is not entirely clear: Spiegel, p. 48, n. 23.

16. For the names bestowed on the text in the manuscripts, see Waquet, p. 2, notes a, c; p. 4, note b; p. 286, note b. For references by Suger himself to the "deeds of Louis," see below, Prologue and *De admin.* 12 (Lecoy, p. 171). Note, however, that Suger in another passage of the *Deeds* writes of himself as "commemorating the history of the king" (below, cap. 28).

17. Odo, p. 3; William, *Vita Sugerii* (Lecoy, pp. 382 twice, 403).

18. That is, against most editors of the text, who have termed or viewed Suger's work as a *Life*, we agree with: Georg Misch, *Studien zur Geschichte der Autobiographie* 4 (Göttingen, 1957), p. 95, n. 5; Hubert Galser, "Sugers Vorstellung von geordneten Welt," *Historisches Jahrbuch* 80 (1961), pp. 93–125 at 96f; and E. Carpentier, "Histoire et informatique: Recherches sur la vocabulaire des biographies royales françaises," *Cahiers de civilisation médiévale* 25 (1982), pp. 3–30 at 6f. Perhaps it should be pointed out that the manuscripts of the text that provide a title style Louis *grossus* (on the manuscripts, see the last part of this Introduction), and that the description was commonly applied to him in the twelfth century (Luchaire, p. 284). On the role of St. Denis in French historiography, consult Spiegel.

19. The separate manuscript is most conveniently available in PL 186:1341–46. On the influence of hagiography, see cap. 1, n. 1, below. For the series of lessons, see *Chron. Mor.*, p. 69.

20. On the lessons as extracts from the *Deeds*, see Lecoy, p. v;

Molinier, p. xvi, n. 1; the question is ignored by Waquet. On Suger's provisions to celebrate Louis's anniversary, see Lecoy, p. 330; on the date see Cartellieri, p. 132 (no. 41). On the date of composition of the *Chronicle of Morigny*, see Mirot's introduction, pp. xii–xv. On Suger's having composed the *Deeds* after 1143, see cap. 32 fin. below, where Suger uses the perfect tense to describe the pontificate of Innocent. And on the earliest reference to the *Deeds*, see *De admin.* 12 (Lecoy, p. 171); this work is to be dated between 1144/45 and 1148/49 (Panofsky, p. 142).

21. This is most recently suggested by Tony Hunt, "L'inspiration idéologique du *Charroi de Nîmes*," *Revue belge de philologie et d'histoire* 66 (1978), pp. 580–606. The crusading works with *Gesta* in their titles that we particularly have in mind are the anonymous *Gesta Francorum et aliorum Hierosolimitanorum* and the *Gesta Francorum Iherusalem peregrinantium* of Fulcher of Chartres, for Suger twice states that his book provides an account of the *gesta Francorum* ("deeds of the French"): see cap. 1 and 10 below.

22. William, *Vita Sugerii* (Lecoy, pp. 382, 389). Aubert, *Suger*, p. 113, suggests that the kings in question were the first Capetians, but surely we are meant to understand the Carolingians, and possibly the Merovingians as well.

23. This has been particularly well brought out by Gabrielle M. Spiegel, to whose ideas on this point we owe much in this paragraph: "History as Enlightenment: Suger and the *Mos Anagogicus*," in *Abbot Suger*, pp. 151–58. It is interesting to compare Suger's method with that of another monastic author, as described by Roger D. Ray, "Bede the Exegete, as Historian," in Gerald Bonner, ed., *Famulus Christi: Essays in Commemoration of the Thirteenth Century of the Birth of the Venerable Bede* (London, 1976), pp. 125–40 at 135.

24. A variation here is supplied by the behavior of popes, at whose feet Louis casts himself (see cap. 10 and 32 below).

25. See for example chapter 7, which is seen as not the first among the chapters dealing with Thomas of Marle but an independent narrative, which begins with troubles caused by Thomas when he obtained a castle by marriage and ends with his loss of the castle when the marriage was annulled.

26. For these events, see in order PL 162:664; *The Historical Works of Simeon of Durham*, trans. Joseph Stevenson (London, 1855), p. 582; and OV 4:195–98.

27. For the brief reference to Louis's wife Adelaide of Maurienne, whom Suger mentions without giving her name, see cap. 27 below; some of the background to the marriage can be gleaned from a letter of Ivo of Chartres (*ep.* 239, PL 162:246f). Louis's activities in bestowing charters is discussed by Walther Kienast, "Der Wirkungsbereich des französchen Königtums in Südfrankreich," *Historische Zeitschrift* 209 (1969), pp. 529–65, who demonstrates heightened activity in the royal chancery during Louis's reign.

28. See cap. 34 below. Charters indicate that Louis was a friend to many religious houses; the evidence is summarized by Luchaire, pp. cl–cliii. In manuscript f of the *Deeds* there is a passing reference to *vir Dei Bernardus* as being among the *intimi* who advised Louis to have his younger son Louis crowned and anointed following the death of Philip, his first son (Molinier, p. 122, n. 2. On this manuscript, see the last section of this Introduction, below). Interesting light on ecclesiastical reform during the period, and Louis's attitude to it, is contained in a letter edited with discussion by Edmé R. Smits, "An Unedited Letter (1132–1133) to Geoffrey de Lèves, Bishop of Chartres, Concerning Louis VI and the Reform Movement," *Revue bénédictine* 92 (1982), pp. 407–17. On Suger's relationship with the house of St. Victor in Paris, see Conrad Rudolf, *Artistic Change at St. Denis* (Princeton, 1990), pp. 34–35.

29. On Suger's debt to Pseudo-Dionysius, consult Panofsky and Otto von Simson, *The Gothic Cathedral: Origins of Gothic Architecture and the Medieval Concept of Order*, 2d ed. (New York, 1964), with modifications proposed by Grover A. Zinn, "Suger, Theology and the Pseudo-Dionysian Tradition," in *Abbot Suger*, pp. 33–40; see too Spiegel, "History as Enlightenment," *Abbot Suger*, pp. 154–56. In general see also Georges Duby, *The Age of the Cathedrals* (Chicago, 1981), pp. 98–108, and, for some comments on his political thought, see Duby, *The Three Orders*, pp. 227–29.

30. Walter Map, p. 442. The most accessible accounts of the political history of the period and Louis's struggles therein are Robert Fawtier, *The Capetian Kings of France*, trans. Lionel Butler and R. J. Adam (London, 1960); Elizabeth M. Hallam, *Capetian France, 987–1328* (London, 1980); and Jean Dunbabin, *France in the Making, 843–1180* (Oxford, 1985). The first of these books, written for publication in France in 1941, has become somewhat outdated in the light of more recent work. Problems occur in delineating and defining both the royal demesne and the royal principality for the

early twelfth century. Hallam, pp. 78–91, with the map on p. 79, and Dunbabin, pp. 162–69, are most helpful. See in general W. M. Newman, *Le Domaine royal sous les premiers Capétiens 987–1180* (Paris, 1937); and on the Ile-de-France, see Marc Bloch, *The Ile-de-France: The Country around Paris*, trans. J. E. Anderson (Ithaca, 1971). See also Charles T. Wood, "*Regnum Francie*: A Problem in Capetian Administrative Usage," *Traditio* 23 (1967), pp. 136–37, where it is stated that in the early thirteenth century the domain was a judicial concept consisting of places where the king employed both his immediate and appellate jurisdiction.

31. Georges Duby, *La société aux XIe et XIIe siècles dans la région mâconnaise* (Paris, 1953), p. 364, quoted by R. I. Moore in the context of a useful evaluation of Duby's work, "Duby's Eleventh Century," *History* 69 (1984), pp. 36–49 at 46. Jean-François Lemarignier has written an excellent synthesis of the period, *La France médiévale, institutions et sociétés* (Paris, 1971). Note as well the discussion of Edward James, *The Origins of France* (London, 1982), pp. 187–96. The best discussion of castles is that of G. Fournier, *Le Château dans la France médiévale: Essai de sociologie monumentale* (Paris, 1978).

32. For the quote and the expedition into Berry, see cap. 25 below as well as Luchaire, nos. 91–92. On the strengthening of royal justice under Louis VI and its connection to Suger's concept of suzerainty, see J.-F. Lemarignier, *Le Gouvernement royal aux premiers temps capétiens, 987–1108* (Paris, 1965), pp. 167–76, whose lead this paragraph follows; see too cap. 29, n. 6, below, for further citations.

33. King Philip I, the father of Louis VI, had himself invaded Flanders after Robert the Frisian had usurped the comital office in 1071. Although the king's side suffered defeat at Cassel and Robert remained as count, Philip soon gained an alliance and a bride, Bertha of Holland, the count's step-daughter and mother-to-be of Louis; on this war of succession in Flanders, see Fliche, pp. 252–68, and Hallam, p. 76.

34. *Chron. Mor.*, p. 21; William of Malmesbury, p. 437f. Note too a reference to Philip's good deeds in the *Chronique de Saint-Pierre-le-Vif de Sens*, ed. R.-H. Bautier and M. Gilles (Paris, 1979), p. 146. The situation in which Capetian monarchy found itself at the accession of Louis is discussed by K. F. Werner, "Kingdom and Principality in

Twelfth-Century France," in Timothy Reuter, ed. and trans., *The Medieval Nobility* (Amsterdam, 1978), pp. 243–90 at 244ff.

35. See Ovid, *Metamorphoses* 15:569.

36. Lecoy, p. 281. Suger's stress on the role of the king as protector of churches and the "poor" is discussed by Andrew W. Lewis, "Suger's Views on Kingship," in *Abbot Suger*, pp. 49–54, esp. p. 51.

37. Guibert, pp. 119–25.

38. See the Prologue below. In his letters and charters, Suger styles himself as "abbot (or servant) of the blessed Dionysius," without the word "Areopagite."

39. Abelard, p. 85f. On the confirmation of the possessions and immunities of the abbey of St. Remigius at Reims, see Luchaire, no. 2.

40. Robert Barroux, "L'anniversaire de la morte de Dagobert à Saint-Denis au XIIe siècle," (Paris, 1945: offprint; originally published 1942–43).

41. Lecoy, p. 406.

42. PL 186:1341A.

43. Helgaud, *Vie de Robert le Pieux*, ed. R.-H. Bautier and C. Labory (Paris, 1965), p. 140.

44. *William, Count of Orange*, ed. Glanville Price (London, 1975), p. 72; see too a comparison made by Suger of people who behave in this way and evil spirits (below, cap. 24).

45. *The Letters of Peter the Venerable*, ed. Giles Constable (Cambridge, Mass., 1967), *ep.* 21, 171, 172, 173 (pp. 42, 405, 408, 410).

46. Waquet, p. xvi. For other modern negative assessments of Suger's style, see Molinier, p. xii; Luchaire, p. lviii; Cartellieri, p. 110; Aubert, *Suger*, p. 117; and Reto Bezzola, *Les origines et la formation de littérature courtoise en occident, 500–1200* 3.2 (Paris, 1963), p. 353. More positive is Max Manitus, *Geschichte der Lateinischen Literatur des Mittelalters* 3 (Munich, 1931), p. 602. For the favorable comparison of Suger to Cicero, see the remarks of his biographer William in Lecoy, pp. 388 and 411.

47. For example, *repulsi . . . repellentes . . . repellere . . . repellentes . . . repellunt . . . impatiens . . . recipiunt . . . recipere . . . arto . . . impatiens . . . arto* (Waquet, p. 72, within the space of twelve lines); *defensionibus . . . defendentes . . . defensabant* (Waquet, p. 74, in two lines).

48. A partial list (page numbers cited from Waquet): *augtivus* (p. 6), *incurtis* (p. 16), *defavillatio* (p. 68), *terrare* (p. 74), *excordatus* (p.

120), *opertura* (p. 138), *interfluctuo* (p. 144), *juvativus* (p. 152), *refugo* (p. 160), *consumptivus* (pp. 168, 268), *damnativus* (p. 174), *devexatio* (p. 176), *superiorites* (p. 182). For whatever reason, such occurrences are not distributed equally throughout the work.

49. Where possible, references to classical authors are supplied in the text. Suger's biographer William mentions his excellent memory for the classical poets, in particular Horace (Lecoy, p. 381); see too the interesting comments of Galser, "Sugers Vorstellung," (cited n. 18 above), p. 97. On Suger's use of Lucan in the *Deeds*, see Jeremy duQuesnay Adams, "The Influence of Lucan on the Political Attitudes of Suger of Saint-Denis," *Proceedings of the Twelfth Annual Meeting of the Western Society for French History* 12 (1985), pp. 1–11.

50. *Chron. Mor.*, p. 24.

51. *De admin.* 33 (Panofsky, pp. 63f). Note too his famous statement: "The dull mind rises to truth through that which is material" (*mens hebes ad verum per materialia surgit* [*De admin.* 28, Panofsky, p. 49]). On twelfth-century monastic art, Georges Duby, *Saint Bernard l'art cistercien* (Paris, 1976), is of wider interest than its title suggests; see too Emile Male, *Religious Art in France, the Twelfth Century* (cited n. 1 above), pp. 154ff, and the speculative study of Erica Deuber-Pauli and Dario Gamboni, "Suger, Théophile, Le Guide du Pèlerin. Elements de théorie de l'art au XIIe siécle," *Etudes des lettres*, ser. 4, vol. 3 (1980), pp. 43–91. But there is no need to see Suger as having been directly influenced by Pseudo-Dionysius: see Peter Kidson, "Suger and St. Denis," *Journal of the Warburg and Courtauld Institutes* 50 (1987), pp. 1–17.

52. For the quote, see *De admin.* 31 (Panofsky, p. 55); and for the formulation, which is implied in the *Deeds* (cap. 32), see *De admin.* 34 (p. 74), with the pun *velat . . . revelat* being typical of our author, although the wording is not original with him. See the brief discussion of E. Male, *Religious Art* (cited n. 1 above), p. 162.

53. Peter the Venerable, *ep.* 160 (ed. Constable, p. 386).

54. *De admin.* 29 (Panofsky, p. 53).

55. Beryl Smalley, *Historians in the Middle Ages* (London, 1974), p. 76; see too Hallam, p. 114.

56. *De admin.* 32 (Panofsky, p. 57); see a very similar phrase below, cap. 20 fin.

57. The abbey, we may note, has been seen as a statement of Carolingian forms of the glorification of monarchy: see Duby, *Cathedrals*, p. 104.

58. See Lecoy, p. 387, for the quote; p. 378 for a statement on Suger's size, and p. 403 for the abbot's *officium* to pray.

59. The standard editions are those of Molinier and Waquet. Each editor discusses the manuscripts at pp. xvii–xxii; for additional manuscript material, see G. M. Spiegel, "History as Enlightenment," in *Abbot Suger*, p. 157, n. 7. We have used Waquet's text as the basis for our translation, although Molinier's preface and notes retain their value. Lecoy de la Marche published the *Oeuvres complètes de Suger* in 1867; while his text of the *Deeds* has been superseded, his work is still useful, as it brings together all of Suger's works and a selection of material about him, in particular the biography of William. Suger's *De consecratione* and part of the *De administratione* (part of chapter 1 and chapters 24–34A) have been edited and translated by Panofsky; the portions of the *De admin.* not contained in this edition are cited from Lecoy. Page references to Panofsky are to the translations, not the Latin texts, although we have sometimes amended the translation, as we have that which Marjorie Chibnall supplies to her text of Orderic Vitalis.

60. That Suger stood behind ms. f, see Molinier, pp. xxii–xxviii; that he did not, see Waquet, pp. xxii–xxiv. The readings of this manuscript are printed by Molinier, p. 12, note n. On the designation of Louis as *rex Francie* in ms. f, see Molinier, pp. 31 note y, 52 note o, 55 note i, 88 note u, 90 note m. On the odd expression "arms as powerful as Hector's," see cap. 19 below and ms. f, ed. Molinier, p. 12 note n. On "we who wrote the history of the lord Louis" in ms. f, see Molinier, p. 25 note e. On the references to Suger in the third person in ms. f, see Molinier, pp. 62 note f and 95 note j.

PROLOGUE

1. See *Thesaurus Linguae Latinae* 5/2 678.72–75 for applications of this term *episcopus episcoporum* to Christ among the church Fathers (although Sidonius Apollinaris applied it to his friend the bishop of Troyes: *ep.* 6.1.1). Bishop Josselin of Soissons (1126–52), the person so described, was a friend of Suger; he owed his advancement to Louis, as the following paragraph indicates. The letters of St. Bernard imply that Josselin and Suger cooperated in affairs of state (*ep.* 298f, 301), and in 1129 Josselin was one of the bishops who testified in favor of the claims of St. Denis over the house of Argenteuil (below, cap. 27, n. 23). In this salutation to Bishop Josselin, Suger has called himself "abbot of blessed Dionysius the Areopa-

gite." On the claims of the abbey of St. Denis to have been founded by St. Paul's disciple Dionysius the Areopagite, see Introduction, above. Peter Abelard, the philosopher and theologian, had entered St. Denis as a monk after his intimate relationship with Heloise ended in 1118; he quickly won notoriety for denying the abbey's claim to have been founded by the biblical Dionysius. The conflict lingered into Suger's abbacy, which began in 1122; see Abelard, pp. 76, 85f; on Suger's election as abbot, see below, cap. 27 with n. 10.

2. The expression used here, "hatred and love," is a form of words that must go back to Catullus's *odi et amo* (carm. 85:1); we do not know how it came to Suger. The quote is from Proverbs 31:23 (Vulgate).

3. See Matthew 5:43f.

4. Horace, *Odes* 3.30.1.

CHAPTER I

1. Louis had been born in 1081, or perhaps 1082; see Joseph Calmette, "L'âge de Louis VI," *Orientalia Christiana periodica* 13 (1947), pp. 36–39. The Latin text of this chapter begins *Gloriosus igitur*. The practice of beginning the body of a biography with a word followed by *igitur* is common in medieval authors (see the biography of Louis VII, Molinier, p. 147), and indicates the influence of hagiography (see Sulpicius Severus, *Vita Beati Martini* 1.2, *Igitur Martinus* . . .; Paulinus, *Vita Ambrosi* 2; Possidius, *Vita Augustini* 1; Ennodius, *Vita Epifani* 70). After referring to Louis as a *puerulus* in this paragraph, Suger frequently designates him as a *juvenis* in the opening chapters of the *Deeds*; on the meaning of such terms in early twelfth-century narratives, see G. Duby, *The Chivalrous Society*, trans. C. Postan (Berkeley and Los Angeles, 1980), pp. 112ff.

2. The connection of St. Denis with earlier French monarchy was celebrated; St. Bernard, for example, wrote that it had been an abbey of royal dignity "from early times" (*ep.* 80). See Gabrielle M. Spiegel, "The Cult of Saint Denis and Capetian Kingship," *Journal of Medieval History* 1 (1975), pp. 19–41.

3. "Greedy for praise" is reminiscent of Horace, *Ars poetica* 324; "a seeker of fame" is a quotation from Lucan, *De bello civili* 1:131. Suger's attitude to William Rufus is set in its historiographical context by Thomas Callaghan, Jr., "The Making of a Monster: The Historical Image of William Rufus," *Journal of Medieval History* 7 (1981), pp. 175–85 at 180, and by Barlow, p. 424.

4. In this sentence Suger has used the word *regnum* ("realm"), which creates problems of definition; on the ambiguities of the term and its possible meanings in medieval terminology, see Charles T. Wood, "*Regnum Francie*: A Problem in Capetian Administrative Usage," *Traditio* 23 (1967), pp. 117–47; in this instance, Suger must mean the royal principality.

On the succession to William the Conqueror discussed in this paragraph, see Barlow, pp. 47–49, who presents the possibility that the youngest son, Henry, may have already fallen heir to the possessions of his mother, Mathilda of Flanders. On Louis's defense of the French Vexin against the incursions of William Rufus, see Barlow, pp. 376–81. The youthful Louis had been invested with the county of the Vexin in 1092 or shortly afterward by his father Philip: see Orderic Vitalis (OV) 3:390. Frequently in these notes we will have occasion to cite the work of Orderic Vitalis (1075–1142), the son of a French father and English mother, who spent most of his life as a monk at the house of Saint-Evroul in Normandy. His sprawling *Historia ecclesiastica* is an important source of information for the period and frequently allows depth to be added to Suger's account; more importantly, Orderic's inclination to see things from a point of view favorable to the English is a useful corrective to Suger, whose bias operated in the opposite direction. See in general M. Chibnall, *The World of Orderic Vitalis* (Oxford, 1984).

5. The wealth of England was proverbial; as Suger goes on to show in this chapter, a practical result of such wealth was the ability of the king to hire mercenaries and to ransom prisoners quickly; for additional comments on England's wealth, see also cap. 19, 26 below; OV 3:254; *Chron. Mor.* 21; and a famous story told by Walter Map, p. 451. For discussions of the topic, see P. H. Sawyer, "The Wealth of England in the Eleventh Century," *Transactions of the Royal Historical Society*, 5th ser., 15 (1965), pp. 145–64, and Edward Miller and John Hatcher, *Medieval England: Rural Society and Economic Change, 1086–1348* (London, 1978), pp. 25f. For the practice of fief rents described here, see Bournazel, pp. 105–10 (esp. n. 38).

6. Suger's report on Louis is scarcely glowing, and Orderic Vitalis in fact says that Louis did not do well (4:20). Writing toward the end of the twelfth century, Walter Map similarly states that in an engagement near Gisors, William Rufus defeated Louis and his proud army and forced him to flee (p. 437).

7. Simon of St. Liz had married the daughter of Earl Waltheof and became earl of Huntingdon and Northampton. Gilbert of L'Aigle possessed estates on both sides of the Channel; for his family, see Barlow, p. 467, table 4. On Pagan of Gisors, lord of an important castle about forty miles northwest of Paris, see below, cap. 16; see also E. Pepin, *Gisors et la Vallée de l'Epte* (Paris, 1939).

8. Matthew of Beaumont held a castle on the Oise about twenty-seven miles north of Paris. On the family of Simon of Montfort, see Barlow, p. 469, table 8; Montfort is Montfort-l'Amaury, Seine-et-Oise, about thirty-five miles southwest of Paris. According to Waquet (p. 11, n. 4), Pagan's true name was Aubry and he could be found among the entourages of both Philip I and Louis VI; Montjay is Montjay-la-Tour, Seine-et-Marne, about fifteen miles northeast of Paris.

9. Referring to Bertrada, Suger has used the Latin word *super-ducta*, which denotes "a wife who has been taken while the first husband still lives," and which we have translated as "irregular union." But later in the *Deeds* Suger refers to Count Fulk IV of Anjou as Bertrada's first husband (cap. 18), which implies some recognition on Suger's part of a subsequent union in marriage to Philip. The problems arising from Philip's conduct in taking Bertrada are discussed by Georges Duby, *Medieval Marriage: Two Models from Twelfth-Century France* (Baltimore, 1978), pp. 29–45, and *The Knight, the Lady and the Priest* (Harmondsworth, 1983), pp. 3–21, and by C. N. L. Brooke, *The Medieval Idea of Marriage* (Oxford, 1989), pp. 122f.

10. A difficult phrase, which could also be translated "nor even the English to the French." We have decided against this rendering, for other French authors of the period point to a belief in the superiority of the French over other peoples: Guibert of Nogent, PL 156: 698; *Historia Karoli Magni et Rotholandi ou Chronique de pseudo-Turpin*, ed. C. Meredith-Jones (Paris, 1936), pp. 220f. See, on this passage, John H. Mundy, *Europe in the High Middle Ages, 1150–1309* (London, 1973), p. 47, and J. Ehlers, "Kontinuität und Tradition als Grandlage mittelalterlichen Nationsbildung in Frankreich," in H. Beumann, ed., *Beiträge zur Bildung der Französischen Nation im Früh- und Hochmittelalter* (Sigmaringen, 1983), p. 26.

11. Suger's assertion that the killing of William was accidental is supported by other sources, although most state that the arrow was shot by Walter Tirel (e.g., OV 4:87; William of Malmesbury, p. 345;

John of Salisbury, *Vita Anselmi Cantuariensis*, PL 199:103); and in modern scholarship: C. Warren Hollister, "The Strange Death of William Rufus," *Speculum* 48 (1973), pp. 637–53. Walter Tirel of Poix, William's unwitting slayer and Suger's informant, appears as a witness to several of Louis's charters (Luchaire, nos. 9, 42, 168). Other twelfth-century sources confirm Suger's gloomy description of William's conduct as monarch (*A-S chron.* 1100, in addition to those just cited).

12. Reminiscent of Job 12:18.

13. On the reign of Henry, the younger brother of Robert and William, see Judith A. Green, *The Government of England under Henry I* (Cambridge, England, 1986); see also in general C. Warren Hollister, *Monarchy*. In the next sentence Suger states that he would enjoy writing about Henry; and according to William, the abbot's biographer, Henry gloried in Suger's friendship and rejoiced to be on familiar terms with him (Lecoy, p. 384). Information concerning the relations between Henry and Suger is provided by Hollister, *Monarchy*, p. 288.

CHAPTER 2

1. In this paragraph Suger has used the adjective "simple" (*simplex*) in reference to Louis. *The Chronicle of Morigny*, p. 11, called him "a man of simple disposition" (*homo simplicis naturae*); Ivo of Chartres described him similarly (*ep.* 238, PL 162:246A); and according to Walter Map, both Louis and his son Louis were men of "simpleness in speech" (p. 44). Elsewhere in this text Suger applies the same word to Hugh of Clermont (cap. 3) and Odo of Corbeil (cap. 15). On the concept of *oratores* and *laboratores* in this passage, consult G. Duby, *The Three Orders: Feudal Society Imagined* (Chicago, 1980), p. 228.

2. As he lay dying, Louis enjoined this practice on his son (see below cap. 33). Poissy is eighteen miles west of Paris.

3. Orderic Vitalis's account of Louis's attack differs from Suger's; he describes it as something of a fiasco (4:286f). Note that Suger differentiates between French and Flemings; his use of the word *Francia* in the *Deeds* is discussed by Charles T. Wood, "*Regnum Francie*" (cited, Introduction, n. 30), pp. 117–47 at 117–19; on Louis's uncle, Robert, see cap. 1, note. f.

4. The campaign against Drogo is discussed by Luchaire, no. 18.

CHAPTER 3

1. This is an expression of interest with regard to feudal tenure: see Bournazel, pp. 61f.

2. Rom. 5:5.

CHAPTER 4

1. Hugh of Clermont was the father-in-law of Matthew of Beaumont. Beaumont is on the river Oise about twenty-five miles north of Paris, and Clermont is about twenty-one miles north of it. On the knights of Senlis, consult Bournazel, pp. 48–50; Senlis is about twenty-six miles north-north-east of Paris. Herluin of Paris had taught the young Louis (Bournazel, pp. 69f). Orderic Vitalis does not mention the storm described here, but attributes the flight of Louis's force to a trick (4:287f).

CHAPTER 5

1. The complex family background of Ebles of Roucy is discussed by B. Guenée, "Les Généalogies entre l'histoire et la politique: La fierté d'être capétien, en France, au moyen âge," *Annales économies sociétés civilisations* 33 (1978), pp. 450–77 at 453.

2. On French campaigns in Spain during this period, see M. Defourneaux, *Les Français en Espagne aux XIe et XIIe siècles* (Paris, 1949).

3. On the Truce of God, consult Hartmut Hoffmann, *Gottesfried und Treuga Dei* (Stuttgart, 1964) (=MGH Schriften 20); this portion of Suger is discussed on p. 245.

4. Reminiscent of Augustine, *In ps.* 118, *serm.* 16.2.

CHAPTER 6

1. Just as the souls of pagans killed in battle in the *Song of Roland* go to hell (see, for example, lines 1268 and 1553), so too do those of some of Louis's enemies (below, cap. 20, 24).

CHAPTER 7

1. Thomas of Marle, the most wicked character in Suger's work, is here introduced. Guibert of Nogent is equally condemnatory, describing him as "the most evil man of all we know in this generation" (p. 170); Orderic Vitalis saw him as "a rebel bandit who ter-

rorized a whole province" (4:377); see too Henry of Huntington, *De contemptu mundi*, ed. Thomas Arnold (London, 1879), pp. 308–10. Of course, all these authors wrote from an ecclesiastical point of view, and a case can be made for a more positive assessment: see Jacques Chaurand, *Thomas de Marle, Sire de Coucy* (Marle-sur-Serre, 1963). Thomas's control over the castle of Montaigu arose from his marriage to his cousin, Ermengarde; as the last sentence of the chapter indicates, Thomas lost the castle when the marriage was annuled because of consanguinity.

2. Louis's intervention on behalf of the villanous Thomas needed some explanation, but there is no need to dismiss the one provided by Suger as a clumsy attempt to whitewash Louis. It is easy to picture the young prince, not yet come into his inheritance, surrounded by an entourage of young knights whose advice could be malign (see *Chron. Mor.*, p. 21; and in the following pages we find Louis opposed to the Garlande brothers); the relationships and alliances that were to characterize the greater part of his reign took time to develop.

3. Lucan, *De bello civili* 1:7.

CHAPTER 8

1. As Suger goes on to explain, Guy Trousseau had returned home after an undistinguished career in the First Crusade (*Gesta Francorum* 23 describes his flight from Antioch). For Guy and his family, see Bournazel, pp. 32–34, 45f, and Fliche, pp. 320–26.

2. After his first reference to Bertrada (cap. 1), Suger avoids mentioning her name and persistently refers to her as *superducta Andegavensis comitissa* (cap. 13 and 18 as well as here). For the meaning of the term *superducta*, see cap. 1, n. 9.

3. The crucial location of the castle of Mantes, between the castles of Meulan and La Roche-Guyon, is indicated by a map in David Crouch, *The Beaumont Twins* (Cambridge, 1986), p. 62.

4. In 1104 Elizabeth, the daughter of Guy Trousseau, married Philip, the elder son of King Philip and Bertrada. The marriage must have followed a reconciliation between Louis and his stepmother. Suger has no need to mention this, as he has avoided mentioning the problems between them (on which see OV 4:195–98, 288). The measures Philip took to settle his various children are helpfully discussed by Lewis, pp. 51f.

5. Suger here introduces Guy the Red, count of Rochefort, castellan of Châteaufort and lord of Crécy (see Fliche, pp. 320–21). Being the younger brother of Guy Trousseau's father, Milo of Montlhéry, he was uncle to the latter Guy. He had served Philip as seneschal before departing for the crusader kingdom in 1101, and on his return from the east was reinstated as seneschal (Bournazel, pp. 33f).

6. The establishment of an alliance by the projected nuptials of Louis and Guy the Red's daughter, Lucienne of Rochefort, was a sign of how far Guy had advanced in the royal favor. But as Suger points out, the girl was not yet of marriageable age; and in 1107 the Council of Troyes dissolved the betrothal on the familiar grounds of consanguinity; but there may have been other reasons. The *Chronique de Saint-Pierre-le-Vif de Sens* (cited, Introduction, n. 34), p. 146, states that Lucienne was not worthy of the royal dignity and not acceptable to the counts of the kingdom: see Lewis, p. 54. By then the pattern of Louis's alliances had changed and, perhaps significantly, Suger states that Louis had undertaken to marry Lucienne on the prompting of his father. On consanguinity, see in general Constance B. Bouchard, "Consanguinity and Noble Marriages in the Eleventh and Twelfth Centuries," *Speculum* 56 (1981), pp. 268–87.

7. Horace, *ep.* 1.2.69f.

8. Milo II, lord of Bray and viscount of Troyes, was the son of Milo I of Montlhéry and his wife Lithuise, viscountess of Troyes. Mentioned in the previous sentence are the Garlandes, rivals of the family of Guy of Rochefort for influence at court; on them see Bournazel, pp. 35–40, and cap. 31, n. 2, below.

CHAPTER 9

1. According to Orderic Vitalis (4:210), Bohemond arrived in Gaul in March 1106, although Luchaire (no. 30) inclines towards a somewhat earlier date. Bohemond's activities in France are described by R. B. Yewdale, *Bohemond I, Prince of Antioch* (Princeton, 1924), pp. 106–12. Suger persistently spells his name Boamund, as does the author of the *Gesta Francorum*. He is silent as to the background of Bohemond's visit. Having been held captive by the Turks (1101–3) and now threatened by a revival of Byzantine power, he was seeking help from a position of weakness. Orderic Vitalis provides the additional information that Bohemond was accompanied by a "son of

the emperor Diogenes" (4:212), who was almost certainly spurious (see Lecoy, p. 429f). The emperor Romanus IV Diogenes died after being blinded following the disastrous Byzantine defeat at the battle of Manzikert in 1071.

2. Suger elsewhere refers to the "riches of Constantinople" (*De admin.* 25, 33; Panofsky, pp. 45, 65).

3. In 1059 Robert Guiscard had sworn fealty to Pope Nicholas II and his successors: see his oath in Brian Tierney, *The Crisis of Church and State* (Englewood Cliffs, 1964), p. 44. During his quarrel with Henry IV ("the emperor"), Pope Gregory VII (mistakenly referred to here as Alexander) sought the assistance of Robert Guiscard; see for example two letters in *The Correspondence of Pope Gregory VII*, trans. E. Emerton (New York, 1932), pp. 181f, 185f.

4. This is not quite accurate. Durazzo fell in early 1082, and Robert Guiscard left subsequently: Yewdale, *Bohemond*, pp. 16f, and D. C. Douglas, *The Norman Achievement* (London, 1969), pp. 63f.

5. Bohemond defeated the Byzantine emperor, Alexius Comnenos, in May 1082, but Robert Guiscard only entered Rome to rescue Pope Gregory from the forces of the German emperor, Henry IV, in May 1084. Again, Suger is clearly in error, but he may have been misled by a source (*Anonymi Vaticani Historia Sicula*, ed. Muratori, *Rerum Italicarum Scriptores* 8:772f).

6. Such a marriage alliance would have been attractive for Bohemond, and the initiative seems to have been his (OV 4:213). There was already a link between the royal family and the crusading enterprise, for the younger brother of King Philip, Count Hugh of Vermandois, had been a participant in the First Crusade. He left the east after the capture of Antioch; he returned in 1101 but died of wounds received in battle before reaching Jerusalem. Never one to refer to Bertrada and her children when not necessary, Suger fails to mention that Philip also gave Cecilia, his daughter by Bertrada, in marriage to Bohemond's nephew Tancred (William of Tyre, *History of Deeds Done Beyond the Sea*, trans. E. A. Babcock and A. C. Krey (New York, 1943), vol. 1, p. 460; Anna Comnena, *The Alexiad*, trans. E. R. A. Sewter (Harmondsworth, 1969), p. 369).

7. The marriage between Constance and Hugh I, count of Champagne and Troyes, had been annulled on the familiar grounds of consanguinity by the Council of Soissons in 1104 or 1105 (Luchaire, no. 30); the case is discussed in a letter of Ivo of Chartres (*ep.* 158, PL 162:163f). Suger's comment that she now sought a husband who

was worthy of her is slightly waspish, and perhaps explained by Hugh's later career of hostility toward Louis (below, cap. 19 fin.; Luchaire, no. 134).

8. Orderic Vitalis (4:213) describes how Bohemond mounted the pulpit of the cathedral at Chartres and urged his hearers to join him in attacking the Byzantine emperor. However, Suger reports that Bohemond, in the company of Bruno of Segni, urged an expedition to Jerusalem rather than an attack on the Byzantines.

9. Bohemond remained in southern Italy until 1107; when he left for the east, Constance stayed behind. Defeated by the Byzantines in 1108, he returned to Italy, where he died in 1109 or 1111: see A. R. Gadolin, "Prince Bohemund's Death and Apotheosis in the Church of San Sabino, Canosa di Puglia," *Byzantion* 52 (1982), pp. 124–53.

CHAPTER 10

1. The standard modern discussion of Pope Paschal is that of Carlo Servatius, *Paschalis II, 1099–1118* (Stuttgart, 1979); see too M. J. Wilks, "Ecclesia and regalia: Papal Investiture Policy from the Council of Guastalla to the First Lateran Council, 1106–1123," in *Studies in Church History* 8, ed. G. J. Cuming and Derek Baker (Cambridge, 1971), pp. 69–85; see also U.-R. Blumenthal, *The Investiture Controversy* (Philadelphia, 1988), pp. 167–70.

2. Later in the *Deeds* Suger praises Louis for not falling out with his father as other young men customarily did (cap. 13). But the emperor Henry IV (1056–1106), like so many other medieval rulers, had cause to grieve when his son Henry grew up. The younger Henry rebelled in 1104, and trouble continued until the death of his father two years later: see the anonymous *Life of the Emperor Henry IV* and some letters of this emperor, translated by Theodore E. Mommsen and Karl F. Morrison, *Imperial Lives and Letters of the Eleventh Century* (New York, 1962), pp. 121–36, 184–89, 190–95. Suger's attitude to German emperors has been discussed by K. F. Werner, "Das hochmittelalterliche Imperium in politischen Bewusstein Franchreiches (10–12 Jahrhundert)," *Historische Zeitschrift* 200 (1965), pp. 1–60 at 38–41. On the lance of St. Maurice, consult Quirin Leitner, *Die hervorrangendsten Kunstwerke der Schatzkammer des Osterreichen Kaiserhauses* (Vienna, 1870–73), pp. 26–28; see also P. E. Schramm, *Herrschaftszeichen und Staatsymbolik*, vol. 2 (Stuttgart, 1955) (=MGH *Schriften* 13), pp. 492f.

3. That the Roman people were venal and avaricious was accepted

by Suger (see too, cap. 27, below) and other authors of the time (e.g., OV 2:57, 3:162, 173, 177, and the biographer of Henry IV, trans. Mommsen and Morrison, p. 115). See in general John A. Yunck, "Economic Conservatism, Papal Finance, and Medieval Satires on Rome," in Sylvia L. Thrupp, ed., *Change in Medieval Society* (New York, 1964), pp. 72–85, orig. publ. in *Medieval Studies* 23 (1961).

4. Trouble between the abbey of St. Denis and bishops of Paris was of long standing: see M. Prou, *Recueil des actes de Philippe I* (Paris, 1908), pp. 114–17, and Fliche, p. 109, for a dispute of 1068. In 1105(?) Paschal had forbidden the monks to engage in various practices without the leave of Bishop Galo (1104–16; J-W, no. 6063). On Suger's appearance before Paschal, consult Cartellieri, no. 7 (p. 128).

5. The word *frigium* is discussed by Schramm, *Herrschaftszeichen*, vol. 1 (1954), pp. 52ff. For the classical background, see Juvenal, *Sat.* 6.516, with the note by E. Courtney, *A Commentary on the Satires of Juvenal* (London, 1980), p. 328. Suger uses the same word below (cap. 32). A twelfth-century drawing of Paschal wearing the *frigium* is reproduced in David Talbot Rice, ed., *The Dark Ages* (London, 1965), p. 340.

6. Paschal's humility before the relics of St. Denis sets up an important theme in Suger's work, although it is more usually a characteristic of Louis: see cap. 28, 34, below and *De consec.*, pp. 6f (Panofsky, pp. 113f, 117). Papal visits were important to monasteries; see the charming account of how Calixtus II came to Morigny in 1119 in *Chron. Mor.*, pp. 31–33. Suger liked to feel that it was customary for popes to spend Christmas at St. Denis if they were in Gaul (*De admin.* 32, Panofsky, p. 59f); in 1147 Eugenius III spent Easter there (Odo, p. 15).

7. Paschal refers to a tradition that the blessed Dionysius was sent to Gaul by Pope Clement, which goes back to the *Passio sanctorum Dionisii, Rustici et Eleutherii* (=*Gloriosae*) 3.15 (MGH: *Auctores Antiquissimi* 4.2, p. 103) of doubtful date and the *Vita Genovefae* 17 (MGH: *Scriptores Rerum Merovingicarum* 3, pp. 221f), the origins of which may be dated around 520. Therefore, Paschal becomes a spokesperson for the claim of the abbey to have been founded by the convert of St. Paul, for Clement was widely believed to have been the second pope in succession to St. Peter.

8. Guibert of Nogent had a similar view of relations between past popes and kings of France (PL 156:697), while Ivo of Chartres wrote in a letter to Paschal that the kingdom of the French had always

been more submisssive to the apostolic see than had other kingdoms (*ep.* 238, PL 162:245D). Looking upon the king as a successor of Charlemagne, Suger is here enlarging Louis's royal duties to include the Carolingian role of protecting the pope; on this see Michel Bur, "Suger's Understanding of Political Power," in *Abbot Suger*, pp. 73–75.

9. Adalbert, a supporter of the young Henry in his struggle with Henry IV, was named chancellor in February 1106. In August 1111 he was invested archbishop of Mainz. On him, see F. Fuhrmann, *Germany in the High Middle Ages* (Cambridge, 1986), pp. 117f.

10. For a brief account of this meeting from the German side, consult Paul Scheffer-Boichorst, ed., *Annales Patherbrunnenses* (Innsbruck, 1870), p. 117; and for a modern discussion, see Monika Minninger, *Von Clermont zum Wörmser Konkordat* (Cologne, 1978), pp. 134–66. The bishops in question are Bruno of Brettheim, archbishop of Trèves (or Trier) (1102–24); Reinhard of Blankenburg, bishop of Halberstadt (1106–23); and Burchard of Holte, bishop of Münster (1097–1118). In 1089 the young Welf of Bavaria had married Matilda of Tuscany, the great ally of successive reforming popes in their struggle with German emperors; but in 1095 the couple separated, opening the way to a reconciliation between Welf and Henry IV in 1096. Following the death of his father in the Holy Land, Welf succeeded him as Duke Welf V of Bavaria.

11. The archbishop's speech raises textual problems; we have followed Robert L. Benson, *The Bishop-Elect* (Princeton, 1968), pp. 243 (n. 53), 264 (n. 7).

12. Following a lengthy description of the meeting at Châlons, Suger passes over the Council of Troyes very quickly, perhaps because it was held in the domain of a prince hostile to the Capetians (Bur, p. 274). It is impossible to miss the anti-German animus of this chapter, but Suger has well caught Paschal's sentiments, for in a letter he refers to the Germans as a *natio prava et perversa* (*ep.* 192, PL 163:198A; =J-W, no. 5971).

13. The quotation is from Lucan, *De bello civili* 2:439f. Other sources support Suger's figure, indicating that the emperor had a large force: K. J. Leyser, *Medieval Germany and Its Neighbors, 900–1200* (London, 1982), p. 206, where it is suggested that English backing may have been responsible.

14. The name *Mons Gaudii* has been discussed by J. Bedier, *Les légendes épiques*, vol. 2, 3d ed. (Paris, 1926), pp. 237–52.

15. An expression possibly borrowed from Florus, *Epitomae* 1.22.39. The reference to the Augusti in the next sentence continues the classical emphasis of this part of the chapter. Suger, however, has put the coronation ceremony described here out of the correct chronological order. The coronation had been planned for February 12, 1111; but when it became clear that Paschal proposed to renounce ecclesiastical regalia on condition that Henry give up investiture, a tumult arose. The coronation took place only after Paschal withdrew his proposal and agreed to let Henry continue with investitures (documents in Brian Tierney, *The Crisis of Church and State*, pp. 89f).

16. *Furor teutonicus*, a phrase borrowed from Lucan, *De Bello civili* 1:255f. Suger displays a Gallic prejudice against Germans; on this and similar sentiments toward other peoples in the *Deeds*, see Jeremy duQuesnay Adams, "The Patriotism of Abbot Suger," *Proceedings of the Annual Meeting of the Western Society for French History* 15 (1988), pp. 19–29.

17. See 1 Samuel 24:11. For "pluvial" mentioned in the previous sentence, consult the article *pluviale* in Du Cange's *Glossarium*.

18. Paschal's *privilegium* allowing Henry to continue performing investitures aroused considerable opposition, particularly in France, where Archbishop Guy of Vienne, who was to become pope in 1119, was vocal in his criticism. At a Lateran synod of March 1112, at which Suger, as he indicates, was present, Paschal backtracked and withdrew the concession of investitures.

19. In July 1111 Paschal retreated to the Pontine Islands in the Tyrrhenian Sea, to return to Rome only in October (J-W, no. 6305; =PL 163:291f). Note too a rhetorical passage in a letter of Hildebert of Lavardin (*ep.* 2.22, PL 171:235Bf).

20. Suger refers to the Council of Vienne, presided over by Archbishop Guy in September 1112. Since Louis had been crowned king in 1108, he was no longer "lord-designate" in 1112 as Suger named him in this sentence.

21. Burchard of Münster has appeared earlier in this chapter as one of Henry's messengers. But Suger is incorrect in asserting that the bishop was deposed by the Council of Vienne. Rather, he had been deposed by a papal legate in 1105 and restored to office in January 1106 (Waquet, p. 68, n. 2).

22. As Henry was childless when he died, the imperial office was indeed transferred. Instead of naming his nephew, Duke Frederick of

Swabia, as his successor, the electors turned to a well-known enemy of the Salian family, Duke Lothar of Saxony; see Otto of Freising, *The Deeds of Frederick Barbarossa*, trans. C. C. Mierow (New York, 1953), p. 48, and *The Two Cities*, trans. C. C. Mierow (New York, 1928), p. 424.

23. In 1136 Lothar went to Italy to help Pope Innocent II against the Normans. He died while returning from Italy the next year "in triumph and victory" (Otto, *Deeds*, p. 53; see also *Two Cities*, p. 428). Count Roger of Sicily had been crowned king by Innocent's rival Anacletus (on whom see cap. 32 below) on Christmas Day 1130; and ms. B of Suger's *Deeds*, which dates from the late twelfth century, reads "King Roger of Sicily" instead of "Count." Suger implicitly denies that Roger was king at the time of Lothar's expedition, although Roger was in reality king. He is known to have been one of those who sought Suger's favor (William, *Vita Sugerii*, in Lecoy, p. 384).

CHAPTER 11

1. Lucan, *De bello civili* 5:525.

2. On Louis's marriage to Lucienne of Rochefort, see cap. 8, n. 6. In no hurry to wed after the annulment at the Council of Troyes in 1107, Louis waited until 1115 before he married Adelaide of Maurienne (Luchaire, no. 192).

3. Hugh's activities are evidence of the difficulties confronting merchants (Bur, p. 301); note the hint, corroborated by other passages in the *Deeds*, that whereas Louis's enemies are attackers of merchants, he is a forwarder of their activities (cap. 21, 31, 33 below). The account of the attack on Gournay contains some of Suger's most detailed military description, complicated by a fair measure of rhetoric.

4. Reminiscent of Vergil, *Aeneid* 6:126.

5. Together with the counts of Flanders and Toulouse, Theobald held the old title of palantine count, by this time honorific (although a document of 1124 appears to distinguish between *palatini* and *optimates*: Tardif, no. 391). *The Chronicle of Morigny* describes him as a wealthy man of high nobility, second to the king in France (pp. 21f). As his estates were near the Capetian demesne, any revival of royal power would obviously mean conflict for him; furthermore, Theobald's mother, Adela, was a daughter of William the Conqueror and so the sister of Louis's rival monarch, Henry I; see further

Dunbabin, pp. 314–18. Suger's portrayal of Theobald is inevitably somewhat negative; but according to his biographer William, Suger was honored in all ways by Theobald, who saw him as his only advocate with Louis (Lecoy, p. 385).

6. Statius, *Thebaidos* 3:255.

CHAPTER 13

1. Some of Suger's contemporaries were not as negative in their portrayals of King Philip. Abbot Hugh of Cluny, for example, saw him to be a potential recruit for the monastic life (PL 159:930–32), while Henry of Huntingdon believed he ended his days as a monk (p. 255). See below, cap. 33, n. 1, for the likely meaning of the phrase "nearly sixty." Philip was probably fifty-six when he died.

2. A respectable gathering of ecclesiastics from the royal demesne assembled for Philip's funeral. The unnamed bishops are Hubert of Senlis (1099–1115) and John of Orléans (1096–1135); the presence of the latter may be significant in view of the events of the following chapter.

3. Orderic Vitalis asserts that because of his sins Philip did not wish to be buried at St. Denis (4:284). Both he and Suger imply that Philip's choice of Fleury for burial was the result of a decision not to be buried at St. Denis; against this we may note that during his lifetime Philip had been benevolent and generous toward Fleury (*Chron. Mor.*, pp. 10f), which argues for at least some positive feelings toward it, and the suggestion that there may have been dynastic and political reasons for seeking burial there rather than at St. Denis: see Alain Erlande-Brandenburg, *Le roi est mort: étude sur les funérailles, les sépultures et les tombeaux des rois de France jusqu'à la fin du XIIIe siècle* (Paris, 1975), pp. 75f, 87.

4. See Fliche, appendix II, pp. 561–62, for a nineteenth-century description of Philip's coffin and tomb.

CHAPTER 14

1. We know that Louis was caused particular trouble by his *cognati* (*Chron. Mor.*, p. 21), and that he feared rebellion after the death of his father Philip (*Chron. Mor.*, pp. 56f), while trouble between Louis and his half-brother Philip was to break out in 1110 (below, cap. 18; see too the last sentence of cap. 15 below for a reference to unnamed "rivals"). Such circumstances dictated the speedy corona-

tion that Suger next describes; Louis's accession to the throne is helpfully discussed by Lewis, pp. 52–54.

2. After describing the burial of Philip in an unusual place, Suger now must discuss the coronation of Louis away from Reims where this ceremony was generally conducted (as in the cases of Henry I in 1027, Philip I in 1059, Louis's own sons Philip and Louis in 1129 and 1131 respectively, and Philip II in 1179). Ivo of Chartres explained in a circular letter that those officiating acted in the way they did because of certain disturbers of the kingdom who sought to have it transferred to another person, or sensibly diminished. He pointed out that there were precedents for coronations in cities other than Reims, that in any case the town was under interdict, and that there was a need for haste because of the state of the kingdom and the peace of the church (*ep.* 189, PL 162:193–6).

3. Those not named by Suger earlier in the text are Archbishop Daimbert of Sens (1098–1122), and Bishops Manasses of Meaux (1103–20), Herveus (not Hugh) of Nevers (1099–1110), and Humbald of Auxerre (1095–1115).

4. Nonliterary evidence from this period suggests that Reims claimed not only the right to crown kings but the subordination of the abbot of St. Denis in the process (R. Hamann-MacLean, in H. Beumann, ed., *Beiträge* [cited above, cap. 1, n. 10], pp. 201ff). It was believed, probably correctly, that the baptism of Clovis occurred at Reims; and when Louis's father Philip had become king, the archbishop of Reims had claimed the right to "elect" and consecrate him (Lewis, p. 46). Suger styles Clovis, as he does Louis, *rex Francorum*, so we have here translated it "king of the French" in the interests of consistency, although Clovis is more generally known in English as "king of the Franks."

5. Another reason for the coronation being held away from Reims emerges. Following the death of Archbishop Manasses in 1106, there were two claimants to the office, the provost Ralph the Green, who enjoyed the support of the majority of the cathedral chapter, and Gervaise of Rethel, who was backed by Louis. In 1107 the Council of Troyes decided for Ralph, but Louis was displeased, and a coronation there would have been difficult. Ivo of Chartres and Lambert of Arras interceded for their episcopal colleague with Louis; and at Christmas 1108 Ralph, acting in a way contrary to the teachings of church reformers, swore fealty to the king.

CHAPTER 15

1. The *Chronicle of Morigny* is also particularly hostile to Hugh of Crécy: "This irreconcilable enemy of the king raged as if he were a servant of the devil" (p. 22). Crécy-en-Brie, Seine-et-Marne, is about thirty miles east of Paris on the Grand Morin.

2. Odo of Corbeil was the son of Adelaide of Crécy by Burchard of Corbeil; following Burchard's death she married Guy of Rochefort and produced Hugh. On Burchard's death, see cap. 20 below.

3. We have sought to bring out Suger's alliteration (*captum comitem et captionis causam*).

4. The ramifications of this family are complex, and one can forgive Suger a slip. Adelaide's husband was Guy of Rochefort, and Hugh her son by Guy.

5. Lucan, *De bello civili* 2:91f.

CHAPTER 16

1. In this chapter Suger again displays his admiration of Henry I (see cap. 1 fin. above). Henry's visit to Normandy may have been connected with the accession of Louis (Henry of Huntingdon, p. 243).

2. With minor variants Suger here reproduces a portion of a prophecy found in Orderic Vitalis (4:490f) and at greater length in Geoffrey of Monmouth, who seems to have invented it: *History of the Kings of Britain*, trans. S. Evans, rev. Ch. Dunn (London, 1963), pp. 139ff; see also the short bibliography in C. N. L. Brooke, "Geoffrey of Monmouth as a Historian," in C. N. L. Brooke et al., eds., *Church and Government in the Middle Ages* (Cambridge, 1976), pp. 77–91 at p. 85, n. 27. The prophecy spread rapidly, for Geoffrey seems to have written his original version not long before Henry's death in 1135; the *terminus ante quem* is discussed by Michael J. Curley, "A New Edition of John of Cornwall's *Prophetia Merlini*," *Speculum* 57 (1982), pp. 217–49 at 219 with n. 12; but see also C. D. Eckhardt, "The Prophetia Merlini of Geoffrey Monmouth: Latin Manuscript Copies," *Manuscripta* 26 (1982), pp. 167–76; the passage in Orderic has been dated similarly (ed. Chibnall, vol. 1, p. 47); for the date of Suger's *Deeds*, see above, Introduction. One wonders from which source Suger drew it. The sentence immediately before the portion quoted by Suger refers to two dragons, taken by Orderic to refer to William Rufus and Robert of Normandy (4:493); he and Suger both

accept that the lion of justice who comes after them is Henry. The round silver half penny of Henry I is illustrated in the *British Museum Society Bulletin* 61 (1989).

3. On the wreck of the White Ship, see also OV 4:411–15; William of Malmesbury, pp. 455f; Henry of Huntingdon, pp. 248f.

4. Henry's famous "coronation charter" of 1100 (mentioned in this paragraph) has been published in *English Historical Documents*, vol. 2, ed. D. C. Douglas and G. W. Greenway, 2d ed. (London, 1981), pp. 432–34.

5. See Vergil, *Aeneid* 6:852. Suger is guilty of a slight overstatement, for Henry was acting with the approval of Louis but not of Philip, who was still king (*Chron. Mor.*, p. 21). Henry won the decisive battle of Tinchebray against his brother Robert Curthose and his followers in 1106 (OV 4:229–31).

6. The first quote is from Ovid, *Ars amatoria* 1:444 and the second from 1 Maccabees 1:3, a text quoted by Suger several times.

7. Normandy had indeed been part of Roman Gaul, and Suger later called Louis the "king of Gaul" (below, cap. 23 at n. 1). Note that he did not consider Normandy to be part of "France" and that he consistently contrasts Normans and French throughout this chapter.

8. Vaguely reminiscent of John 11:50.

9. For relations between Henry and Louis, see C. Warren Hollister, "War and Diplomacy in the Anglo-Norman World: The Reign of Henry I," *Anglo-Norman Studies VI*: Proceedings of the Battle Conference 1983, ed. R. Allen Brown (Suffolk, 1983), pp. 72–88; reprinted in Hollister, *Monarchy*, pp. 273–90.

10. Count Robert of Flanders and the palatine count Theobald have been introduced above. The count of Nevers was William II (1100–1148) and the duke of Burgundy, Hugh II (1102–42). On the dilemma of the counts of Meulan, Norman magnates but vassals of the king of France, consult D. Crouch, *The Beaumont Twins* (Cambridge, 1986), pp. 71–74; Louis's activities in this instance are discussed at p. 60.

11. Without doubt, Louis regarded Normandy as a fief, but homage was not done for it until 1120 (below, n. 18).

12. Suger uses the unusual word *palestrita*, literally a wrestler or the director of a wrestling school.

13. *Non est michi tibia tanti*, presumably a proverb, although we have not been able to trace it. The expression defies literal transla-

tion; see Waquet, p. 109, n. 1. Henry complained of the worthlessness of his negotiations with Louis in a letter to St. Anselm (Anselm, *ep.* 461, *Opera omnia*, vol. 5, ed. F. S. Schmitt [Edinburgh, 1951], p. 410f).

14. Lucan, *De bello civili* 4:661.

15. Reminiscent of Vergil, *Aeneid* 5:42.

16. Statius, *Thebaidos* 3:255 (also quoted above cap. 11 at n. 6).

17. Suger is misleading here, for following his interview with Louis, Henry spent two years in England: see C. Warren Hollister, "Normandy, France and the Anglo-Norman *Regnum*," *Speculum* 51 (1976), pp. 202–42 at p. 224, n. 2.

18. As it stands this statement is also a little misleading. The events described in the chapter began in 1109 (Luchaire, no. 72). Suger describes the war that developed out of the incident at Planches-de-Néaufles as having gone on for nearly two years, and locates William's homage immediately after the war. But William only performed homage in 1120: see Luchaire, no. 298; J.-F. Lemarignier, *Recherches sur l'hommage en marche et les frontières féodales* (Lille, 1945), pp. 91f. William's homage is also mentioned by William of Malmesbury (p. 439f), although not by Orderic Vitalis. It constituted a breakthrough for the king of France, as William the Conqueror, William Rufus, and Henry had all apparently not rendered homage. On the question of the performance of homage and the nature of the feudal relationship between the Norman dukes and the Capetian kings of the period, see David Bates, *Normandy before 1066* (London and New York, 1982), pp. 59ff, and C. Warren Hollister, *Monarchy*, pp. 41f.

CHAPTER 17

1. Some idea of the site of La Roche-Guyon can be obtained from a photograph in C.-L. Salch, *Dictionnaire des châteaux et des fortifications du Moyen-Age en France* (Strasbourg, 1979), p. 977, although the fortifications are of a later date.

2. Lucan, *De bello civili* 6:651–53. On the castle Suger describes in such menancing language, see Edward A. Freeman, *The Reign of William Rufus*, vol. 2 (Oxford, 1882), pp. 180f. Suger is our only source for these events.

3. Psalm 7:15 (altered). This chapter presents several problems, the most important of which is the difficulty of establishing the relationship between Guy and his slayer William. In the title of the

chapter William is called the brother-in-law of Guy, but here he is Guy's father-in-law; two lines further down in the text William is called Guy's *gener*, a word which may be translated either as "son-in-law" or "brother-in-law," but can mean only "brother-in-law" in its context. But in the lamentation of Guy's wife over his death, the two men are called *gener* and *socer* in the very same line, which in this context can mean only "son-in-law" and "father-in-law." The precise relationship between the two men is impossible to determine; we have translated the words in the context in which they appear and have not followed the psycho-historical interpretation of Waquet (note a, p. 114), who has decided that William and Guy must be brothers-in-law. Some of the problems could possibly be overcome if we understand Suger to mean that Guy's unnamed father-in-law conceived the plot while his son William, Guy's brother-in-law, committed the murder. But the story remains unclear and Suger's imprecise use of language in several other instances (such as line 5 up, p. 78) suggests that he failed to revise this chapter.

4. The speech of Guy's widow began with a jerky sequence of phrases; now it ends with a rhyme (*insania . . . mania*) which we have not been able to express in translation.

5. See Matthew 2:16; this is also reminiscent of Psalm 137:9 (=136:9).

6. Lucan, *De bello civili* 1:695 (a particularly apt quotation).

7. At the time of these events, Louis may have been involved in preparations for an expedition to Barcelona (Luchaire, no. 72); but it is curious to find him standing off, particularly in view of Henry's potential intervention.

8. On the issues raised by cruelty here and elsewhere in Suger's text, see C. Warren Hollister, "Royal Acts of Mutilation: The Case against Henry I," *Albion* 10 (1978), pp. 330–40; reprinted in Hollister, *Monarchy*, pp. 291–301.

CHAPTER 18

1. Philip, the half-brother of King Louis, continued to pose problems. He had obtained the castle of Mantes from Louis in 1104 (above, cap. 8; Luchaire, no. 32; see too above, cap. 14, n. 1). Amalric of Montfort, Philip's uncle, had inherited his estates from his brothers Richard and Simon; Bertrada, Philip's mother, was Amalric's younger sister. Philip's half-brother, Fulk V the Young, the son of Bertrada by Fulk IV of Anjou, succeeded his father in 1109,

thereby inaugurating a rise in Angevin power; he became king of Jerusalem in 1131.

2. The correspondence of Bishop Ivo of Chartres casts light on Louis's problems with the succession: we find Ivo explaining the need for haste in arranging the coronation of Louis (*ep.* 189, PL 162:93–96; see also above, cap. 14); he also describes dukes and marquises awaiting the chance to separate themselves from the king (*ep.* 209, PL 162:214B, written in 1109); and when congratulating Louis on finally deciding to marry, he states that this would help strengthen his kingdom (*ep.* 239, PL 162:246f, presumably written in 1115). Louis had clearly brought some of these problems on himself by failing to contract a respectable marriage that would produce legitimate heirs.

3. The ballista (*mangunellum*) and catapult (*fundibalarium*) are discussed with illustrations in Camille Enlart, *Manuel d'archéologie française*, vol. 1, Architecture 2 (Paris, 1904), pp. 440–47.

4. On the marriage of Hugh of Crécy to Amalric's daughter Lucienne, see *Chron. Mor.*, p. 24.

5. See Terence, *Andria* 4.4. line 39f.

6. Before his death in March 1108, Guy Trousseau had left his estate of Montlhéry to Louis (Luchaire, no. 53). Milo II of Bray, the brother of Guy Trousseau and cousin of Hugh of Crécy, is now putting forward his hereditary claim to the fortress; on Milo, see cap. 8, above, and *Chron. Mor.*, pp. 23f. On the complex branchings of this family, see Fliche, p. 321.

CHAPTER 19

1. A play on 3 Kings (= 1 Chronicles) 12:11. Hugh of Le Puiset was the son of Evrard, who took part in the First Crusade, as Suger indicates. He died in the siege of Antioch when Hugh was still a small boy; so his uncle Hugh II, who had married a daughter of Ebles of Roucy, exercised control over the estates on his behalf. But Hugh II was one of those whom Bohemond persuaded to follow him to the East in 1106; so control passed to Guy, viscount of Etampes, another brother of Evrard, before it finally devolved upon Hugh. Consult on this family J. L. La Monte, "The Lords of Le Puiset on the Crusades," *Speculum* 17 (1942), pp. 100–118.

2. Psalm 35:13 (= 36:12).

3. Adela's husband, Count Stephen of Blois and Chartres, participated in the First Crusade [a touching letter from him to Adela is

translated in Edward Peters, ed., *The First Crusade* (Philadelphia, 1971), pp. 225–28]; but he fled from Antioch, and on his return home Adela gave him no peace until he departed again for the east, where he was killed in 1102. Theobald, the second son of Stephen and Adela, succeeded to the estates in 1107 and governed them personally from 1109, but Adela continued to be influential until she entered a convent in 1122.

4. On these events, see Fliche, pp. 314f.

5. These activities of Constance, the third wife of King Robert the Pious, can be dated to shortly after Robert's death in 1031. But Constance does not seem to have erected Le Puiset with the dependencies of St. Denis in mind; rather, it was part of a campaign she waged against King Henry; on this see Jean Dhondt, "Sept femmes et un trio de rois," *Contributions à l'histoire économique et sociale* 3 (1964–65), pp. 50–52. On the castle of Le Puiset's importance in military history, see G. Fournier, "Le château du Puisset du XIIe siècle et sa place dans l'évolution de l'architecture militaire," *Bulletin monumental* 122 (1964), pp. 355–74.

6. The meeting at Melun about twenty-seven miles southeast of Paris occurred on March 12, 1111 (Luchaire, no. 110). Suger also describes the opposition to Hugh in *De admin.* 12 (Lecoy, pp. 170f).

7. On the land of the priests free under pharaoh, see Genesis 47:22–26.

8. The letters of Ivo of Chartres, who had supported Louis during the succession in 1108, allow the events occurring here to be followed in large part; in one of them he refers to Hugh as "ever returning evil for good" (*ep.* 111, PL 162:129C). Present at Melun with Ivo were Daimbert of Sens, who had officiated at Louis's coronation, and John of Orléans, who had attended Philip's funeral and in whose cathedral Louis's coronation occurred (above, cap. 13, 14).

9. Psalm 75:4 (=76:3).

10. The activities of these communities of the people seem to have been outgrowths of earlier peace movements, on which see H. Hoffmann, *Gottesfried* (cited cap. 5, n. 3), pp. 104–25, 195–206; the reign of Louis is discussed on pp. 207–16. The parish is among the communities discussed by Susan Reynolds, *Kingdoms and Communities in Western Europe, 900–1300* (Oxford, 1984), pp. 79ff; this incident is touched on at p. 98.

11. Suger uses *castrum* and *castellum* interchangeably here; see J. F. Verbruggen, "Note sur le sens des mots *Castrum, Castellum* et quelques autres expressions qui désignent des fortifications," *Revue*

belge de philologie et d'histoire 28 (1950), pp. 147–55. See Sheila Sancha, *The Castle Story* (New York, 1979), pp. 21–33 on fortifications.

12. Pride comes before a fall, states Suger, perhaps with Scripture at the back of his mind (Prov. 16:18). Earlier in this chapter, he pointed out pride as a characteristic of Hugh and his family.

13. Allaines is the modern Allaines-Mervilliers, Eure-et-Loir, a few miles southwest of Le Puiset. For the second time in the *Deeds*, a judicial combat is proposed as a way of settling a dispute (cap. 16 above). On Theobald's behalf will fight his steward (*procurator*), Andrew of Baudement (on whom consult Bur, pp. 431f), and on Louis's behalf his own seneschal (*dapifer*), Anselm of Garlande. Perhaps significantly, on neither occasion did the combat occur.

14. With Hugh imprisoned in the castle of Château-Landon about forty miles east of Le Puiset and conveniently out of the way, Theobald begins causing trouble again; and for the second time in two paragraphs, Suger applies the verb *machinare* ("to scheme") to his activities. Theobald's mother, Countess Adela, was the sister of King Henry of England, thus making Theobald his nephew.

15. On the activities of Count Robert of Flanders during the First Crusade, see M. M. Knappen, "Robert II of Flanders in the First Crusade," in *The Crusades and Other Historical Essays Presented to Dana C. Munro by His Former Students*, ed. Louis J. Paetow (Freeport, New York, 1968 reprint), pp. 79–100.

16. Another example of battle scenes stimulating Suger to classical allusions, for there are echoes here of Horace, *Odes* 3.2.28 and 3.1.7. Meaux is about twenty-seven miles northeast of Paris.

17. A play on Matthew 19:30 and Luke 13:30.

18. The reference to baptism which almost became baptism by triple immersion affords a nice example of Suger's humor; on the ritual of triple immersion in the writings of Pseudo-Dionysius and the use of it in the art of the abbey church, see Pamela Z. Blum, "The Lateral Portals of the West Façade of the Abbey Church of St. Denis," in *Abbot Suger*, pp. 215–17. But just as Suger tells of a victory won by Louis, so Orderic Vitalis describes an engagement won by Theobald in which Robert of Flanders was so severely wounded while fleeing that he died shortly afterwards (4:290; see too *A-S Chron.* 1111). Louis accompanied the body of the dead count to Arras (Luchaire, no. 122). Typically, Suger does not mention the death of Robert.

19. Pagan of Montjay has been mentioned above (cap. 1 at n. 8).

Hugh "the great," the younger brother of King Philip, had married Countess Adela of Vermandois; their daughter Mahaud married Ralph of Beaugency, the son of Lancelin of Beaugency (mentioned above in this chapter) and one of Theobald's vassals. Beaugency is on the Loire, about thirteen miles southwest of Orléans.

20. On Louis's awarding of the castle of Montlhéry to Milo of Bray, see cap. 18 above. For this proverb (*stimulus anum accelerat* = "the prod speeds the old woman along"), Molinier cites Leroux de Lincy, *Livre* 2:2247, *Besoing fait vieille trotter*. Consciously or otherwise, Suger here lapses into language with double meanings and sexual connotations. The vulgar drift of the word *stimulus*, meaning "prod," is obvious, while *anus* can mean either an "old woman" or the "human posterior." In addition, the paragraph concludes with the ambiguous word *copulavit* (Waquet, p. 148).

21. We assume that Suger meant to write "arcebant," and that the passive form found in all the manuscripts was a slip on his part.

22. Lucan, *De bello civili* 5:336.

CHAPTER 20

1. Hugh's mother Alix was Odo's sister.

2. Suger uses a similar expression in *De admin.* 32 (Panofsky, p. 57).

CHAPTER 21

1. The affair broadens. Louis probably wished to visit Flanders to plan activities against Henry with Count Baldwin VII, who succeeded Count Robert in 1111. (As noted above, cap. 19, n. 18, Suger suppressed the death of Robert; on the later cooperation between Louis and Baldwin, see cap. 26, below.) Orderic Vitalis sets the events of this chapter in a different context, asserting that Theobald's warfare here against Louis was designed to keep the king of the French from attacking the Norman possessions of Henry, who was then embroiled elsewhere (OV 4:303f). Likewise, C. W. Hollister, *Monarchy*, p. 284, points out that the three assaults of Louis on the castle of Hugh of Le Puiset occurred during hostilities with the king of England (1111, 1112, and again in 1118) and must be viewed in a context wider than that of simple movements against Hugh, one of those who have been called "robber barons" of the Ile-de-France.

2. On Louis and merchants, see cap. 11, n. 3; on this case see as well Gabriel Fournier, *Le château dans la France médiévale* (Paris, 1978), pp. 128f.

3. Suger has used his words cleverly: *impugnantes expugnare*.

4. Reinforcements arrive in the persons of William of Garlande, the brother of Anselm, and some of Louis's household knights (mentioned above, cap. 12, n. c).

5. On Ralph, see cap. 19, n. 19.

6. Battle again prompts Suger to classical expressions; the pillars of Hercules were fixed and immutable. Established at the Straits of Gibraltar, they marked the boundary between Europe and Africa; see the comments of Pliny, *Naturalis historia* 3.1.4, and Martianus Capella, *De nuptiis Philologiae et Mercurii* 6.624.

7. The quotations are from Lucan, *De bello civili* 2:601–3 and 1:212. The first one is particularly elegant, for not only is it apt when read in its original context, but also it allows Suger to indulge in another pun, between "Toury" (*Tauriacum*) and "bull" (*taurus*).

8. Ralph, the son of Louis's uncle Hugh "the great" and Countess Adela of Vermandois, became count of Vermandois in 1117. The most frequent witnesser of charters among Louis's lay magnates, he came to the fore toward the end of the reign, becoming senseschal following the fall of Stephen of Garlande in 1127 (below, cap. 31, n. 2).

9. See Sallust, *Catilina* 60.

10. Literally "from the top of the wheel," but Suger clearly has in mind the wheel of Fortune, familiar to medieval writers from a famous poem in the *Consolation of Philosophy* by Boethius (book 2, met. 2), as later references make clear.

11. In these notes we have occasionally pointed out instances where Suger glosses over failures of Louis. In this case, it is Orderic Vitalis who is silent about Theobald's final withdrawal and the destruction of the castle (see 4:304).

CHAPTER 22

1. Lucan, *De bello civili* 1:326.

2. The third campaign of Louis against Hugh of Le Puisset took place between January 16, 1118, when Anselm of Garlande was alive and witnessed a charter (Luchaire, no. 231) and May 1 when the king abolished evil customs established by the lords of Le Puiset

at Toury (Luchaire, no. 237). Concerning Hugh's mysterious end, consult La Monte, "The lords of Le Puiset" (cited cap. 19, n. 1), pp. 101f.

CHAPTER 23

1. An unusual title for Louis, who is almost always styled by Suger "king of the French." The odd formation is presumably influenced by the immediately preceding "king of England," while the word "Gaul" was free of the ambiguity inherent in "France," which could mean merely the Ile-de-France.

2. Waquet (p. 172, n. 1) observes that Lancelin of Bulles was a vassal of the church of Beauvais, which is about forty-five miles north of Paris. The castle of Livry was about seven miles northeast of Paris.

3. Suger shows how the peace of Gisors concluded in March 1113 between Louis and Henry redounded against a group of barons who had been causing Louis trouble. To this extent the settlement was without doubt to his advantage, but the more detailed account of Orderic Vitalis indicates that Henry did better. Orderic describes the peace as having been sought by Louis and reached by the two kings at a meeting between them, and states that Louis ceded Bellème, the county of Maine and all Brittany to Henry (OV 4:307); see Hollister, "Normandy, France," Monarchy, p. 39. Molinier has suggested (p. 80) that the concluding quotation is from a Carolingian capitulary; Waquet believes (p. 172) that it comes from canons relating to the Peace of God. Neither has been able to identify it; nor have we.

CHAPTER 24

1. The complaints made by the clergy against Thomas are mentioned by other sources (OV 4:377; Guibert, p. 203f, an account that complements Suger's). A feature of this chapter is Suger's sustained use of religious rather than classical imagery. The papal legate Cono, bishop of Palestrina, mentioned here held four councils in France during 1114–15: Beauvais, Soissons, Reims, and Châlons-sur-Marne; on the Council of Beauvais, see Robert Somerville, "The Council of Beauvais, 1114," *Traditio* 24 (1968), pp. 493–503, reprinted in Robert Somerville, *Papacy, Councils and Canon Law in the 11th-12th Centuries* (Great Yarmouth Norfolk, 1990), cap. X; Cono would later be involved in the Council of Soissons in 1121

(Abelard, p. 79); for details of his activities, consult the article in the *Dictionnaire d'histoire et de géographie ecclésiastiques* 13, pp. 461–71. The word *honor*, translated as "honor" in the last sentence of the paragraph, is unclear, and could mean "fief."

2. Suger uses the vague word *exercitum* to describe Louis's force, and contrary to his usual practice does not name the vassals who cooperated. Guibert is more direct and states that Louis "received hardly any help from the knightly order" (p. 204).

3. Suger has used a similar expression in cap. 17.

4. Wisdom 5:21.

5. 1 Samuel 24:11. Elsewhere Suger applies this text to Pope Paschal (cap. 10 at n. 17); Guibert also applies it to Gaudry (p. 176).

6. The events of the commune are described by Guibert; Louis had inititially been bribed to support it (p. 168) but was prevailed upon by Bishop Gaudry to turn against it (p. 171). Following the murder of Gaudry on April 25, 1112, the citizens of Laon called in Thomas of Marle to defend them against Louis (p. 184).

7. Louis's attack on the tower occupied by Adam is also described by Guibert (p. 203). On Adam, see Waquet, pp. 178f, n. 3. Amiens is about eighty miles north of Paris.

CHAPTER 25

1. Ovid, *Heroides* 17:166.

CHAPTER 26

1. The quotes are from Lucan, *De bello civili* 1:135 (Suger reads *suffere* for *iam ferre*) and 1:92f respectively. The claims here are somewhat misleading, as Henry never performed homage to Louis for Normandy; his son William did so only in 1120 (above, cap. 16, n. 18).

2. The wonderful abundance of England's wealth has been discussed above (cap. 1, n. 5).

3. In 1115 trouble had broken out over the capture of Count William of Nevers on the orders of Count Theobald (Ivo of Chartres, *ep.* 275, PL 162:277f; Luchaire, no. 203). Henry crossed to Normandy shortly after Easter 1116 (*A-S chron.* 1116); in 1117, according to the same chronicle, Louis crossed into Normandy with the count of Flanders, but stayed there only one night (see too Henry of Huntingdon, p. 246).

4. The strategic significance of Gasny can be gauged from John Le

Patourel, *The Norman Empire* (Oxford, 1976), map 2, p. 386, which also gives an idea of the line of castles. The story of the capture of Gasny is also told by Orderic Vitalis, but he claims that Louis entered it disguised as a monk. The occupation of the church prompted from him the scathing remark that a den of robbers had been established in the house of the Lord (OV 4:311, citing Luke 19:46; see below, cap. 30 at n. 4, for use of this text by Suger).

5. Also joining Louis's forces was Count Fulk V of Anjou who has been introduced above (cap. 18, n. 1). According to a spurious later document, Louis obtained Fulk's help only by conceding him the seneschalate as a hereditary possession: see *De majoratu et seneschalia Franciae*, pp. 239–46, in *Chroniques des comtes d'Anjou*, ed. L. Halphen and R. Poupardin (Paris, 1913); but this is to be rejected as absolutely apocryphal (Luchaire, pp. 325f). As Suger goes on to explain, Fulk sided with Louis only for a short while, for in 1119 his daughter Matilda was married to William, the son of King Henry (below, cap. 26; William of Malmesbury, p. 454).

6. As he often does, Orderic Vitalis provides complementary information. He states that Henry built not one but two castles, Malassis and Trulla Leporis (4:311); but he fails to mention any success by Louis against the former.

7. Another reference to the top of the wheel (see above, cap. 21, n. 10); we have supplied the word "fortune" from the top of the paragraph.

8. Fulk V of Anjou had married Eremburge, the daughter of Count Elias of Maine, and he had taken over Maine following his wife's death in 1110 (*Chroniques*, ed. Halphen and Poupardin, p. 111).

9. Suger passes from the major vassals of France to the petty barons of Normandy. Hugh of Gournay, Count Henry of Eu, and Count Stephen of Aumale were among a group who sought the installation of Henry's enemy William Clito, the son of Robert of Normandy, as duke of Normandy (OV 4:315). Suger ignores the association between Louis and William until the installation of William as count of Flanders following the murder of Charles in 1127 (below, cap. 30), but Louis has been supporting William's endeavors for some time (OV 4:310, 376, 472f).

10. Manuscript g of Suger's *Deeds* names "Henry" as the conspirator, but it is of sixteenth-century provenance; the translation of the *Grandes chroniques* offers "Hugh," but this dates from 1274. C. Warren Hollister identifies Henry's assailant with Herbert the Chamberlain: "The Origins of the English Royal Treasury," *English*

Historical Review 93 (1978), pp. 262–75 at 267f (*Monarchy*, pp. 214f). The assailant, one of Henry's *intimi* who had been elevated by royal authority, would have been one of Henry's "new men" (see OV 4:164–67), perhaps not totally dissimilar to Suger. Such men are discussed by Judith A Green, *The Government of England under Henry I* (Cambridge, 1986), pp. 139ff. William of Malmesbury describes him as "a chamberlain who was born of a plebeian father but became prominent as keeper of the royal treasures": *Gesta Regum Anglorum*, ed. Thomas D. Hardy, vol. 2 (London, 1840), V:411, p. 642. Elsewhere Henry is said to have dreamed that the peasants, knights, and clergy of the kingdom attacked him: see the illustration in Christopher Brooke, *The Structure of Medieval Society* (London, 1971), p. 47.

11. The affair of Alençon is described in much more detail by Orderic Vitalis (4:331–33), who confirms the losses suffered there by Henry and Theobald. Alençon is about one hundred miles southwest of Paris.

12. Orderic Vitalis attributes the fatal sickness of Count Baldwin VII of Flanders not so much to the wound as to his having eaten freshly killed meat, drunk mead, and slept with a woman on the following night (4:316), while William of Malmesbury was of the opinion that his disorder was worsened by his having eaten garlic with goose and engaging in intercourse (p. 437). The last words of this paragraph could also be translated "not only the king of England but everyone else thereafter."

13. Henry's situation continues to improve with the death of another of his enemies. According to Suger, Enguerrand died because he had attacked lands belonging to Mary; but Orderic Vitalis, more pragmatic in this instance, attributes his death to a wound in the eyebrow (4:354).

14. In 1119 Matilda, the daughter of Louis's vassal Fulk of Anjou, married William, the son of his enemy Henry. In the following year William was drowned in the White Ship disaster (above, cap. 16, n. 3).

15. 1 Maccabees 1:3. Louis's region was the Ile-de-France; it is implicitly distinguished from the areas from which the count of Flanders, Enguerrand of Chaumont, and the count of Anjou were operating.

16. On Burchard see above, cap. 2; Guy was the son of Hugh of Clermont, on whom see above, cap. 3.

17. Suger has here minimized Louis's defeat on August 20, 1119,

at the battle of Brémule, about sixteen miles southeast of Rouen; compare the *A-S chron.* 1119: "The King of France was routed and all his best men captured." Other sources provide more detailed accounts, among them Orderic Vitalis, according to whom 140 French knights were captured, together with Louis's standard (4: 359–63; see Henry of Huntingdon, pp. 247f). It is a little surprising to find Walter Map describing Louis as having been cheerful after the battle (p. 457). See in general Luchaire, no. 259.

18. Orderic Vitalis's account of the events following the engagement at Brémule is slanted quite differently. He states that Louis, having come to Breteuil, "failed to achieve anything but dishonour and loss" (4:370). Ivry is the modern Ivry-la-Bataille, about fifty miles west of Paris, and Breteuil is about twenty-seven miles west of there.

19. The cathedral church of Chartres claimed to possess the tunic that the Virgin had worn when giving birth to Christ: see Guibert, p. 85, and von Simson, pp. 160–64.

20. Following the death of Count Baldwin in 1119, Charles "the Good" had become count of Flanders; another source, however, states that part of the town was burned (*Chron. Mor.*, p. 31). Suger ends this chapter on a note of continuing hostilities, and this allows him to imply later that war was still going on in 1124 (cap. 28, n. 7); but peace was effected in 1120 (OV 4:403–5; Luchaire, no. 298).

CHAPTER 27

1. On the *conducticia* ("propensity for being bribed") of the Roman people, see above, cap. 10, n. 3. Paschal II had travelled to France in similar circumstances, but Suger is probably thinking of the eighth century for his "popes of old" (see the opinions of Guibert of Nogent and Ivo of Chartres, cited above, cap. 10, n. 8).

2. The history of the island of Maguelonne as a Christian site is surveyed in *Dictionnaire d'archéologie chrétienne et de liturgie* 10:1030.

3. Suger has again created problems of definition with his use of the word *regnum*, for it is not clear whether these first fruits were simply from the churches under the king's direct rule or from others as well: see Charles T. Wood, "*Regnum Francie,*" (cited above, cap. 1, n. 4), p. 118.

4. The pope arrived in Marseilles on October 23, 1118, and died at Cluny on January 29, 1119, so Louis can hardly have been "hurrying

to meet him." We know that Louis was probably in Paris on January 14 (Luchaire, no. 232).

5. On the significance of the election of Archbishop Guy of Vienne as Pope Calixtus II, consult Stanley A. Chodorow, "Ecclesiastical Politics and the Ending of the Investiture Controversy: The Papal Election of 1119 and the Negotiations of Mouzon," *Speculum* 46 (1971), pp. 613–40.

6. Calixtus opened the Council of Reims on October 20, 1119. The site of Reims may have prompted Suger to say little about this council, although Louis, in the presence of Calixtus, made a speech of which Orderic Vitalis supplies a version (OV 4: 376–78). On this council, see Robert Somerville, *Papacy, Councils and Canon Law in the 11th-12th Centuries* (Great Yarmouth Norfolk, 1990), cap. 12.

7. On the term "antipope," see M. E. Stroller, "The Emergence of the Term *Antipapa* in Medieval Usage," *Archivum historiae pontificae* 23 (1985), pp. 43–61, esp. 47f, 59f.

8. Burdinus was captured on April 10, 1121, and thereafter held at a number of prisons. A sixteenth-century sketch of frescoes that used to be in the old Lateran Palace survives; see the reproduction in Geoffrey Barraclough, *The Medieval Papacy* (London, 1967), p. 102. It depicts the scene described here, and Molinier makes the attractive suggestion that the fresco was seen by Suger on one of his trips to Italy (p. 95).

9. See Matthew 5:14f.

10. Suger travelled to Italy on Louis's business; the embassy is therefore a sign of the close relations that existed between them immediately before Suger's election as abbot of St. Denis. Suger describes his travelling companion Hugh, the abbot of St. Germain-des-Pres, as his *connutritus*, literally one who had been nursed or brought up with him (see two paragraphs below, where Abbot Adam is described as Suger's *nutritor*). In other words, Hugh had been a monk at St. Denis. Calixtus issued a bull in favor of St.-Germain-des-Pres on January 28, 1122 (J-W, no. 6947); Suger became abbot on March 12. The rest of this chapter can be seen as exemplifying an autobiographical tendency in the works of Suger, which has been discussed by K. L. Weintraub, *The Value of the Individual Self and Circumstance in Autobiography* (Chicago, 1978), pp. 68–70. It can also be seen as revealing Suger's vanity (Panofsky, p. 29).

11. The word *crepusculum* must mean "dawn," as it seems to in the second paragraph of cap. 17.

12. Adam had died on February 19, 1122. The description of him as being "of good memory," and the sentiments Suger details at the end of the paragraph seem rather conventional; Abelard, for one, was scathing in condemnation of what he considered Adam's evil ways (pp. 77, 86). The relationship of Adam and Suger was the subject of an interesting discussion between A. Graboïs and L. Grodecki at the conference *Pierre Abelard, Pierre le Vénérable* held at Cluny in 1972 (proceedings published in Paris, 1975), pp. 285f.

13. Waquet suggests that the two destroyers were the king and the pope (p. 210, n. 1), but the passage remains difficult to understand.

14. The archbishop of Bourges was Vulgrin (1121–36); the bishop of Senlis was Clairembald (1117–33). The king's anger had quickly blown over, and he confirmed the privileges and possessions of the monastery (Luchaire, no. 315).

15. Psalm 112:7f.

16. These activities of Suger are described in his *De consec.* and *De admin.*

17. The reform of St. Denis is well known from a letter of Bernard of Clairvaux (*ep.* 80). However, Bernard stresses Suger's achievement in freeing the abbey from secular involvement, but the abbot here emphasizes his reform of the religious life at St. Denis. Suger's genuine concern for the religious life is indicated in a letter from Peter the Venerable of Cluny, in which he refers to himself as Suger's *intimus amicus* (*ep.* 166, ed. Constable, p. 399). In addition, Peter is known to have praised Suger's style of life (William, *Vita*, ed. Lecoy, p. 392).

18. *Apostolici*, could also be translated "bishops." Later in the sentence we translate *felicitates* as "presents," a little freely.

19. Wisdom 7:11. On the ideas here, see Giles Constable, "Suger's Monastic Administration," in *Abbot Suger*, pp. 17–32 at p. 22. On Suger's view of beauty as a pathway to God, see Introduction above.

20. Suger now emerges as an inveterate traveller to Italy. In this passage he speaks of himself using both singular and plural forms of the first person. We have not sought to bring this out in our translation.

21. It may not be coincidental that the churches of St. Benedict at Monte Cassino and St. Nicholas at Bari had been the sites of recent building programs. Perhaps Suger was not only a pious pilgrim but used this travel, undertaken so recently after he had become abbot, to gather ideas for the works he was to undertake at St. Denis.

22. This is another trip to Italy, undertaken in 1124 (Cartellieri, no. 40) and hence scarcely some years later. A letter of Calixtus, simply dated "March 20" with no indication of year and addressed to all the archbishops and bishops of France, asks them to help the abbot of St. Denis against all evildoers (J-W, no. 7113).

23. Argenteuil is a few miles downstream on the Seine from St. Denis. This incident has been studied in detail by Thomas G. Waldman, "Abbot Suger and the Nuns of Argenteuil," *Traditio* 41 (1985), pp. 239–72, who concludes that "the charters of kings of old" were forged by Suger; see as well M. Groten, "Die Urkunde Karls des Groben für St.-Denis von 813 (D. 286), eine Fälschung Abt Sugers?" *Historisches Jahrbuch* 108 (1988), pp. 1–36. A forgery perpetrated by an English religious community at almost exactly the same time has been the subject of wise words by Richard Southern, *Saint Anselm and His Biographer* (Cambridge, 1963), pp. 308f.

CHAPTER 28

1. The Council of Reims occurred in October 1119 (above, cap. 27), or almost five years before the planned invasion described in this chapter. But in the interval Henry and Calixtus had come to an agreement (above, cap. 27, n. k). In the light of this, Suger's explanation of motive should perhaps be rejected, and the planned attack should rather be seen as a move in support of Henry I of England: see Ekkehard, *Chronicon*, MGH: *Scriptores* 6, p. 262; Geoffrey Barraclough, *The Origins of Modern Germany* (Oxford, 1947), p. 164; Hallam, p. 118; and H. Fuhrmann, *Germany in the Middle Ages* (Cambridge, 1986), p. 94.

2. Other writers of the period, Guibert of Nogent for one, described the blessed Dionysius as "lord of all France" (PL 156:962). It is noteworthy that Suger's account of the planned invasion of 1124 is centered on St. Denis, although the attack threatened Reims, on whose church he looked with no favor (Bur, p. 208, n. 48).

3. One of the most difficult passages in the book. Louis had been made count of the Vexin in 1092 (Luchaire, no. 4); and in his *De administratione* Suger asserts that in 1124 Louis stated, in a full chapter of St. Denis, that he held the county as a fief of St. Denis, and that if he had not been king he would have performed homage (*De admin.* 4). From this it would follow that Louis was a vassal of St. Denis. Similarly, according to ms. f of the *Deeds*, which may

represent a revision of the text by Suger himself (above, Introduction), Louis declared that he would be required to make an act of homage to the church, had not his royal office prevented it (Molinier, p. 142). These statements are stronger than the wording of this passage of the *Deeds* but do not contradict it, for even here the high status Suger claimed for St. Denis is clear. It has even been asserted that Suger forged a charter according to which Charlemagne gave all France to St. Denis: Robert Barroux, "L'abbé Suger et la vassalité du Vexin en 1124," *Le moyen âge* 64 (1958), pp. 1–26; but the evidence for this position is not strong: C. van der Kieft, "Deux diplômes faux de Charlemagne pour St. Denis, du XIIe siécle," *Le moyen âge* 64 (1958), pp. 401–36; see too Spiegel, "Cult of Saint Denis" (cited above, Introduction, n. 5) at 59f; Dunbabin, p. 258.

It became customary for French kings departing for war to pick up a banner at St. Denis, as did for example Louis VII when going on the Second Crusade in 1147 (Odo, p. 17). A centuries-old tradition has seen the *vexillum* described by Suger and Odo as having been identical with the famous *oriflamme*; a useful conspectus of opinions is provided by Philippe Contamine, "L'Oriflamme de Saint-Denis aux XIVe et XVe siècles," *Annales de l'est* 25 (1973), pp. 179–244 at 180–85; see too Spiegel, "Cult of Saint Denis," at p. 58. But the identification has been denied in an important study by L. H. Loomis, "The Oriflamme of France and the War-Cry Monjoie," in *Studies in Art and Literature for Bella da Costa Greene*, ed. Dorothy Eugenia Miner (Princeton, 1954), pp. 67–82; see further R. Hamann-MacLean in Beumann, ed., *Beiträge* (cited above cap. 1, n. 10), p. 222, where there is an intriguing discussion of Suger and national sentiment.

"France" here probably has the sense of "the territory within the sphere of influence of the French king": Margaret Lugge, *"Gallia" und "Francia" im Mittelalter* (Bonn, 1960) (=*Bonner Historische Forschungen* 15), p. 173, where other twelfth-century examples are cited.

4. How could France be said to be "the mistress of these lands"? It is likely that Suger is again suggesting a comparison with the past, in this case along the lines that territories controlled in his day by the Germans had formerly been controlled by Charlemagne, who was a Frank: see Walther Kienast, *Deutschland und Frankreich in der Kaiserzeit* I (Stuttgart, 1974), pp. 195f.

5. Suger elsewhere applies the word *barbari* ("barbarians") to non-

French people (*De admin.* 33, Panofsky, p. 61), whereas Guibert of Nogent refers to some English as *barbari* (p. 195), although admittedly they were behaving very badly. Suger has been found guilty of xenophobia by J. Ehlers, "Elemente mittelalterlicher Nationsbildung in Frankreich (10.–13. Jahrhundert)," *Historische Zeitschrift* 231 (1980), pp. 567–87 at 568.

6. The numbers provided for the forces involved here are by far the largest in the book; even the "astonishing host" which Henry V led to Rome is credited with only 30,000 knights (above, cap. 10). Suger seems to be using multiples of 60 to indicate size, with 60,000 in this instance obviously meaning "huge." (We are indebted to Professor Charles T. Wood of Dartmouth College for pointing this out.) The estimate Suger gives of the numbers in this one contingent alone is considerably larger than Steven Runciman's estimate of the total manpower of the First Crusade: see *A History of the Crusades*, vol. 1 (Cambridge, 1951), pp. 336–41. See too below, cap. 33, n. 1, for Suger's use of sixty to indicate old age for Louis.

7. Theobald's first uncle mentioned here was Hugh I, count of Champagne and Troyes (see too above, cap. 9, n. 7). But the most recent hostilities between Louis and Theobald described by Suger had occurred in 1120 (above, cap. 26, n. 20).

8. Suger sees Henry's withdrawal as a retreat, and indeed according to ms. f it was preceded by French attacks on his position (Molinier, p. 144). Perhaps it is not surprising that German sources see the matter differently. According to Ekkehard, Henry withdrew because of a Germanic distaste for attacking other lands, and because he had heard that the people of Wörms were planning a revolt (MGH: *Scriptores* 6, pp. 262f). Otto of Freising states that Henry proceeded as far as Metz, where he learned that the people of Wörms were already revolting, and so returned (*Two Cities*, trans. Mierow, p. 423). Doubtless such matters can be interpreted differently on different sides of a frontier, particularly when pride is at stake. Hollister raises the interesting possibility that the Germans turned back in terror at an eclipse of the sun (*Monarchy*, p. 287).

9. Louis did indeed give the crown of his father to the abbey of St. Denis, but the act is clearly dated 1120 (Tardiff, no. 379), four years before the German threat. Perhaps Suger's memory played him false, or perhaps he wished this event to be seen as occurring in his abbacy rather than Adam's, but for a more likely explanation see below, n. 11. On the general significance of the handing over of the

crown, see P. E. Schramm, *Der König von Frankreich* 1, 2d ed. (Darmstadt, 1960), pp. 132–37, and von Simson, p. 77.

10. On the famous Lendit fair, held each June between St. Denis and Paris, consult Anne Lombard-Jourdan, "Les foires de Saint-Denis," *Bibliothèque de l'Ecole des Chartes* 145 (1987), pp. 273–338, esp. p. 300, for Louis's renunciation of the fair. See also in general L. Levillain, "Essai sur les origines du Lendit," *Revue historique* 155 (1927), pp. 241–76; Germaine Lebel, *Histoire administrative, économique et financière de l'abbaye de St. Denis* (Paris, 1935); von Simson, pp. 78f (plate 13a reproduces a fourteenth-century representation of a bishop of Paris blessing the fair).

11. Again, Louis's act survives; but it was issued when Louis was at St. Denis on his way to the front, and not after Henry's withdrawal (Tardif, no. 391). This error can be linked with the erroneous dating of the return of Philip's crown (above, n. 9). In both cases we seem to be confronted with a manipulation of the evidence to highlight Louis's thankful feelings towards the blessed Dionysius on his return from Reims. Perhaps Louis's affection for the saint and his abbey did indeed grow warmer, but a passage in Abelard warns against portraying too favorable a view of such feelings on the part of Louis's advisors, if not the king himself, during the early years of Suger's abbacy (p. 88). See also Eric Bournazel, "Suger and the Capetians," in *Abbot Suger*, pp. 62f.

It was a common practice for crosses to be set up indicating boundaries. For the Pillars of Hercules, see above, cap. 21, n. 6.

12. Suger has written *collum*, which means "neck" and which we have translated as "shoulders," which must be what he intended to convey. He is here emphasizing the king's performance of a function of service.

13. This paragraph is somewhat tendentious. Theobald had not made war on Louis for several years (above, n. 7); and according to the *Anglo-Saxon Chronicle* (1124) trouble between King Henry of England and Amalric broke out shortly after the feast of the Annunciation, and hence could not have been caused by the emperor's advance. Even if Amalric's victory could not be dated to a period before the German advance, the hyperbole of this paragraph would make it suspicious, particularly when it is compared with the rhetorical claims of the following paragraph. Here, as elsewhere in this chapter, we see evidence of Suger's creativity as a historian. But the anti-German feeling displayed in this chapter and elsewhere in the

Deeds (e.g., in cap. 10) doubtless accurately reflects contemporary French sentiment. It is also to be found in the Old French epic *The Crowning of Louis* (in *William of Orange: Four Old French Epics*, ed. Glanville Price [London, 1975], pp. 47–55, a passage which is interesting in the light of contemporary German expeditions to Rome) and in a delightful story of Walter Map. According to this tale Henry V, annoyed that Louis was doing well in a war against Theobald, sent messengers threatening that unless he made peace within a month Paris would be besieged. Louis mysteriously replied "Tpwrut, German" (p. 459, referring to an unspecified time).

14. The quote in the previous sentence is from 1 Maccabees 1:3; this one is from Lucan, *De bello civili* 1:348f.

CHAPTER 29

1. Lucan, *De bello civili* 1:427, although Suger reads *Latios* for *Latio*.

2. This expedition of Louis into the Auvergne was distinguished by the presence of three counts: Fulk of Anjou, Conan of Brittany (count since 1112, here named for the first time as helping Louis) and William of Nevers (called by his name neither here nor in cap. 16). All three were to join the host at Reims in 1124. Suger applies to them and the other members of the force the expression *regni debitores*, implying feudal obligation. The events described in this chapter are briefly discussed by Reinholt Kaiser, *Bischofsherrschaft zwischen Königtum und Furstenmacht* (Bonn, 1981), p. 186.

3. Coming after the unsatisfactory conclusion to his most recent troubles with Henry I (above, cap. 26), Louis had reason to be pleased with this result; and a document of 1122 refers to him at Paris with his magnates, seeing himself triumphant over all his enemies and in possession of a glorious peace: see Martène, *Amplissima collectio* 1 (Paris, 1724), p. 678.

4. Despite the words with which this paragraph opens (*Verum temporum lustro peracto* = "but five years had hardly passed"), this second expedition of Louis should probably be dated 1126. *Lustrum* can also have the sense of "four years" (see Ovid, *Fasti* 3.163), which would yield better sense here.

5. This is the first clear reference to Louis's weight (see below, cap. 31, 33 for additional ones). Louis was notorious for his fatness: see also OV 4:376; William of Malmesbury, p. 439; and J. Vielliard, ed.,

Le Guide du pelerin de Saint Jacques de Compostelle, 5th ed. (Paris, 1984), p. 118. According to Henry of Huntingdon, Louis and his father Philip were such that "their God was their belly" (*Epistola de contemptu mundi* 13, ed. Thomas Arnold, 1879, p. 312); Henry here alludes to Phil. 3:19. See further Luchaire, p. 284.

6. The question of feudal hierarchy in the period is examined by J.-F. Lemarignier in two works, *Le Gouvernement royal* (cited above, Introduction, n. 32), pp. 167–76, and *La France médiévale* (cited above, Introduction, n. 31), pp. 143–48; *Le Gouvernement royal* concludes with reference to this passage; but note also the points of view expressed by two contributors to *Abbot Suger*, Andrew W. Lewis, "Suger's Views on Kingship," pp. 50–54, and Eric Bournazel, "Suger and the Capetians," pp. 55–72, esp. p. 60.

CHAPTER 30

1. The plot against Charles was the work of the Erembald clan, which, despite its great power, was of servile origin (hence the distinction between *servus* and *dominus* at the end of the next paragraph). The ringleader of the plot, Bertold ("Bertulf" in Galbert of Bruges), was provost of Bruges and chancellor of Flanders, and his brother Desiderius Hacket was castellan of Bruges. The evil role played throughout Suger's *Deeds* by people at this level of the feudal hierarchy needs no emphasis, and in the following paragraphs Suger's language describing them is unsparing. The contemporary account of the happenings in Flanders by Galbert of Bruges has been splendidly translated and annotated by James Bruce Ross; the French translation by J. Gengoux, *Le meurtre de Charles le Bon* (Angers, 1978), is worthy of note for its excellent illustrations. The history of the Erembalds and the background to the murder of Charles has been studied in great detail by E. Warlop, *The Flemish Nobility before 1300* (Kortrijk, 1975), pp. 185–200; see too J. Dhont, "Medieval 'Solidarities': French Society in Transition 1127–1128," in F. L. Cheyette, ed., *Lordship and Community in Medieval Europe* (New York, 1968), pp. 268–90, orig. publ. in French in *Annales économies-sociétés-civilisations* 12 (1957), pp. 529–60.

2. See Psalm 7:15.

3. We have not been able to identify this quotation.

4. See Luke 19:46.

5. An ambiguous expression, which could mean either that Louis did not let a war detain him, or that there was no war to detain him.

Suger may well have wished to imply the former, but the latter was true, for in 1127 there was peace between Louis and both Henry and Theobald. Louis arrived in Bruges at twilight on April 5, 1127 (Galbert, p. 201). His expedition to Flanders took place in a mood of religious exultation, which seems to have been caught in a secular version of a famous Palm Sunday hymn: Joseph M. De Smet, "Le 'Vexilla regis prodeunt' du cod. brux. 6837–40, composé pour l'expédition de Louis de Gros contre les meurtiers de Charles I le Bon (1127)," *Revue d'histoire ecclésiastique* 46 (1951), pp. 165–69.

6. Count Charles of Flanders had died childless, so there was need for the succession to be established. Suger's account naturally emphasizes the role of Louis, but Galbert indicates that there was both a designation by Louis and an election "by all his barons and those of our land" (pp. 94f); see too F. L. Ganshof, "Le roi de France en Flandre en 1127 et 1128," *Revue historique de droit française et étranger*, 4th ser., 27 (1949), pp. 204–28, although according to Herman of Tournai the office of count was given (*datus est*) by Louis to William (PL 180:120D). William the Norman's father, Robert Curthose, enjoyed notoriously bad relations with his brother Henry I of England. The selection of William was therefore an anti-English act, and indeed William had been used by Louis on earlier occasions against Henry, although Suger does not refer to them (see above, cap. 26, n. 9).

7. *Turrim tantum ut eos turris retineret retinuerunt.*

8. See Job 30:31.

9. Galbert's version of the death of Burchard ("Bursiard") is not as full (p. 249).

10. Galbert supplies a more detailed account of Bertold's end, and a less grisly version of the story of the dog (pp. 208–12). It is significant that Suger has Bertold exposed to the judgment of Louis, but Galbert refers to him as submitting to the judgment of William of Ypres, an enemy of Louis. Presumably, Galbert was in a better position to know the facts.

11. The subject of these two sentences, lacking in the Latin, must be Louis, although Galbert represents the choice of punishment for the traitors as having been jointly made by Louis and William Clito (p. 251).

12. The chamberlain Isaac had escaped from Bruges but was captured and hanged, contrary to what one would understand from Suger, several weeks before his comrades were thrown from the tower (Galbert, pp. 171f, 189, 255).

13. Suger has written "Bruges"; but as Waquet indicates (p. 248, n. a), Ypres makes more sense here.

14. According to Galbert, William of Ypres was captured on April 26, 1127, while the execution at the tower took place in May after Louis's return to Bruges (pp. 248–52). It is pleasant to find Suger's figure of 300 knights in William's forces supported by Galbert (p. 248).

15. Indeed, William of Ypres's attempt to become count failed. But Suger does not mention the later career of William Clito. Despite the vigorous support of Louis, his power was challenged by Thierry of Alsace, a grandson of Robert the Frisian. In July 1128, William was killed in battle (Galbert, pp. 307f) and at some later date Louis recognized Thierry as count of Flanders (Galbert, p. 312).

CHAPTER 31

1. Thomas had been declared anathema in 1114 (above, cap. 24; see Guibert, pp. 198f). Presumably he had subsequently been restored to the communion of the church, but dying without the sacrament was fitting for a former excommunicate, and it is not difficult to detect a note of relish in Suger's description.

2. Under Louis, much power at court passed to the four Garlande brothers, Anselm, William, Gilbert, and Stephen. In particular Stephen, who became chancellor in 1106 and seneschal in 1120, wielded a great deal of authority; there were suggestions that the office of seneschal, which involved military command, was not compatible with that of archdeacon, which he also filled. Further, the brothers were of non-noble family, so that Suger never describes them as *nobilis*, although he is able to describe an earlier seneschal, Guy of Rochefort, as such (cap. 10). Inevitably they attracted resentment, especially Stephen, "the most intimate counsellor of the king," by whose judgment the kingdom of the French was said to be governed (*Chron. Mor.*, p. 27; see also pp. 33, 34; it should be noted that Stephen was hostile to Morigny). But strong currents were flowing against him. In 1115 Louis had belatedly married Adelaide of Maurienne; in 1119 her uncle became pope, and her sister subsequently married Louis's ally William Clito; so the king was building up connections in other directions. Stephen was opposed by various streams of ecclesiastical opinion, represented by Ivo of Chartres (*ep.* 260, PL 162:264f) and Bernard of Clairvaux. In a famous letter to Suger, probably to be dated to 1127, St. Bernard congratulated Suger

on the reform of St. Denis, but then turned to a vehement attack on Stephen, and concluded with a cryptic message: "By the grace of God you have received a robe of many colors; see that it covers you, for it is no use beginning a work if you do not persevere to the end. Let my letter end with this warning to you to make a good end of what you have begun" (*ep.* 80). Finally, the *Chronicle of Morigny* notes the marriage of Stephen's daughter to the important baron Amalric of Montfort (on whom see above, cap. 18, n. 1) and his claim that the office of seneschal was hereditary (*Chron. Mor.*, p. 43; also Luchaire, no. 399; on the question of hereditary succession, consult Bournazel, pp. 112–15).

It now seems impossible to evaluate totally the roles played by political jealousy, social antagonism, clerical opinion, marriage alliance, and the claim to hereditary succession in the fall of Stephen in August 1127 (Luchaire, no. 399). Perhaps weight should also be given to fears arising from the murder of Charles the Good earlier in the year by an alienated faction of lowly extraction in Charles's court (above, cap. 30; see cap. 26 for similar worries of Henry I). But Stephen was driven from court, and together with Amalric of Montfort he concluded an alliance with Louis's old enemies Henry I and Theobald. As Suger explains, Louis and Count Ralph of Vermandois attacked Livry in 1128; but he does not explain that the war dragged on until 1130 and that Stephen was reinstated at court in 1132 (Luchaire, pp. 303–4). The evidence of charters suggests, however, that his power after 1132 was much less than it had been before 1127. The balance of power at court had decisively swung in favor of Suger and Count Ralph of Vermandois. Suger's handling of the entire affair is understated and free of the passion animating the Morigny chronicler and St. Bernard; it has recently been suggested that Suger was indebted to the patronage of Stephen of Garlande for his rise in royal favor: Eric Bournazel, "Suger and the Capetians," pp. 55–72, in *Abbot Suger*, at p. 56. It is quite in keeping with the character of Suger's work, aiming as it does to recount the deeds of Louis, for his treatment of the fall of Stephen of Garlande to concentrate on the siege of Livry.

CHAPTER 32

1. For another application of this figure for unity, consult Boso's *Life of Alexander III*, intro. by Peter Munz and trans. by G. M. Ellis (Oxford, 1973), p. 45.

2. The quotation is from Lucan, *De bello civili* 1:127. A schism broke out in the Roman church immediately following the death on February 13, 1130, of Honorius II (the pope who had recently confirmed the claims of St. Denis over the monastery at Argenteuil: see above, cap. 27), for on the following day two rival groups each elected a pope. One of the claimants to the pontifical title, the deacon Gregory (Innocent II), seemed likely to continue the policies of Honorius, while the other, the priest Peter Leo (Anacletus II), followed a tradition of thought and practice going back to the Gregorian reform of the eleventh century. Suger's treatment of these events is curious. He asserts that the party that elected Anacletus comprised "the senior and wiser among the members of the Roman church," that they planned to elect him "according to Roman practice," and that his election was approved by "many bishops, cardinals, clergy, and Roman nobles." A reading of the text of the *Deeds* could lead one to suspect that Suger sympathized with Anacletus, and indeed he may have had more in common with the traditions represented by Anacletus than with the currents of ecclesiastical thought in tune with reformed monasticism that Innocent represented. But Suger was scarcely the man to go against the decision of the Council of Etampes to recognize Innocent II as pope. See, in general, A. Graboïs, "Le schism de 1130 et la France," *Revue d'histoire ecclésiastique* 76 (1981), pp. 593–612, and Mary Stroll, *The Jewish Pope* (Leiden, 1978); on the attitude of Orderic Vitalis, see the interesting comments of Marjorie Chibnall in the general introduction to her edition (pp. 94f).

3. Suger does not refer to the presence of St. Bernard at the Council of Etampes, and we need not take at face value the assertion of a biographer of Bernard that Louis particularly wished him to be there (PL 182:270 C). Louis's early support for Innocent is indicated by a letter published by T. Reuter, "Zur Anerkennung Papst Innocenz II: Eine neue Quelle," *Deutsches Archiv für Erforschung des Mittelalters* 39 (1983), pp. 395–416.

4. A decision taken on the basis of *electio* need not have favored Innocent. Suger emphasizes the criterion of *persona*, as do other writers who support Innocent (*Chron. Mor.*, p. 52; Bernard, *ep.* 124).

5. A striking expression of how Suger perceived the relationship between the pope and St. Peter. On solemn crown-wearings by monarchs, consult Schramm, *Der König von Frankreich* (cited cap. 28, n. 9), pp. 124–28.

6. Chartres was in the territory of Henry's nephew and ally Theobald. The *Chronicle of Morigny* agrees that Henry was following Louis's example (p. 52).

7. The kings of France and England cast themselves at Innocent's feet, but the emperor Lothar offered himself as the pope's squire (*strator*) on greeting him. In a famous incident that occurred in June 1155, Frederick Barbarossa caused ill-feeling by his reluctance to perform this duty when he met Pope Hadrian IV: see Peter Munz, *Frederick Barbarossa* (London, 1969), pp. 8of. Just as Lothar led the pope about "as if he were his lord," so Louis took a standard "as if from his lord" (p. 128) and the duke of Aquitaine addressed Louis "as his lord" (p. 136), a form of words with feudal implications in all cases.

8. This church is discussed by Sumner McKnight Crosby, *The Abbey of St. Denis, 475–1122*, vol. 1 (New Haven, 1942), pp. 68–70. The following passage brings out Suger's great interest in the externals of worship.

9. Innocent's words represent a neat play on 2 Corinthians 3:15f; see too *De admin.* 34 (Panofsky, p. 75). In medieval art the figure of a woman in a blindfold is often used to represent *Synagoga*: see a clear example from this period in Gertrud Schiller, *Iconography of Christian Art*, trans. Janet Seligman, 2 (London, 1972), ill. 446. There may also be a covert reference here to the Jewish origins of Anacletus who, according to Orderic Vitalis, looked more like a Jew or Saracen than a Christian (4:385).

10. The *Chronicle of Morigny* supplies the interesting detail that Philip's companions fled in terror after the accident, so that the dying youth was carried to the nearest house by the hands of poor people (p. 56). The same chronicle (p. 57) adds weight to Suger's charge that the pig was diabolical. It reports that the animal was never found, whence it was considered as "something from the enemy power." See too OV 5:26f; Walter Map, p. 457.

11. Suger is now among the inner circle of Louis's advisers. As early as 1124, a document of Louis's had described him as *fidelis et familiaris* (Tardif, no. 391); see cap. 33 fin., 34 below for the good relations between them. On Louis, the second son of Louis VI and his successor, see Marcel Pacaut, *Louis VII et son royaume* (Paris, 1964); information concerning the date of his birth is given at p. 31. Insurrection from rivals is hinted at by Orderic Vitalis (5:27).

12. Louis VI had been anointed and crowned at Orléans, much to

the disgust of the church at Reims (above, cap. 14). However, in accordance with traditional practice, his son underwent these formalities at Reims, arguably to the distress of Suger, for although he states that he was one of those whose advice Louis was following, he deals with the ceremony in a few lines, quite unlike the *Chronicle of Morigny* (pp. 57–60). Presumably Suger's dislike of the church of Reims is operating again. Pope Innocent was on hand; one gets the feeling from this chapter that he was at loose ends for much of his stay in France.

CHAPTER 33

1. Suger elsewhere suggests that Louis was nearly sixty when he died (below, cap. 34). Louis was probably born in 1081, or perhaps in 1082: Joseph Calmette, "L'âge de Louis VI," *Orientalia Christiana periodica* 13 (1947), pp. 36–39; and, as he died in 1137, he never reached the age of sixty. But Suger could refer to Louis's father Philip at his death as "nearly sixty" when he was certainly younger (above, cap. 13); so perhaps he simply intended sixty years to stand for old age; see too cap. 6 above for a group of "about sixty" who died by fire and cap. 28, n. 6, for an army of 60,000, a multiple of sixty that obviously means "huge."

2. Louis's desire to become a monk was mentioned above, in a passage that is also part of the lessons (cap. 1). According to a document of 1120, issued when Louis handed over the crown of his father to St. Denis, the insignia of dead kings were to be given to the abbey (Tardif, no. 379, and above, cap. 28 with n. 9). This passage shows the pious Louis wishing to "lay down the crown and the kingdom, and profess the monastic way of life" in anticipation of death. For centuries rulers had sometimes entered monasteries to die; some eleventh-century examples were Count Burchard of Vendôme and Count Geoffrey Martel of Anjou: see Eudes de Saint-Maur, *Vita Domni Burchardi*, ed. C. Bourel de la Roncière (Paris, 1892), pp. 26ff, and *Chroniques*, p. 237; Count William of Nevers was to do likewise in 1147 (Bernard, *ep.* 230f); see too above, cap. 13, n. 1, for the case of Philip I. By Louis's time such conduct was becoming perhaps a little old-fashioned, but his wish would have caused no surprise. Note Suger's stress that Louis sought to enter the abbey of St. Denis, even though Montraër was close to the abbey of St. Benedict on the Loire, where his father had been buried.

3. On Anna of Kiev, see B. Lieb, *Kiev et Byzance à la fin du XIe siècle* (Paris, 1924), pp. 150–52, and R. Hallu, *Anne de Kiev reine de France* (Rome, 1973). The abbey of St. Denis claimed to possess the crown of thorns that had been placed on the head of Christ at the Crucifixion: see Joseph Bedier, *Les légendes épiques*, 3d ed., vol. 4 (Paris, 1929), pp. 122–30. The goods Louis left to St. Denis from the royal chapel are discussed by P. Verdier, "La Politique financière de Suger dans la reconstruction de Saint-Denis et l'enrichissement du trésor," in *Artistes, artisans et production artistique au moyen âge* (Paris, 1987), pp. 167–82 at pp. 176f.

4. Louis's statement of belief consists of two portions of roughly equal length. The first closely follows the Apostles' Creed, although the verb "judges" is here in the present tense rather than the future and the phrase "the last and great judgment" is an addition. Perhaps we have here two indications of the state of mind of a dying king who felt that he had governed sinfully. The second portion is a declaration of faith in the Eucharist expressed in the first person plural. The teaching of the church on the Eucharist was then being challenged by heretics; but it may be that this powerful passage on Louis's devout belief in the sacrament, concluding as it does with another intensified word (*praeoptans*), together with the stress on Louis's devout reception of it, is intended to suggest a contrast with the death of Thomas of Marle, recounted above, cap. 31. For "every power of the air," see Ephesians 2:2.

CHAPTER 34

1. Suger here describes the dying William entrusting all his land and his daughter Eleanor to Louis "for the purpose of marriage" (*desponsandam*); and in the next sentence he explains how Louis promised his son to her. But two other sources explicitly state that the dying William ordered that his daughter be given in marriage to the younger Louis (*Chron. Mor.*, p. 67; OV 5:81). As Fawtier has pointed out, we simply do not know whether William intended marriage with the younger Louis or merely wardship for Eleanor (R. Fawtier, *Capetian Kings*, p. 21). Perhaps the statements of the *Chronicle of Morigny* and Orderic should be accepted. Suger would have deemed it more proper for the initiative to have been taken by Louis, rather than display the marriage, however desirable, as having been foisted upon him.

2. Proverbs 8:15.

3. According to Orderic Vitalis, Louis died on August 4 (5:88); but the date supplied by Suger is to be preferred (Luchaire, nos. 590, 595).

4. As Suger was still on the expedition to Bordeaux, the administration of the abbey was in the hands of the prior Herveus, on whom see William, *Vita Sugerii*, Lecoy, p. 386.

5. Suger earlier used the same phrase *more regio* ("in accordance with royal custom") to describe the burial of Louis's son Philip (above, cap. 32). In opposition to King Philip's choice of the abbey of St. Benedict on the Loire for interment, he is emphasizing that the abbey of St. Denis is the appropriate place for royal burials: on this, see Eric Bournazel, "Suger and the Capetians," in *Abbot Suger*, p. 62.

6. Lucan, *De bello civili* 4:393f.

Index

215

The Deeds of Louis the Fat
was composed in 9.5/13 Trump Mediaeval by
Keystone Typesetting, Inc., Orwigsburg, Pennsylvania;
printed and bound by Braun-Brumfield, Inc., Ann Arbor,
Michigan; and designed and produced by Kachergis Book
Design, Pittsboro, North Carolina

CPSIA information can be obtained at www.ICGtesting.com
Printed in the USA
BVOW010032090112

279869BV00001B/2/P